ACHIEVING QUALITY AND DIVERSITY

ACHIEVING QUALITY AND DIVERSITY

Universities in a Multicultural Society

RICHARD C. RICHARDSON, JR.

ELIZABETH FISK SKINNER

Sponsored by the
NATIONAL CENTER FOR POSTSECONDARY GOVERNANCE AND FINANCE

American Council on Education 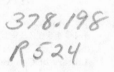 Macmillan Publishing Company
New York
Collier Macmillan Canada
Toronto
Maxwell Macmillan International
New York   Oxford   Singapore   Sydney

Macmillan Publishing Company
866 Third Avenue, New York, N.Y. 10022

Collier Macmillan Canada, Inc.
1200 Eglinton Avenue East, Suite 200
Don Mills, Ontario M3C 3N1

Library of Congress Catalog Card Number: 90-38074

Printed in the United States of America

printing number
1 2 3 4 5 6 7 8 9 10

Library of Congress Cataloging-in-Publication Data

Richardson, Richard C.
Achieving quality and diversity: universities in a multicultural society/Richard C.
Richardson, Elizabeth Fisk Skinner.
p.   cm. — (American Council on Education/Macmillan series on
higher education)
Includes bibliographical references and index.
ISBN 0-02-897342-9
1. Minorities–Education (Higher)–United States–Case studies.
2. Academic achievement–Case studies. 3. Universities and
colleges — United States — Admission — Case Studies. 4. Educational
equalization–United States–Case studies. 5. Universities and
colleges — United States — Case Studies. I. Skinner, Elizabeth Fisk.
II. American Council on Education. III. Title. IV. Series: American
Council on Education/Macmillan series on higher education.
LC3727.R52 1991
370.19′342′0973–dc20   90-38074
                                                                              CIP

CONTENTS

ILLUSTRATIONS

FIGURE

TABLES

PREFACE

Policymakers, college and university officials, and researchers have given considerable attention to defining the dimensions of the problem of low participation and graduation rates for African-Americans, some Hispanic groups, and American Indians. Much less attention has been given to why some institutions have been effective in helping underrepresented minority students overcome the barriers that cause high attrition rates in other institutions. Most discussions of institutional efforts have focused on the need for more financial aid, "model interventions," or "administrative commitment." Reports addressed to policy and institutional audiences have been largely anecdotal and prescriptive.

As a context for more productive discussions of issues related to access and quality, this book presents a comprehensive model of how institutions adapt to improve the environments they provide for more diversely prepared students without relinquishing the standards to which they have been historically committed. The model is grounded in the experiences of institutions that have graduated higher than average numbers of these underrepresented students, as compared to their states and the nation. The model explains institutional effectiveness in terms that are meaningful to less successful colleagues and to those who make the policies that guide public higher education at the state level.

We began the work that led to the model by asking faculty and administrators what they had learned from their experiences as relatively successful institutions. We expected them to describe key strategies and model interventions; they did not. Some expressed surprise that they had been selected as examples of success and argued that their outcomes with minority students could not reasonably be attributed to any institutional commitment or identifiable set of practices. Others pointed to strategic planning and systematic activity by administrators and student affairs staff in the face of faculty indifference and disengagement.

Many special programs were described. Most were funded by federal or state grants, but a significant number were also supported by scarce discretionary dollars from institutional budgets. All the programs were able to provide evidence that they worked, at least in terms of the purposes for which they had been established. But none of the case-study institutions attributed effectiveness to the impact of special programs alone, and approaches were as diverse as the populations served.

Increasingly we came to understand minority participation and achievement as a complex phenomenon that is influenced by the state policy environment, characteristics of the minority and majority populations served, and institutional mission and selectivity, in addition to the more obvious variables related to administrative leadership and institutional programming.

To place the case-study institutions in the context of historically Anglo public four-year institutions, we developed outcome measures using nationally available data. With the aid of more sophisticated ways of estimating outcomes, we became increasingly aware that while all ten of the institutions we studied made important contributions to the nation's pool of college-educated minority citizens, there was considerable variance in the outcomes they attained and in the ways they went about achieving such outcomes.

By examining their experiences in relation to the literature describing the national experience with minority participation and achievement during the past quarter century, we came to believe that many of the problems minority students experienced can be traced to policy decisions of the 1960s which created two sets of institutions: one with open access to provide for diversity, and another with selective admission standards to provide for quality. This approach reinforced pre-civil rights beliefs that quality and access were mutually exclusive goals.

The belief that quality and diversity conflict is correct only to the extent that institutions accommodate greater diversity in student participation without changing their learning environments or the amount of time they provide for students to achieve learning competencies. Quality can be preserved if time and instructional methods are varied to take into account differences in student preparation. Resistance to placing additional emphasis on helping university students learn should be attributed more to the corresponding additional demands on faculty time than to any inherent incompatibility with relevant concepts of quality.

The model outlined in chapter 1 and elaborated upon in chapters 2 and 3 suggests that all institutions must accept responsibility for both quality and diversity. Within this model, *quality* is defined as student achievement, and *diversity* as increased racial and ethnic participation and completion in the student bodies of institutions in which minority groups remain underrepresented. The key to improved outcomes, in the form of participation and graduation rates, is a balance between the emphasis an institution places on diversity and the attention it gives to helping diverse students achieve the institution's traditional standards for graduation. The model suggests that open-access institutions reduce race- and ethnicity-related differences in participation and achievement by increasing emphasis on helping students achieve. For selective institutions, the process requires systematic attention to increasing diversity while concurrently altering time constraints and learning environments to enable diverse students to meet existing standards.

While the model presented in chapters 1 to 3 draws from the literature on organizations, it is firmly grounded in the experiences of the case-study institutions. The ten case studies presented in chapters 4 to 13 provide concrete evidence of how model variables interact to produce institutional outcomes. They also provide examples of the ways in which experienced institutions have adapted to the differing circumstances of historic context, mission, location, and clientele. Since the case studies are undisguised, they furnish relevant examples of the strategies institutions have used to respond to the diversity that will increasingly characterize student populations in the next decade and beyond.

The research described in this volume was intended from its inception to impact public policy. To that end, chapter 14 provides a process and a series of instruments through which institutions and the states that fund them can assess and improve the environments they provide for minority participation and achievement. The instruments and process grew out of a successor study to the one that produced the model and the ten cases. In the current study, we have operationalized the model and are testing it statistically with 143 institutions in ten states.

The data collection phase for the case studies presented in this book ended in 1987. Since then, there have been important changes in all ten institutions. Because the case studies are undisguised, institutional representatives are anxious to have readers understand that institutional progress in accommodating diversity and achievement did not end with the second site visit. We promised to emphasize that much excellent progress not reflected in these reports has been made in the more than two years between the end of data collection and the publication of this book.

The choice of terminology in referring to the racial and ethnic groups that make up the nation's population is a difficult one. We try consistently to use the term "African-American" to refer to the nation's black citizens. The only exception is where the use of the term would contradict popular usage, as in "historically black institutions." We refer to whites of Western European extraction as "Anglos" to distinguish them from white Hispanics. In speaking of Hispanics, we distinguish between major population groups, such as Cuban Hispanic and Mexican-American, where these distinctions are important to an understanding of a case. "American Indian" has been used consistently in preference to "native American."

ACKNOWLEDGMENTS

The list of those to whom we are indebted is very long. We particularly appreciate the senior researchers who helped to design the study, participated in the debates that led to the development of the model, and most important, conducted the case studies on which the model is based. They are the authors of the case-study chapters, so we will not repeat their names here. The study could not have been completed without their commitment and wisdom, nor without the multicultural and interdisciplinary perspectives they brought to the effort.

Our design called for cooperating researchers appointed by chief executive officers of the participating institutions. Cooperating researchers arranged the site visits of the senior researchers, helped them to obtain documents and data, checked case-study reports for accuracy, and served as members of the team that critiqued the initial model developed to explain outcomes. Cooperating researchers are also introduced at the beginning of the case with which they assisted. While cooperating researchers played a critical role in the conduct of the study, they are not responsible for the value judgments or structure imposed on the data by the senior researchers and the editing process.

The chief executive officers of case-study institutions who agreed to publication of undisguised case studies in a volatile and highly sensitive area deserve particular commendation for commitment and courage. Two of the ten institutions originally invited refused to participate—a statistic that indicates the level of risk taken by the eventual participants. The ten that participated believed that the importance of the issues outweighed any potential embarrassment that might result from the discovery of occasional warts on institutional physiognomies. We hope that this volume justifies their expectations and support.

Also deserving of commendation are the state higher education executive officers who helped in selecting the institutions invited to participate, gave their own time, and provided access to key members of their staff. Their assistance helped us to understand the importance of the state policy environment as an influence on institutional policies and practices.

Special thanks are also owed to a new set of cooperating researchers from state and institutional settings who are helping us with the current study and whose efforts in large measure produced the format and items for the self-assessment instruments provided in Chapter 14. Currently cooperating state researchers include: Stephen Bragg, Illinois; Frank Carrasco, New Mexico; Lewis Dars, Massachusetts; Rosario Martinez, Texas; Ann Moore, Ohio; Charles Ratliff, California; Regina Sofer, Florida; Julia Wells, South Carolina; Mattielynn Williams, Tennessee; and Diane Yavorsky, New Jersey.

Both studies have benefitted from the advice of Technical Advisory Committees and others who have taken a special interest in these issues. We appreciate the contributions of James Blackwell, University of Massachusetts at Boston Harbor; Alfredo G. de los Santos, Jr., Maricopa Community Colleges; Sara Melendez, University of Bridgeport, Connecticut; James Murtha, City University of New York; Keith Pailthorp, Portland State University; Samuel Peng, Center for Education Statistics; Julie Smith, University of Illinois at Chicago; David Spence, Southern Regional Board; Elaine El-Khawas, American Council on Education; James Mingle, State Higher Education Executive Officers; Jeffrey Gilmore, Office of Educational Research and Improvement (OERI) of the U.S. Department of Education; Theodore Marchese, American Association of Higher Education; Alison Bernstein, Princeton University; Michael Nettles, University of Tennessee at Knoxville; and Monique Clague, University of Maryland, College Park.

No study can proceed without competent research staff. We have been particularly blessed by the support of an unusually able corps of doctoral students at Arizona State University, including Michael Pavel, Tanzella Gaither, Brian Murphy, and Dewayne Matthews. Most important of all is our administrative assistant, Alice Shepard, who spent untold hours on the manuscript, shaping it to its final form. To all these and others unnamed, we express our sincere appreciation.

PART ONE

Minority Participation and Achievement in Context

1

UNDERSTANDING MINORITY PERSISTENCE AND ACHIEVEMENT

In the 1960s and early 1970s a combination of legislative, executive, and judicial influences placed pressure on colleges and universities to increase the participation rates of underrepresented minority groups. The rapid influx of new students , many admitted under differential admission standards, improved participation rates but failed to produce anticipated gains in college-educated minority citizens. In the 1980s race- and ethnicity-related attrition rates, along with continuing concerns about the public schools, led to higher college admission standards, the assessment movement, and a newly protective attitude toward the curriculum. These quality initiatives have had an adverse impact on the participation and achievement of African-American, Hispanic, and American Indian students in many majority institutions.

In this book we draw on case-study data from ten public universities to develop a model for understanding the complex relationships among variables influencing minority persistence and achievement in majority institutions. We then use the structure provided by the model to describe the policies and practices identified by state and institutional administrators, faculty members, community representatives, and graduates as contributing to degree achievement by African-American, Hispanic, and American Indian students. Our analysis of the meaning of the experiences of the case-study institutions is followed by the edited case studies to provide "real-life" examples of the differing combinations of variables within the model that produce the results recorded by the institutions. Since the case studies are undisguised, they also provide an inventory of approaches that may be consulted by institutions interested in improving their own outcomes.

While it is impossible to discuss success without contrasting failure, the focus of this book is on state and institutional behaviors that remove barriers and promote achievement. The case-study institutions were chosen for their experience in graduating underrepresented minority groups. The primary objective of the study was to explain organizational success in ways that would be helpful to others concerned about reducing race- and ethnicity-related barriers to college attendance and graduation. As a result of the study we have come to believe that further progress toward proportional representation and comparable achievement for African-Americans, Hispanics, and American Indians requires fundamental changes in institutional practices and priorities as these influence faculty and staff attitudes about the compatibility of quality and student diversity. In the remainder of this chapter we explore this thesis in some depth after providing a brief overview of the study.

THE STUDY

In 1985 the National Center for Postsecondary Governance and Finance, with support from the Office of Educational Research and Improvement (OERI) of the U.S. Department of Education, undertook ten undisguised case studies following a common protocol. Each case involved collection of detailed descriptive information about minority achievement in natural contexts. The emphasis was on holistic data that preserved the processes involved and the complex interrelationships among factors. Each case included several components representing varying levels of analysis: (1) the institution, (2) the state policy environment, and (3) the student. For each component, information was collected through several methods and from several perspectives to permit triangulation of findings. Triangulation was also enhanced by using a multiethnic, multiracial, and multidisciplinary research team and by receiving input from cooperating researchers at the case-study institutions, including a member check on the accuracy of interim and final reports (Lincoln and Guba 1985, 314).

This approach to data collection has received increasing attention from educational researchers over the last ten years (Rist 1970; Lincoln and Guba 1985). Related approaches have long been an integral part of policy research (Noblit 1986) as well as the qualitative traditions of research in sociology and anthropology. The use of such techniques produces a richer and better-balanced understanding of how environments influence the achievement of college students. The case-study institutions were selected because their records for graduating African-American, Hispanic, or American Indian students were above average for their states and for the nation, and because they were willing to share experiences without disguising data. All were public, historically Anglo institutions. While similar in control, the universities provided important contrasts in outcomes, state contexts, institutional missions, community settings, and proportions of specific populations enrolled. Table 1.1 provides selected information about the case-study institutions.

TABLE 1.1. Selected 1986 Data: Ten Case-Study Institutions

Institution	Carnegie Classification[a]	Selectivity	Enrollment	% African-American	% Hispanic	% American Indian
Brooklyn	Comp I	High	14,625	21.3	8.9	1.2
CSUDH	Comp I	Low	7,327	34.3	10.5	0.8
FIU	Comp I	Medium +	16,744	8.4	38.3	0.1
FSU	Res II	Medium	22,990	7.0	3.0	0.2
MSU	Doc-G I	Low	20,043	17.7	0.3	0.1
Temple	Res II	Medium	30,615	13.9	2.0	0.3
UCLA	Res I	High	34,419	6.2	10.1	0.6
UNM	Res I	Low	24,124	1.8	22.5	3.3
UTEP	Comp I	Low	13,753	2.3	51.3	0.3
Wayne	Res II	Low	28,764	21.9	1.7	1.0

Note: Case-study institutions were as follows: Brooklyn College of the City University of New York; California State University, Dominguez Hills (CSUDH); Florida International University (FIU), Miami; Florida State University (FSU), Tallahassee; Memphis State University (MSU), Memphis, Tennessee; Temple University, Philadelphia, Pennsylvania; University of California, Los Angeles (UCLA); University of New Mexico (UNM), Main, Albuquerque; University of Texas at El Paso (UTEP); and Wayne State University, Detroit, Michigan.

[a] Classifications from *A Classification of Institutions of Higher Education*, by The Carnegie Foundation for the Advancement of Teaching, Princeton, N.J.: Princeton University Press, 1987.

Individuals interviewed at each institution during two extended site visits included the president, chief academic officer, deans of academic units, admissions officer, financial aid officer, faculty members, and student support staff. Interviews were open-ended and designed to gain historical perspective as well as varying views of current policies and practices related to student achievement. The researchers who are the authors of the case studies described in subsequent chapters were interested in detailed descriptions of specific programs and activities as well as the interviewees' interpretations of institutional strategies.

At the state level, interviews were conducted with representatives of state governing and/or coordinating boards, including chief executive officer, affirmative action officer, planning and research officer, chief academic administrator, and financial aid administrator. The purpose of these interviews was to develop a view of the state policy environment as a context for the university's approach to serving minority students. Topics included financial aid practices, visible evidence of state-level commitment to diversity, and specific initiatives related to access and quality in higher education (whether legislative, executive, or judicial).

Community visits were used to obtain an overview of economic, political, and demographic characteristics. While we began with a wide net of interest in community influences, logistics and the process of data analysis ultimately led us to concentrate on public schools, community colleges, and community-based programs that exhibited a direct and obvious relationship to student attendance and persistence at the case-study institutions.

To obtain a student perspective, open-ended telephone interviews, averaging 40 minutes, were conducted with 108 African-American, Hispanic, and American Indian graduates of the ten universities. The graduates varied in educational characteristics of parents, age, number of years taken to complete their degrees, major field of study, and whether they had transferred from another university or college. Students were encouraged to provide detailed, descriptive information to allow their own perspectives of college-going to emerge (Spradley 1979). Topics used as stimuli included motivation, influence from family and community, high school experience, and work experience, as well as activities on campus, course work, and selection of major. Interviewees were also asked specifically about organizational sources of help and whether they felt members of their racial or ethnic group experienced the university differently from their majority counterparts.

Data from all sources were treated exhaustively (Mehan 1978) through a careful coding and collating process to preserve multiple perspectives and ensure that all information was accounted for in the model. A site-ordered, predictor-outcome matrix (Miles and Huberman 1984, 167) served as an aid to cross-case analysis and as a check to ensure that all relevant data had been collected at each site. Using a suggestion from Yin (1988), an explanatory model was developed using a single case. The model was then tested on each of the remaining cases and modified as necessary to explain the relationships among variables and outcomes. The process of model testing and modification continued until all the data for all of the cases were satisfactorily explained.

The most significant limitations of the study involved lack of prolonged engagement at each site, difficulties in coordinating the activities of multiple researchers, and selection of cases for inclusion. The research design partially compensated for the first limitation by requiring multiple site visits spaced over two years and by including cooperating researchers on the team. These "natives" of the institutional setting were able to provide a perspective informed by prolonged involvement at the site. The use of a detailed protocol, along with meetings of the research team, kept the problems of coordination within acceptable limits while ensuring input from multiple perspectives at all stages of the study.

The model that evolved from analysis of the case studies furnishes the structure for introducing the evidence upon which our conclusions were based. We explore state influences on institutional behaviors in chapter 2 and the institutional change process in chapter 3, as a prelude to the case studies reported in chapters 4 to 13. Chapter 14 synthesizes the insights furnished by the cases and suggests an approach for using the results to assess and alter institutional environments to make them more responsive to the academic and social needs of underrepresented groups without relinquishing standards.

QUALITY AND DIVERSITY: CONFLICTING OR COMPLEMENTARY?

Quality is a complex concept with at least four distinct meanings (Astin 1985). The first two, reputational ratings and available resources, are based on the same variables assessed somewhat differently: undergraduate selectivity, per-student revenues and expenditures, scholarly visibility of staff, library size, student/faculty ratios, and faculty salaries. In order to achieve quality according to either of these two meanings, selective admission standards are necessary. Admission of students who vary from these standards is a threat.

Quality may also be viewed in terms of student outcomes, an approach that is more problematic than the reputational and resource views because there is little agreement about desired outcomes and how they should be assessed. Such student outcomes as low attrition rates, high proportions attending graduate schools, number listed in *Who's Who*, and percentages making good salaries are highly correlated with reputation and resources. When quality is judged by these student outcomes, it remains an attribute of institutions with the highest ratings for reputation and resources.

A fourth definition of *quality* emphasizes talent development or value added. This view can be understood as a variation or extension of the student outcomes perspective. As Astin notes (1985, 77), the great merit of the talent development approach is its consistency with diversity and academic standards. An institution that maximizes development of the talents of all its students will also maximize the number of students who attain minimum performance levels as well as the number who exceed these levels.

While these four meanings are conceptually distinct, they have become intertwined in practice, and all but the last are often seen to be in conflict with broadened access to minorities. Institutions that provide good access are assumed to have poor educational quality (Seneca and Taussig 1987), while an institution that emphasizes quality begins by raising admission standards. As institutions work to raise quality ratings, they push onto other institutions the task of serving students who cannot contribute to this goal. Such students are disproportionately African-American, Hispanic, and American Indian.

In opposition to this perspective, this book proposes a grounded model for altering institutional environments so that diversity is no longer perceived as a threat to quality. The model suggests that institutions can achieve both quality and diversity through adaptations that support achievement by more diverse learners. As evidence we present the experiences of ten historically majority universities that have found ways of adapting their practices to improve participation and achievement rates for African-Americans, Hispanics, or American Indians without diminishing the rigor of the experiences they provide to other groups.

Our emphasis on changing institutions should not be interpreted as advocacy for any reduction in the number or intensity of interventions aimed at helping underrepresented students cope with majority institutions. To the contrary, we believe that practices such as school and college collaboration in early outreach, bridge programs, aggressive recruitment, targeted student financial aid, and academic support services are indispensable to attainment of equity goals. The importance of these activities, however, may lie as much in the pressures they create for institutional adaptation as in the buffer they provide between diverse students and institutional practice.

EQUITY ISSUES IN HISTORICAL PERSPECTIVE

Schlesinger (1986) has summarized the cyclical swings that characterize American history as a fundamental tension between public action and private interests. The emphasis on access that began in the early 1960s coincided with the public action phase of a thirty-year cycle that had shifted to an emphasis on private interests by 1978. The development of open-access institutions and the initiation of state and federal programs of need-based student financial aid served as the principal policy instruments of the democratizing period of public action, while admission standards and assessment practices have assumed increasing importance in the quality-oriented, conservative 1980s.

The tension between access and quality has been a continuing part of the evolution of American higher education since the founding of Harvard by a group of Cambridge- and Oxford-trained gentlemen who "stoutheartedly refused to yield an inch to pioneer prejudices or frontier values" (Rudolph 1965). In each cycle we have argued about who and what should be taught, aligning ourselves for or against such threats to quality as inclusion of agriculture and the mechanical arts, admission of female students, and, in the most recent cycle, accommodation of minorities both within institutions and in the curriculum. Hansen and Stampen (1988) have traced patterns of student financial aid in relation to overall financing of higher education for the period 1947–1985. The patterns they report conform closely to the cycles proposed by Schlesinger and translate, in their judgment, into alternating mandates for access and quality.

Aaron (quoted in Wildavsky 1979, 22) places the current cycle in sharper perspective when he notes that the civil rights movement created a coalition between those who sought a fair process or equal educational opportunity and those concerned about fair outcomes or distributive justice. Title VI of the Civil Rights Act of 1964 prohibited distribution of federal funds to colleges and universities that discriminated on the basis of race, color, or national origin. Progress toward fair outcomes was the legal test for compliance. A series of court decisions, beginning with *Adams v. Richardson* in 1973, placed pressure on the federal government to enforce the provisions of Title VI by withholding funds from states not in compliance, but overall the success of Title VI activities was disappointing to those who sought fair outcomes (Williams 1985, 4).

By the early 1980s the leading edge of a broad-scale retreat from concerns with fair outcomes could be discerned in declining rates of minority participation and graduation, and in the growing disparities between college costs and the availability of need-based financial assistance. The prospects for achieving fair outcomes with "color-free" strategies in a society where unequal treatment as a function of race, color, or national origin had been the law of land for ten times as long as equal opportunity seemed increasingly dim. The trend lines of the 1980s suggest that open-access institutions and need-based financial aid will not change outcomes sufficiently in the near term to avoid polarization and conflict along racial and ethnic lines. And in the long run, as someone has observed, we are all dead.

Schlesinger suggests that cycles of public action and private interest are not automatic; it takes people to make them work.

> There is no mathematical determinism in history . . . those who believe in public purpose must interpret events, press issues and devise remedies. (1986, 45)

State and institutional policymakers constantly face the task of finding an appropriate balance between, on the one hand, the private interests of individuals in a fair process that allows them to retain and enjoy educational benefits that may in part be a consequence of past advantages of race or ethnicity and, on the other hand, public action to achieve the fair outcomes essential to preserving cohesion and economic viability in the multicultural society we are destined to become.

In the late 1980s the widening gap between fair process and fair outcomes foreshadows the beginning of a new cycle of public action focused on improving participation and graduation rates for citizens whose current circumstances clearly relate to past legal discrimination. Previous experience with quality and access initiatives must be assessed and the results applied to the development of public policy if any new cycle is to produce results different from its predecessors.

Wildavsky argues that political preferences are molded through social relationships which give rise to shared values and changed preferences:

> When individuals make important decisions, these choices are simultaneously choices of culture—shared values legitimating different patterns of social practices. (1987, 5)

According to this view, the preference for specific institutional arrangements and instruments of policy at any point in time is a function of the historical context in which the shared meanings that support them were worked out.

The concept of political culture as the social relationships through which "opposed visions of the good life are selected, sustained, altered, and rejected" (Wildavsky 1987, 17) provides a means of understanding the changes in process and outcomes essential to altering the view that access and quality must remain as mutually exclusive objectives. State governments and the systems of higher education they support are linked in multiple relationships through which existing environments for minority access and achievement were created, and through which any new balance between fair process and fair outcomes must be sought. Institutions bear no greater share of the responsibility for current process and outcomes than the state governments they work with to define the preferences that govern current practice. And they cannot reasonably be expected to achieve different outcomes in the absence of appropriate changes in state policy.

The quality initiatives of the current private interest cycle have produced unintended consequences for access just as the access initiatives of the earlier public action cycle affected quality in unintended ways. What lessons are suggested by this historical synopsis? One would seem to be the necessity of considering both quality and diversity when developing any policy to change either. A second involves the importance of encouraging all institutions, regardless of mission, to accept responsibility for both expanding diversity and strengthening achievement. A third relates to the need to improve student-institutional fit by changing institutional environments, as well as by designing programs to change or buffer individuals from discouraging elements in the environments as currently experienced. These insights are supported by the experiences of the states and institutions profiled in this volume.

A THEORETICAL MODEL OF ACCESS AND ACHIEVEMENT

The experiences of the case-study institutions suggest a systematic way of looking at the process through which institutions adapt to resolve tensions between quality and diversity. Minority students experience frustration when they are recruited by institutions on the strength of previous achievements and cultural affiliations and then expected to behave like Anglo students with whom they may have little in common. Their frustration deepens as differences in preparation and learning preferences translate into often insurmountable barriers to graduation. Minority students and staff, with external allies, seek to influence public opinion and exert pressure on institutional leaders for change by obtaining support from governors, the courts, and the legislature. When states take an active interest in minority students, campus administrators respond by developing better coordinated strategies for improving diversity and achievement.

As faculty and staff adapt their behaviors to respond to initiatives from campus administration, the organizational culture shifts to provide a more productive academic and social environment for students who differ in preparation or culture from those an institution has traditionally served. Figure 1.1 portrays the relationships among these influences.

Adaptation is defined within the model as changes in an organization's behaviors, values, and beliefs to improve the fit with its environment (Goodman and Dean 1982). From this perspective, the culture of any organization, the assumptions and beliefs shared by its members (Kuh and Whit 1988; Tierney 1988), develop as learned responses to the problem of maintaining effective relationships with external agencies that provide essential resources (Pfeffer and Salancik 1978) and the need to achieve a working consensus among those whose cooperation is essential to achieving institutional goals (Schein 1985).

A Model of Institutional Adaptation to Student Diversity*

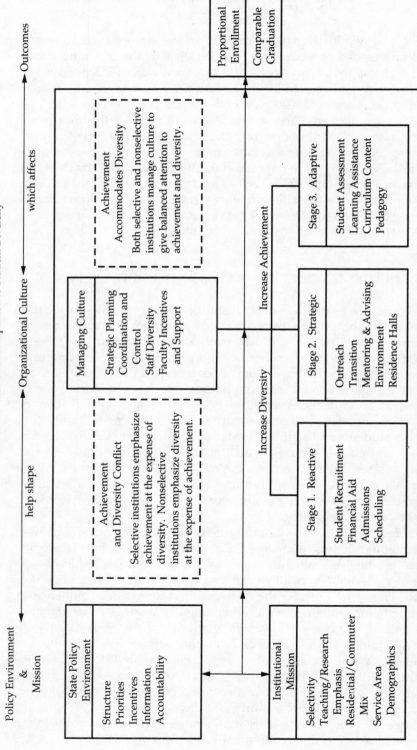

FIGURE 1.1. A Model of Institutional Adaptation to Student Diversity*

* Student diversity has three major dimensions: (1) preparation, (2) opportunity orientation, and (3) mode of college-going. African-Americans, Hispanics, and American Indians share these dimensions with other groups, but are distributed differently as a function of historic discrimination and socioeconomic status.

The environment an institution provides for minority participation and achievement can be viewed as the observable product of an invisible culture. Analysis of outcomes related to minority participation and graduation yields clues to the nature of an institution's culture. The study of institutional interventions provides an index of the progress an institution has made in changing its culture to accommodate students who will make up the college-going population in 2025. The assessment of management strategies offers a way of evaluating the effectiveness of institutional leaders in using the tools at their disposal to reshape the cultures of their institutions.

Quality and diversity conflict in two types of organizational cultures: a selectivity culture (low concern for diversity, high concern for achievement) and an open-access culture (high concern for diversity, low concern for achievement). The model can be used to understand organizational culture as it is influenced by the state policy environment and mission and, in turn, influences institutional outcomes.

In a society where race and ethnicity are unrelated to opportunity, minority groups should participate in the undergraduate programs of any institution to the extent of their representation in the population from which the students come. We refer to this condition within the model as "proportional enrollment." Minority groups should also graduate at rates comparable to their representation among undergraduates. Both outcomes must be considered concurrently since comparable graduation rates can be attained by restricting admissions to a minority elite, at the cost of limiting participation. Conversely, high participation rates can be generated through open admissions and subsequent screening that makes the open door a revolving door for the underprepared. In order to contribute to equal educational opportunity, institutions must attain both proportional representation and comparable graduation.

While this sounds like a simple enough proposition, its attainment is complicated by differences in the ways that potential African-American, Hispanic, and American Indian college students are distributed in terms of preparation, belief in the value of higher education, and financial resources. To meet participation and graduation goals for these groups, institutions must adapt their environments to accommodate greater diversity without relinquishing their commitment to high standards of achievement for all students. They do this by moving through three stages that have been labeled within the model as "reactive," "strategic," and "adaptive," following loosely the scheme for categorizing the kinds of leadership involved suggested by Chaffee (1985). We see these stages as way stations along a continuum that stretches from the pre–civil rights era into the present.

Historically, the measure of an institutions's success in achieving affirmative action targets has been participation. Institutions under pressure to improve their equity performance have reacted by stressing recruitment, financial aid, and special admission procedures. Open-access institutions typically attain this stage as a consequence of their mission. When the effects of these reactive measures on student achievement become apparent, institutions develop outreach, transition, and academic support strategies designed to help a more diverse student population adapt to expectations geared to the clientele the institution has traditionally served. These strategies, especially as they become more systematic and better coordinated, characterize the strategic stage of adaptation. The emphasis is on changing students, and most of the interventions are carried out by student affairs personnel.

Institutions enter the adaptive stage when they realize that participation and graduation goals cannot be attained in a system in which students are expected to do all the changing. The focus in the adaptive stage is on assessment, learning assistance, and curricular renewal. Faculty members become involved in this stage to change educational practices, curriculum content, and teaching practices to make them reflect the students actually served rather than the historic clientele.

The task of administrators in the model is to manage organizational culture so that institutions progress through the stages instead of remaining locked in a pre–stage 1 setting, in which achievement is stressed at the expense of diversity, or in a stage 1 environment, in which diversity is accommodated at the expense of achievement. Administrators manage culture by using the same tools they employ to address other priorities: strategic planning, coordination and control, staff hiring practices, and faculty incentives and support.

Within public institutions there are always competing priorities. Increasing diversity has a low institutional priority under the best of circumstances because it involves the cause of groups either not present or seriously underrepresented in internal decision-making forums. Under such circumstances, institutions are most likely to pay attention to diversity as a priority if they are held accountable for improving outcomes by their state policy environments. States can have a significant influence on the degree to which administrators use culture management strategies to pursue diversity and achievement by setting priorities, offering incentives, and enforcing accountability. The impact of these influences varies as a function of such mission characteristics as selectivity, emphasis on teaching or research, and service area demographics.

STUDENT DIVERSITY IN CONTEXT

In 1986 more than eight out of ten students attending an American college or university were Anglo. In that same year, Anglo enrollment in public schools was about seven in ten. By 2020 the proportion of Anglo school children will decline to one out of two (Palas, Natriello, and McDill 1989). Despite the message in these changing demographics, predominately Anglo, four-year colleges and universities were serving proportionately fewer minority students in 1986 than they were a decade earlier.

Much of the responsibility for this decline in participation rates for African-Americans and American Indians, as well as the failure of Hispanic participation rates to keep pace with their growing presence among high school graduates, must be attributed to initiatives that seek quality by excluding diversity. African-American, Hispanic, and American Indian youth have reading and writing skills substantially below those of Anglo children and are far more likely to drop out of school, especially in the inner cities. Those who do graduate are significantly more likely to attend college after intervening military or work experience. Because proportionately fewer plan, while attending high school, to go to college, they are less likely to take appropriate courses. Because more minorities attend college as adults, the proportions with family and job responsibilities are higher. In 1984 Hispanic and African-American children represented one-quarter of the 0 to 17 age group but one-half of children in poverty. They were disproportionately likely to live with mothers who had not completed high school. More than one-fourth of Hispanic children in public elementary and secondary schools in 1983 spoke a primary language other than English in the home, compared with about 2 percent of all students (Pallas, Natriello, and McDill 1989).

Race or ethnicity is one dimension of student diversity, but it is less important to college success than three other dimensions: (1) preparation, the development of expectations about higher education and participation in experiences that approximate college-going; (2) opportunity orientation, the beliefs students develop about valued adult roles and the part played by education in structuring access to those roles; and (3) mode of college-going, which distinguishes between students who follow traditional full-time patterns of college attendance and those who enter college with adult roles and responsibilities. The particular mix of these characteristics within the minority populations served by an institution has important implications for the student outcomes produced by its organizational culture.

Perhaps the most often cited reason for minority underachievement is lack of preparation. The graduates we talked with explained their difficulty or lack of difficulty in getting a degree in terms of the adequacy of their preparation, but their treatment of the issue was broader than the usual superficial discussion of academic background. From a student perspective, preparation involved complex cognitive, physical, and social aspects of the college-going experience.

Graduates emphasized the importance of developing accurate expectations about course content and necessary academic skills, as well as readiness for the more general cognitive development usually associated with a college education. Preparation to attend a predominantly Anglo university was directly related to family educational experience. Students with the most accurate and detailed expectations came from families where a tradition of college-going already existed. Preparation was also affected by association with present and past college-goers in school, the community, and the workplace. Positive models helped students prepare for the college experience by providing indirect simulation of college-going through the stories they recounted. The more experience that was shared and the more recent the stories, the more specific and accurate students' expectations became.

Many of the graduates we interviewed, especially at selective institutions like UCLA, were second- or third-generation college students and well prepared for most aspects of the academic environments they confronted. Others overcame the trials of first-generation college status and inadequate preparation, but they were more likely to have attended such institutions as UTEP or CSUDH where long-standing commitments to providing opportunities for upwardly mobile first-generation college students provided organizational cultures responsive to the preparations they brought.

For most graduates career opportunities were the primary basis for judging the validity of their college experience. Students devalued "just going to college" as drifting. They advised future students to have a strong goal and not worry about whether they liked the experience itself or whether they encountered discrimination. The graduates knew that, as minorities, they had "beaten the odds" in attaining a college degree and invariably attributed their success to "determination." Unlike many of their contemporaries, they had at some time in their lives accepted a connection between a college degree and their potential for a "good" job. Some had always believed college was the route to employment opportunity, while others adopted this belief later in life as a result of experiences in the workplace or the military.

Yet many minority graduates remained somewhat skeptical about the opportunities associated with college. Some came from communities where a college education was not an important element in becoming an adult and were discouraged by the stories of college graduates they knew who had remained in the same jobs they held before entering college. An American Indian student from New Mexico spoke of the absence of jobs for college-educated people on her reservation. Others, concerned about examples of discrimination in hiring and promotion they had observed or heard about, were uncertain whether college could overcome the negative effects of minority status. An African-American graduate of Wayne State reported persisting despite his family's and his friends' continually telling him he was wasting his time.

The problem of minority underachievement is further complicated by the fact that African-Americans, Hispanics, and American Indians are more likely to attend college in nontraditional ways, while current retention strategies are based largely on traditional concepts of college-going (Tinto 1987). The striking contrasts between traditional and non-traditional modes of college-going evident in our student interviews help to illustrate why differential access to one mode over the other has significant consequences for equity goals and why support strategies based on the traditional mode are ineffective for nontraditional students.

While a number of our interviewees did attend college directly after high school as full-time students with no outside responsibilities, many others described an experience which differed dramatically from this classic picture. These nontraditional students maintained significant outside roles and responsibilities. Their college-going was characterized by shallow connections with the university, complemented by extensive connections with the workplace or the home. For these students, being a college student was just one, and often not the most important, of many roles. As one African-American graduate of Memphis State commented, "I was a full-time student; I was employed full time; and I was a full-time daddy and husband."

Differences in opportunity orientation, preparation, and mode of college-going influence degree attainment rates for all students but impact with particular force on minorities because more attend less competitive high schools, fewer have college-educated parents, and greater proportions find their way into the college experience only after first entering the military or holding a job. All these differences turn out to be significant liabilities in institutions where quality and diversity are perceived as conflicting.

RECONCILING QUALITY AND ACCESS

Quality, as traditionally defined, relies upon admission standards to produce students capable of coping with the demands of an institutional environment designed around the assumption that future students will resemble their predecessors in preparation, opportunity orientation, and mode of college attendance. Colleges and universities operating according to this definition provide quality without access when they waive regular admission requirements for minority students without offering the support services essential to their success.

Access, as traditionally defined, relies upon overall institutional participation rates as the appropriate measure of success in achieving affirmative action goals. Institutions that restrict minority access to high-demand programs and fail to provide the assessment and remediation services necessary to guarantee attainment of equivalent outcomes in all programs provide access without quality. Quality redefined to accommodate the growing diversity that will characterize America's college-going population in the next quarter-century emphasizes teaching and support strategies for promoting comparable achievement among a student body selected to ensure fair representation of all races and ethnic groups. In different ways and from different historical and political contexts, the case studies illustrate the way this process is operating in ten experienced institutions.

2

THE STATE ROLE
IN PROMOTING EQUITY

Higher education is a responsibility of the states, but those concerned with equity issues have focused on federal leadership for most of the past century. The Morrill Act of 1890, closely followed by *Plessy v. Ferguson* six years later, encouraged seventeen states to create the dual systems of public higher education that have figured so prominently in the desegregation actions of the past twenty years. The record of efforts to achieve equal educational opportunity during the past quarter-century is largely the story of Title VI enforcement of the Civil Rights Act of 1964 in only nineteen states (Williams 1988). Most of the policy discussions of minority participation and achievement in higher education have implicitly or explicitly accepted the preeminent role of the federal government (Newman 1985).

A recent report of the State Higher Education Executive Officers represents a significant departure from this perspective. While acknowledging the critical importance of the maintenance of a strong federal role, SHEEO leaders called for the states collectively to assume a larger share of the moral and practical leadership (State Higher Education Executive Officers 1987). Each SHEEO leader was urged to develop and implement a comprehensive and systematic plan based on the needs and deficiencies of their particular state. Among the state actions recommended were:

- Establish the issue as a preeminent concern.
- Remove economic barriers.
- Seek involvement with elementary and secondary education.
- Disseminate information regularly about opportunities for minority students and progress in meeting their needs.
- Search creatively for resources to improve minority programming.
- Ensure that opportunities are available to minorities at both two- and four-year institutions.

The report also included a number of recommendations clearly designed to strengthen the state role in shaping institutional policy toward minority access and achievement in such areas as planning and reporting, assessing students for admission, increasing diversity among professional ranks, and changing institutional environment. Going well beyond the traditional oversight states have exercised for budgets, accounting procedures, purchasing, personnel, and construction, these recommended state interventions also limit unplanned growth and distribute available resources equitably (Millett 1984).

Justification for these proposed measures, already in operation in some states, can be found in the experiences of the past decade. The level of participation in public four-year colleges and universities, never proportional for black, Hispanic, and American Indian students, has either declined or failed to improve as rapidly as high school graduation rates. African-American, Hispanic (except for Cuban-Americans), and American Indian students who do gain admission to traditionally Anglo, four-year institutions lag behind their Anglo classmates in progress toward the baccalaureate.

National statistics understate the changes historically Anglo institutions of higher education must accommodate during the next quarter-century. Eighty percent of degrees earned by African-American, Hispanic, and American Indian students have been awarded by 20 percent of institutions, many of which have historically served a minority clientele (Deskins 1983). Currently, minorities are concentrated in institutions with the fewest resources, and they are less likely to graduate or transfer than their majority colleagues. Within public four-year institutions, responsibilities for educating minority citizens have not been equitably distributed. Many of the more selective institutions enroll small numbers of African-American or Hispanic students and graduate relatively few of those they do enroll.

OVERVIEW OF THE PROBLEM

The shape of the challenge is clear from comparing the composition of the enrollments in public schools with those in colleges and universities. Table 2.1 shows the race and ethnicity of students enrolled in the public schools for the United States and for states participating in the study in fall 1984. All of these students will have completed high school or dropped out by 1996, less than a decade from now. While minorities will constitute "one-third of the nation" shortly after we enter the twenty-first century (Commission on Minority Participation in Education and American Life 1988), the impact will not be felt uniformly across states. Three of the states shown in Table 2.1 had Anglo populations in their public schools in 1984 ranging from 7 to 13 percent above the U.S. average. At the other extreme, three—California, New Mexico, and Texas—already had or were approaching public school systems in which

TABLE 2.1. Fall 1984 Enrollment in Public Schools: Case-Study States
Percentage of Enrollment by Race or Ethnicity

AREA	ANGLO	AFRICAN-AMERICAN	HISPANIC	ASIAN OR FILIPINO	AMERICAN INDIAN
United States	71.2	16.2	9.1	2.5	1.1
California	52.0	10.1	29.2	8.1	0.6
Florida	67.7	23.1	8.1	1.0	0.1
Michigan	79.5	16.7	1.9	0.8	1.0
New Mexico	44.9	2.2	43.4	0.7	8.7
New York	64.4	18.7	13.6	3.2	0.1
Pennsylvania	84.6	12.6	1.6	1.1	0.1
Tennessee	78.5	20.9	0.1	0.5	–
Texas	56.6	13.9	27.9	1.4	0.1

Source: U. S. Department of Education, Office of Civil Rights.

the majority of the students were African-American, Hispanic, Asian-American, and American Indian. There are also marked differences in the composition of minority public school students across states. The rapidly growing Hispanic population is strongly concentrated in four southwestern and western states. While African-Americans remain strongly represented in the public schools of southeastern states, they are also well represented in the more urban midwestern and eastern states such as Illinois, Michigan, New Jersey, and New York.

Comparing public school enrollments for 1984 with the ethnic and racial composition of fall 1986 enrollments in higher education (table 2.2) provides a rough approximation of the changes colleges and universities must accommodate in the next decade if their enrollments are to reflect the composition of public schools 12 years earlier.

In three states African-American and Hispanic students must increase their representation from 17 to 21 percent by 1996 in order to be as well represented in colleges and universities as they were in the public schools more than a decade earlier. Two additional states from this set need changes on the order of 13 to 14 percent. The remaining three need changes of approximately 7 percent. Table 2.2 understates the changes needed because the data include community colleges and historically black institutions which currently bear a disproportionate share of the responsibility for educating African-American, Hispanic, and American Indian students in many states.

The problem is not exclusively or perhaps even primarily educational. To the extent that socioeconomic inequalities are defined as an educational problem, the roots are clearly in the public schools. Higher education is involved to the extent that it serves either as part of the problem or as part of the solution. Quite clearly, colleges and universi-

TABLE 2.2. Fall 1986 Enrollment in Higher Education: Case-Study States *Percentage of Enrollment by Race or Ethnicity Compared to Fall 1984 Public School Enrollments*

	ENROLLMENT IN HIGHER EDUCATION				
AREA	Anglo	Black	Hispanic	Asian or Filipino	American Indian
United States	81.6	8.9	5.1	3.7	0.7
	(+10.4)	(−7.3)	(−4.0)	(+1.2)	(+0.4)
California	68.6	7.0	11.6	11.5	1.2
	(+16.0)	(−3.1)	(−17.6)	(+3.4)	(+0.6)
Florida	78.3	9.6	10.3	1.6	0.3
	(+10.6)	(−13.5)	(+2.2)	(+0.6)	(+0.2)
Michigan	87.0	9.2	1.3	1.4	0.6
	(+7.5)	(−7.5)	(−0.6)	(+0.6)	(−0.4)
New Mexico	63.9	2.4	26.2	1.2	6.3
	(+19.0)	(+0.2)	(−17.2)	(+0.5)	(−1.7)
New York	77.5	11.3	6.9	3.7	0.5
	(+13.1)	(−7.4)	(−6.7)	(+0.5)	(+0.4)
Pennsylvania	90.6	6.6	1.0	1.6	0.2
	(+6.0)	(−6.0)	(−0.6)	(−0.5)	(+0.1)
Tennessee	84.0	14.3	0.8	0.7	0.2
	(+5.5)	(−6.6)	(+0.7)	(+0.2)	(+0.2)
Texas	72.3	8.9	15.7	2.8	0.3
	(+15.7)	(−5.0)	(−12.2)	(+1.4)	(+0.2)

Source: National Center for Education Statistics, *Digest of Education Statistics*, 1988, tables 38 and 149. U.S. Department of Education, Office of Educational Research and Improvement.

Note: Figures in parentheses indicate comparative (plus or minus) public school enrollments.

ties have served in the last quarter-century both as promoters of upward mobility and as defenders of prevailing social privilege.

Policy issues surrounding higher education access and outcomes are further complicated by differences within minority groups. Asian-Americans outperform all other groups. Yet many of them resent the characterization of "model minority" and correctly point to recent immigrant groups that exhibit many of the same problems experienced by some African-Americans and Hispanics. In Florida, Cuban Hispanics have higher participation and graduation rates than Anglos. African-American immigrants from Africa or the Caribbean and those whose parents graduated from college perform in ways not significantly different from the majority population. And the educational experiences of American Indians from the urban Northeast have little in common with their counterparts from rural western reservations.

State policy initiatives during the past quarter-century reflect the difficulties in characterizing and understanding the correlates of minority status. They also reflect the problems inherent in devising public policy that improves opportunities for some to the possible detriment of others. Hsia (1987) has focused the dilemma. Should public policy aim for equality of educational opportunity or for distributive justice? Equality of educational opportunity is a concept that links access to academic qualifications without making allowances for race or ethnicity. Distributive justice, by contrast, seeks proportional representation among minority groups as its operational measure.

Anglo and minority children with educated parents, those who reside in affluent school districts, and minorities from high-performing groups are the principal beneficiaries of policies emphasizing equality of educational opportunity. Groups traditionally underrepresented in higher education benefit the most from policies based on distributive justice. Before 1965 meritocratic criteria largely determined access to most of higher education. The creation of open-door community colleges as the major access point for populations previously excluded or underserved was, in the minds of most policymakers, a major effort to give greater attention to distributive justice. The development of state and federal need-based financial aid programs also promoted values related to distributive justice since African-Americans, Hispanics, and American Indians were more likely to meet the eligibility criteria than Anglos or Asian-Americans. Both of these strategies were distinguished by their "color-free" character, an important political consideration in gaining public support.

The policy of designating one set of public institutions to pursue distributive justice, while maintaining a second relatively free to pursue the meritocratic principles of equality of educational opportunity, has produced system discontinuties which now threaten public policy goals in states undergoing significant demographic change (Brint and Karabel 1989). The stable or declining minority enrollments of the 1980s, the troubled transfer function in the community colleges most frequently attended by minorities, the failure of graduation statistics to keep pace with minority enrollment increases, and the continuing concentration of African-Americans, Hispanics, and American Indians in institutions with the fewest resources suggest that all institutions need to pursue both equality of educational opportunity and distributive justice.

What is the appropriate balance between equality of educational opportunity and distributive justice? What kinds of goals should states establish with respect to each? What is the role of colleges and universities in state efforts to achieve such goals? How can progress toward their attainment be reasonably estimated? What are the policy options that might encourage all institutions to emphasize both quality and diversity? In this chapter and the next we will explore some of the possible answers to these questions, using as our frame of reference the conceptual scheme outlined in chapter 1 and the experiences of the ten case-study institutions reported in chapters 4 to 13.

DEFINING AND ASSESSING STATE OUTCOMES

Any policy approach that seeks to improve educational opportunities for underserved minority students presumes the existence of a method for assessing current status and keeping track of improvements. While fair outcome goals must remain proportional representation and comparable achievement (any alternative would imply implicit recognition of race and ethnicity as legitimate determinants of educational opportunity and achievement), many of the variables that contribute to current differences are not under the control of institutions of higher education or the state agencies that oversee them. Even though it is tempting to place the blame at lower levels of the educational system or elsewhere in society, colleges and universities can make their most important contribution to equity by working with the variables they control.

Two separate indicators are needed to measure state or institutional progress toward fair outcomes. The first is an estimate of the differences between majority and minority participation rates. The second is an estimate of differences in graduation rates attributable to the effects of race and ethnicity. Both indicators need to be assessed over time to provide trend information to help policy leaders set attainable goals, assess progress, and determine the need for corrective actions.

As part of the study described in chapter 1, we have been working on indicators to permit tracking progress across states and across institutions using data collected by the National Center for Educational Statistics. Since 1966 most colleges and universities have periodically provided race- and ethnicity-specific data on enrollments and graduates, first through the Higher Education General Information Survey (HEGIS), and more recently through the Integrated Postsecondary Education Data System (IPEDS). While the HEGIS data base is flawed by missing and inaccurate information, it is the only record we have of institutional and state performance during the most important period in the history of higher education for equity objectives.

The process of constructing and interpreting equity scores from an existing data base not designed for this purpose is highly complex. Comparing scores across states is like comparing golf scores without information about players' handicaps. Florida is home to a high-performing Cuban Hispanic population whose educational attainments exceed those of their Anglo counterparts. California's population includes many Hispanics who lack the preparation and orientation of the Cuban Hispanic population. Given the same level of effort, the two states may achieve significantly different outcomes. Most southern states rely heavily on historically black institutions to achieve very respectable participation and graduation rates, an alternative that is not available in most northern states. State equity scores are most useful in tracking progress over time within the same state. Comparisons across states should be interpreted with caution.

The information in tables 2.3 and 2.4 was developed using data from HEGIS and the U.S. Bureau of the Census for the period 1980–1986. The African-American Equity Score for Enrollment was calculated for each state by dividing the proportion of African-American students in public four-year institutions in 1986 by the proportion of African-Americans in the population estimates for 1985. A score of 100 indicates "proportional representation," meaning that in 1986 African-Americans were as well (or better) represented among four-year college students as among the estimated population for the state.

The African-American Equity Score for Graduation was calculated by dividing the proportion of African-Americans who graduated from public four-year colleges in a state in 1986 by the proportion present in the undergraduate student bodies of the same institutions four years earlier. A score of 100 indicates "comparable achievement," meaning that African-Americans were as well (or better) represented among graduating seniors in 1984 as among undergraduate students in the same institutions four years earlier.

Similar calculations were done for Hispanics and American Indians and are shown in tables 2.3 and 2.4 as Hispanic or American Indian Equity Scores for Enrollment or Graduation. Progress toward proportional representation for the period 1980–1986 among public four-year colleges and universities within the study states is placed in sharper perspective by table 2.3.

This table understates the need for improved access to most majority four-year institutions in several of these states because the data include historically black institutions which in southern and some border states enroll one-third or more of all African-American students. In Tennessee, for example, the Desegregation Monitoring Committee reported that 36 percent of African-American undergraduates enrolled in public colleges and universities in fall 1985 attended historically black Tennessee State University (TSU). For the preceding year TSU awarded 28 percent of the baccalaureates earned by African-Americans from public institutions in the state.

The data in table 2.3 reflect the national experience for this period (Wilson and Melendez 1987), but there were important differences among states and across populations. African-American students lost ground during these six years in seven of the eight states. Gains in participation were recorded only in New Mexico, where African-Americans represented less than 2 percent of the population. Only California lost ground with Hispanics, and the decline was largely a function of rapid growth in representation (in 1980, Hispanics constituted 19 percent of the population; in 1985, 22 percent). New Mexico, the only state where American Indians exceeded 1 percent of public school enrollments, experienced an increase in representation during the period, but American Indians remained significantly underenrolled in 1986.

TABLE 2.3. Fall 1980 and 1986 Equity Scores for College Enrollment:
Case-Study States
(A Score of 100 Indicates Proportional Enrollment)

| | AFRICAN-AMERICAN | | HISPANIC | | AMERICAN INDIAN | |
STATE	1980	1986	1980	1986	1980	1986
California	86	61	43	40	100	100
Florida	76	62	67	89	50	50
Michigan	62	54	51	69	100	100
New Mexico	100	100	71	71	31	44
New York	45	37	22	25[a]	100	100
Pennsylvania	100	83	69	70	100	100
Tennessee	94	88	49	100	100	100
Texas	72	68	54	63	100	71

Source: The equity scores were calculated by the authors utilizing HEGIS data (as explained
in text) and census data. All the 1980 scores used data from the 1980 census (as cited).
For 1986, American Indian scores also used the 1980 data. However, African-American
and Hispanic 1986 scores utilized population estimates from the following source: U.S.
Bureau of the Census, *Current Population Reports*. Series P-25, No. 1040-RD-1, "Population Estimates by Race and Hispanic Origin for States, Metropolitan Areas, and Selected
Countries: 1980 to 1985," pp. 11, 50.

[a] These equity scores should be interpreted with caution because of reporting practices
in the City University of New York during this period.

Low participation rates for all groups and losses in proportional
representation by the African-American population are in themselves
adequate causes for concern. An equally critical part of the problem,
however, is revealed by examination of graduation rates for the same
period. Table 2.4 reports an estimate of the extent to which African-
Americans, Hispanics, and American Indians earned baccalaureate degrees in 1980 and 1986 as a function of their participation rates four
years earlier. For this ratio the numerator was the proportion of a particular racial or ethnic group earning a degree in a given year and the
denominator was the proportion represented in the undergraduate student population four years earlier. Undergraduate enrollment was used
rather than first-time-in-any-college (FTIAC) freshmen, to take into consideration the substantial numbers of transfer students present in the
public four-year institutions of most states. While the equity graduation
scores in table 2.4 should not be interpreted as cohort survival rates,
the method used in calculating the scores yields results similar to institutional studies of graduation rates where these extend over six years
or more.

Only New York appeared to have better graduation rates for African-
American students in 1986 than 1980, and this change is impossible to

TABLE 2.4. Fall 1980 and 1986 Equity Scores for Graduation:
Case-Study States
(*A Score of 100 Indicates Proportional Graduation*)

STATE	AFRICAN-AMERICAN		HISPANIC		AMERICAN INDIAN	
	1980	1986	1980	1986	1980	1986
California	65	45	87	83	92	72
Florida	70	58	100	100	78	77
Michigan	60	55	85	99	67	74
New Mexico	72	87	84	88	99	94
New York	59	66[a]	63	100[a]	100	71[a]
Pennsylvania	67	55	25	83	82	30
Tennessee	84	62	100	100	100	61
Texas	59	58	92	87	99	81

[a] These equity scores should be interpreted with caution because of reporting practices in the City University of New York during this period.

interpret because of the reporting practices at City University of New York (CUNY) during this period. All others reported declines, some of which were very large. The situation was very different for Hispanics, with most of the states reporting results that approached parity. From tables 2.3 and 2.4, as well as the data analyzed for chapter 14, it was apparent that the problem for Hispanics is primarily one of access, while the problem for African-Americans involves both access and achievement. New Mexico, the only state with an American Indian population of 1 percent or greater, experienced a modest decline in graduation rates. The problem for American Indians who have not been assimilated into non-reservation populations appears to involve both access and achievement, as it does for African-Americans.

While some of these differences can be explained by the populations served or the presence of historically black institutions, case-study data suggests that other influences were at work as well. How can states convince their colleges and universities that improving minority participation and graduation rates ought to be high on institutional agendas? What changes in mission emphasis need to occur if all institutions are to share responsibility for access and quality? What accountability measures are needed to reward success and discourage failure? Who are the important state actors and what range of actions can they reasonably take without sacrificing an appropriate balance between institutional autonomy and institutional accountability? Possible answers to these questions are suggested by an overview of the experiences of the eight states on which our study focused. In chapter 14 these experiences are presented in greater detail as part of a suggested framework for state self-assessment.

SHAPING INSTITUTIONAL AGENDAS

The final report of the Carnegie Council on Policy Studies in Higher Education underscored the fundamental dilemma states face in trying to foster greater institutional responsiveness to changing demographics and economic development. Colleges and universities prize historic continuity, as evidenced by the fact that 62 of the 66 institutions that have been preserved in recognizable form since 1530 are universities. But as the council noted, colleges and universities do change and the process is instructive (Carnegie Council on Policy Studies in Higher Education 1980).

Public higher education is a resource-dependent enterprise. In 1984–1985 slightly more than 45 percent of the current fund revenues of public institutions of higher education came from the states, almost all in the form of appropriations for salaries, operating support, and capital projects. In that same year the federal government provided less than 11 percent of current fund revenues, but almost two-thirds of that amount was in the form of restricted grants and contracts excluding Pell funding[1] (U.S. Department of Education 1986). These figures suggest that it might not be too great an oversimplification to conclude that states have funded historic continuity while the federal government has concentrated on change. Students, whose tuition payments produced 15 percent of the revenues for the same period, also influence priorities by "voting with their feet," but they can vote only for the choices available.

It is against this largely passive state role in determining higher education priorities that the 1987 SHEEO report speaks. States can promote the inclusion of new clientele through the educational opportunity programs many have initiated. They can alter the ground rules for assessment of outcomes and eligibility to advance to junior standing as demonstrated in Florida, Texas, and elsewhere. They can challenge their institutions to improve undergraduate instruction and minority services as in Tennessee. They can require information about institutional progress toward achieving equity objectives and they can make that information publicly available, as in California and Texas. They may not win many awards for popularity from institutions in the process.

College and university leaders prefer to establish institutional priorities through administrative interpretation of institutional mission. They seek appropriations based on negotiated formulas that allow broad discretion in use of available resources. They respond most readily to new priorities accompanied by new funding which is designed ultimately to be subsumed within the base. Administrators, with the full support of their faculties, resist assessments designed to measure their progress

---

1. Pell grants succeeded the Basic Educational Opportunity Grants as the primary need-based federal financial aid program for college students.

toward achieving state priorities, particularly when these involve comparisons with other institutions. They actively dislike schemes that link funding support to attainment of prescribed outcomes, as in Tennessee's performance funding program. None of these preferences are in themselves wrong or bad. In aggregate they protect institutional autonomy at the expense of limiting the impact of state actions designed to cause institutional change. That is, of course, their intended purpose.

The development of new institutions is an unlikely scenario in most states, so added importance will attach to changing existing institutions to make them more responsive to diversity. Attempts to improve student preparation probably need to begin earlier and to involve much greater interinstitutional cooperation. While the emphasis on removing economic barriers through need-based student financial aid will remain a key component of any effort to improve equity outcomes, the major gains from this strategy have probably already been recorded.

The actions states take to increase the attentiveness of their public institutions to issues involving minority participation and achievement can be divided into four major categories. The first involves identifying state priorities and planning in ways that create a public policy agenda. The second is concerned with use of inducements and capacity building to systematically alter faculty and administrative priorities and their professional preparation for addressing new issues. The third has to do with mandating programs and practices designed to address the consequences of past discrimination. The fourth relates to use of evaluation and accountability measures to inform coordinating and governing boards as well as the general public of institutional progress toward achieving priorities.[2] The same four categories apply whether the priority is economic development or minority participation and achievement.

States vary in their arrangements for coordinating and governing public higher education. In Florida a single governing board provides administrative oversight and coordination for the state's public four-year colleges and universities. In Michigan the coordination that occurs is largely voluntary. Where statewide coordinating or governing boards are absent or weak, the responsibility for carrying out state priorities falls to institutional governing boards. The ability of these boards to support state priorities can be problematic if the priorities run counter to the preferences of the senior administrators they employ. While no one has been able to demonstrate convincingly the superiority of any particular approach to state governance, it is clear that the process of getting institutions to cooperate in achievement of state priorities is dif-

2. This classification of state actions draws upon a conceptual scheme suggested by Lorraine M. McDonnell in "Policy Design as Instrument Design," a paper delivered at the Annual Meeting of the American Political Science Association, Washington, D.C., September 1988, as well as on our analysis of the range of policy actions exhibited by the case-study states.

ferent in Michigan and in Florida. Any attempt to define and implement systematic strategies to improve institutional performance in specified areas must take into account differences in state governance arrangements.

The character of the state policy environment for minority participation and achievement varied dramatically among the study states, as did the governance arrangements. In Michigan and New Mexico the responsibility for determining appropriate levels of participation rests with the institutions and their respective governing boards. By contrast, a combination of legislation and court decrees has charged public institutions in Florida, Texas, and Tennessee with specific responsibilities for increasing minority participation. New York, Pennsylvania, Tennessee, Texas, and California provide extensive need-based student financial assistance programs augmented by opportunity programs providing counseling, academic support, and cultural activities.

State policies designed to strengthen quality also influence access. In Pennsylvania, Michigan, California, and New Mexico quality is the responsibility of individual institutions and their respective governing boards. Mission differentiation and admission standards are the major strategies for improving quality. In Florida, New York, Texas, Tennessee, and some other states, admissions criteria and mission differentiation are augmented by statewide efforts to assure quality by assessing entry and exit competencies. All except Florida also fund remedial work in baccalaureate-granting institutions.

The emphasis a state places on articulation between baccalaureate-granting institutions and other segments of education, especially two-year colleges where minority students are overrepresented, also has important consequences for diversity. Transfer between two- and four-year institutions in New Mexico and Pennsylvania is governed solely by voluntary articulation agreements individually negotiated between pairs of institutions. In Florida a statewide agreement addresses the status of transfer students with associate degrees, course numbering, academic calendars, and the desired distribution of baccalaureate students between two- and four-year public institutions. Students experience fewer problems in transferring in Florida than they do in New Mexico and Pennsylvania.

Some states have also emphasized articulation with primary and secondary schools. In Tennessee the educational competencies required by entry-level college courses have been defined and articulated with the K-12 sector. Results of assessment tests of educational competencies of entering college students, as well as their subsequent performance, are reported to the high schools from which students graduated.

States also vary in the information available for monitoring minority participation and achievement. While policymakers in Michigan and Pennsylvania had information related to state funding formulas, they did not make use of it to produce regularly available reports on student participation or achievement by race and ethnicity. In New York City there were no current data on minority participation and graduation rates except for occasional studies based on samples. By contrast, state agencies in California, Tennessee, Texas, and Florida routinely maintained and disseminated information on institutional progress in meeting affirmative action goals for students, faculty, and administrators. In Tennessee the information was used in the state's performance funding program.

State-funded, need-based student financial assistance also contributes to the environment for diversity and achievement, as does tuition policy. Where test scores are used to award merit scholarships, few go to African-Americans, Hispanics, and American Indians unless scores are adjusted to qualify the same proportion of students from each racial or ethnic group, as is done in Tennessee. Finally, the presence of public, historically minority institutions in close proximity to majority institutions influences both participation and graduation rates. Several states in this study, through legislative or judicial actions, responded to the presence of historically minority institutions by encouraging or mandating cooperative or shared programs (Florida and Pennsylvania), by incorporating historically minority institutions into systems that included both minority and majority institutions (Texas), and by merging historically white and black institutions (Tennessee).

A STATE AGENDA FOR IMPROVED EQUITY

State policymakers act by establishing priorities, offering incentives, mandating actions, and instituting accountability measures to encourage or require institutions to change their practices and outcomes. In many of the study states, statements from chief executives, legislative resolutions, and incentive funding measures sent the clear message that improved minority participation and achievement were among the criteria by which institutional effectiveness would be judged. Executive and legislative concerns for fair outcomes received the most attention in states in which coordinating and/or governing boards reinforced them by setting priorities, monitoring outcomes, and tying resource allocation to the adequacy of institutional planning.

States move toward achievement of equity goals in higher education as they convince their institutions that removing race and ethnicity as a factor in participation and graduation should be an important concern for everyone. The first step is simple. Someone to whom institutions listen must say that equity is important and attainable. The initiator can be a governor, the legislature, or a coordinating or governing board. Because influences are cumulative, ideally all three deliver the same message.

Once equity has been defined as a priority, the methods for its attainment are not fundamentally different from those used to achieve other priorities. Because there are many actors who must coordinate their efforts, planning is essential, as is good information. A governor, a legislator, or board members can reasonably require development of a plan that provides at a minimum current status, proposed objectives, strategies for achieving them, time lines, and estimated costs. The process of developing a plan should include participation by those upon whose efforts the plan's success will ultimately depend. Particularly important is strong involvement from the minority community to ensure that their aspirations and frustrations push institutional planners beyond the "safe objectives" they might otherwise prefer.

The most important contribution of the plan is to provide state policymakers and institutional representatives with a sense of the range of variables that must be addressed in a systematic way if results are to equal expectations. The plan also provides a framework within which governors, legislators, board members, and institutional staffs can cooperate effectively. Governors can ensure that the issue remains high on the public agenda and receives appropriate consideration in budget development. Legislators can fund interventions aimed at getting selective institutions to become more concerned about diversity and open-access institutions to give greater attention to academic achievement for all students. Coordinating and governing boards can develop accountability measures to promote an appropriate balance between quality and diversity in all institutions and to ensure that administrators and the institutions they lead make acceptable progress toward planned objectives.

Colleges and universities must admit and graduate more minority students without compromising standards in order to satisfy state and national requirements for a trained work force and a cohesive society. The lack of progress during the past decade suggests the need for a more active state role in defining minority achievement as a priority and in monitoring institutional progress toward its attainment. The strategies through which a more active state role can be implemented without excessive interference in institutional governance can be discovered by observing the experiences of states that have already wrestled with the issue. Creative alternatives must be found to accommodate differences among the states in governance patterns, but little remains to be invented.

3

INSTITUTIONAL CLIMATE AND MINORITY ACHIEVEMENT

THE MODEL APPLIED TO THE CASE-STUDY INSTITUTIONS

In the early stages of our work we searched for model interventions and committed leadership. But faculty and staff at some institutions were surprised to learn their institution was doing better than others and were unable to identify special practices that might account for their success. In other apparently successful institutions, leadership was described as ambivalent about minority initiatives and concerned about the adverse impact on reputation of too much success in attracting a more diverse clientele.

The search for patterns that might explain success in graduating minority students revealed considerable diversity across the ten institutions. Some appeared to be successful because they attracted well-prepared minority students who, with fairly limited assistance, overcame gaps in academic preparation and feelings of marginality and cultural isolation. In others, a multicultural environment and extensive support services helped very diverse students achieve respectable graduation rates. In a few, strong state and system interventions seemed to explain outcomes better than institutional practices or administrative commitment.

The response of public institutions to pressures for greater diversity is influenced by mission, selectivity, and proximity to minority population centers. Comprehensive teaching-oriented institutions, especially those in multicultural settings, have priorities and enrollment pressures that enhance their readiness for working with students who need help in learning. Established research universities with high selectivity search for well-prepared minority students whom they expect to succeed with little assistance beyond the standard learning format available to all students. Part of their investment in this approach is philosophical: university students should be well prepared and self-directing. And part is practical: improvements in the learning environment come at the expense of resources otherwise directed to the support of research. Research universities of low selectivity with a long-standing commitment to diversity may rely on selectivity in high-demand majors and differential attrition rates to preserve acceptable academic standards. Because such universities have high participation rates, they may escape the pressures experienced by other research universities in the absence of state monitoring of graduation rates by major. Institutions that serve commuting populations depend primarily on their academic environments to help minority students achieve, since that is the only aspect of the institution most encounter with any regularity.

By 1980, California State University, Dominguez Hills (CSUDH), a small teaching-oriented institution with low selectivity, had achieved proportional representation for all groups except Hispanics and comparable graduation rates among all groups. It was regarded within the California State University system as an institution with quality problems. Since 1980, quality initiatives have reduced graduation rates while participation rates have been maintained.

Wayne State University and the University of New Mexico, research institutions with low selectivity, have faced fewer pressures to address the achievement side of adaptation because they have had high minority participation rates in states where lack of monitoring information, along with weak or nonexistent coordinating structures, have left institutions free to determine their own priorities. In contrast, the comprehensive or doctorate-granting universities with medium to low selectivity—Florida International University (FIU), University of Texas at El Paso (UTEP), and Memphis State University (MSU)—have given greater attention to achievement strategies, partly because of local and state pressures.

Brooklyn College of the City University of New York and the University of California at Los Angeles (UCLA), as highly selective institutions, have both benefitted from systemwide strategies to improve participation rates. Brooklyn, as a teaching-oriented institution, has easily adapted in ways that enable it to increase graduation rates, while research-oriented UCLA has developed extensive support programs to address race and ethnicity-related disparities in achievement. Temple and Florida State University (FSU), research-oriented institutions with moderate selectivity, have used strategies similar to those at UCLA. Florida State has the added advantage of a largely residential campus. Substantial resources and solid reputations have contributed to the adaptation process in these four institutions. State or system influences have also been important.

Minority representation, socioeconomic status, and participation in civic and business activity in the service areas from which commuting institutions draw the majority of their students also influence the process of institutional adaptation. In Miami and El Paso, dynamic local economies provide employment opportunities for Hispanics attending FSU and UTEP. Although such opportunities may compete with college attendance in the short run, they also contribute to formation of positive attitudes about the relationship between education and a rewarding career. The economies of Memphis and Detroit are less dynamic, as reflected in unemployment patterns, the incomes of college graduates, and the attitudes toward the value of a college education among the graduates we interviewed.

African-American students are heavily dependent on public schools, many of which enroll few nonminority students. When public schools are inadequate, discrepancies in academic preparation must be corrected through remedial work in the university, contributing to the temptation for faculty members to view increases in minority enrollments as threats to quality. In Memphis, where the public schools were described as "improving" after the disrupting effects of desegregation, one in four white students attended a private secondary school. The ratio for African-Americans was one in fifty. In Detroit all but two highly selective public high schools were described in the case study as "terribly deficient." Both Wayne State and Memphis State drew most of their freshmen from local schools.

While the institutions in our study tried to eliminate problems of underpreparation and uncertain objectives before students showed up on campus, many also worked to change their organizational cultures to help the more diversely prepared student meet institutional expectations for an educated person.

INSTITUTIONAL ADAPTATION IN CONTEXT

The process leading to greater emphasis on minority access followed three differing scenarios among case-study institutions. In several the change was abrupt and far-reaching. Florida State and Memphis State, previously segregated institutions, enrolled their first African-American students. California State University, Dominguez Hills, a new institution apparently headed for the suburban seclusion of the Palos Verde peninsula, suddenly found itself in the heart of a heavily minority population basin, partly as a result of the Watts riots. Brooklyn College of the City University of New York, along with its sister institutions, experienced the revolutionary effects of open admissions in 1970. Even when the university was forced to retreat from open admissions for financial reasons, revised admissions procedures guaranteed continuing participation for previously underrepresented groups.

UCLA, FIU, and UTEP experienced significant but evolutionary change. At UCLA a combination of student activism, legislative mandates, and system pressures kept affirmative action consistently on the institutional agenda from the early 1960s to the present. Florida International University, from its authorization in 1965, was expected to respond to a Cuban Hispanic exile population that prized education and was among the most culturally and economically advanced in the western hemisphere. Like UCLA, UTEP has been the target of student and community activism, as well as state initiatives stemming from court-mandated and voluntary efforts to desegregate the state's systems of colleges and universities.

At Wayne state, Temple University, and the University of New Mexico, the social context has changed more slowly. Because of location and admission policies these three institutions have had environments more consistently receptive to minority student participation than most other institutions in the study. Both Wayne State and Temple have long-standing commitments to working-class students with widely varying levels of preparation. The University of New Mexico, described in the case study as a "multicultural institution in a multicultural state," operated under virtually an open-admissions policy until very recently. Partly because of success in providing access, the pressures on these three institutions to improve minority achievement have been more recent and less systematic than those influencing other institutions in the study.

ASSESSING OUTCOMES AS INDICATORS OF ORGANIZATIONAL CULTURE

Against what standards should institutions be assessed in determining their relative contributions to state equity objectives? The Ohio Board of Regents (1988) has argued that the goals should be proportional enrollment and comparable achievement, the outcomes specified by our model. To argue otherwise requires defense of the proposition that race and ethnicity should be factors in determining who goes to college and where.

Proportional enrollment occurs when minorities are as well represented in a college-going population as they are in the larger base from which that population is drawn. The base can be defined as the adult population of a service area or a state, or more restrictively as the population of 18- to 24-year-old high school graduates. Comparable achievement occurs when minorities are as well represented among the baccalaureate graduates of an institution as they are among its undergraduate students. Taken together, these two measures suggest a way of estimating the culture of an institution by considering how far it has progressed toward the ideal. Rough estimates of participation and achievement can be calculated by using census data and the information institutions have been providing to the federal government since 1966 in a way similar to the calculations used to generate equity scores for enrollment and for graduation for states in chapter 2.

Given the necessary data, any institution can be categorized in terms of its progress toward proportional representation and comparable achievement for any racial or ethnic group. Because of the difficulty in determining appropriate service area demographics for public institutions located in metropolitan settings, we have used the proportions enrolled in 1980 and 1986 as the measure of institutional progress. We have also provided state demographics for both years, but the proposition that the contributions of Wayne State or Memphis State to equity should be judged on the basis of state demographics rather than those of their surrounding metropolitan statistical areas appears questionable.

We have calculated equity scores for graduation for each public college and university in the United States for the period 1980–1986 by dividing the proportion of African-Americans and Hispanics in the 1980 and 1986 graduating classes by the proportion in the undergraduate student body four years earlier. The methodology is based on the premise that an institution with comparable achievement for its minority students should have a graduating class in any given year that resembles in composition its undergraduate student body four years earlier. As was true for the state equity scores, 100 indicates comparable graduation. A score of 50 suggests that African-Americans or Hispanics were only half as likely to enroll or to graduate as Anglo and Asian-American students.

Table 3.1 provides the results of this assessment for African-American students for the case-study institutions. Table 3.2 provides comparable information on Hispanic participation and achievement for the same institutions, excluding Tennessee where the representation of Hispanics is less than half of 1 percent.

TABLE 3.1. African-American Participation and Achievement: Case-Study Institutions
A Comparison of Equity Outcomes Using 1980 and 1986 HEGIS Data

INSTITUTION	ENROLLMENT (%)		GRADUATION EQUITY SCORE		STATE (%)	
	1980	1986	1980	1986	1980	1985
UNM	2	1	49	99	2	2
FIU	9	7	63	59	14	14
Temple	20	14	61	64	9	9
Wayne	27	25	77	62	13	14
MSU	19	19	89	66	16	14
FSU	10	7	98	50	14	16
UCLA	6	6	57	75	8	8
Brooklyn	23	21	100	100[a]	14	15
CSUDH	40	35	100	71	8	8
UTEP	2	2	100	88	12	12

[a] Calculated from data furnished by the institutions.

TABLE 3.2. Hispanic Participation and Achievement: Case-Study Institutions
A Comparison of Equity Outcomes Using 1980 and 1986 HEGIS Data

	ENROLLMENT (%)		GRADUATION EQUITY SCORE		STATE (%)	
INSTITUTION	1980	1986	1980	1986	1980	1985
UNM	23	23	85	84	37	38
FIU	32	38	100	100	9	10
Temple	2	2	31	48	1	1
Wayne	2	2	76	60	2	2
FSU	2	3	100	100	9	10
UCLA	6	11	72	100	19	22
Brooklyn	7	9	100	100[a]	9	11
UTEP	44	54	100	100	21	23
CSUDH	10	11	100	100	19	22

[a] Calculated from data furnished by the institution.

The cases have been organized within the tables according to where they seem to fall along the stage continuum presented in the model outlined in chapter 1. The first six appear to be predominantly reactive/strategic, while the last four seem more on the strategic/adaptive side of the continuum. This judgment was made primarily on the basis of the culture management strategies at work and the relative influence of student affairs–coordinated interventions as distinct from those that involved the academic program and faculty.

The University of New Mexico and Florida International, presented in chapters 4 and 5, achieve much of their success as a result of the Hispanic populations they serve and their multicultural environments. There is relatively little evidence, however, that these two institutions have employed strategic planning to extend the benefits of their environments to the American Indian population in the case of UNM or the African-American population in the case of Florida International.

Temple, Wayne State, and Memphis State (chapters 6 to 8) serve large African-American populations as a function of their locations and because of their commitment. In each, however, the institutional approach seems to place greater emphasis on participation than on achievement. The differences in outcomes seem more a function of populations served than differences in institutional approach. Florida State (chapter 9) might be grouped with either cluster of institutions, but declining participation and graduation rates for African-Americans would suggest that the linkage between FSU's largely student affairs–led interventions and the demands of the academic program remain tenuous.

UCLA and Brooklyn College (chapters 10 and 11), in contrast, focused most of their attention during the study on addressing the transition between extensive support strategies, the content and structure of academic programming, and the involvement of faculty. California State University, Dominguez Hills and the University of Texas at El Paso (chapters 12 and 13), both institutions in which Anglo students now represent less than a majority, seemed to have moved furthest toward the adaptive stage. In these institutions, strategic planning and comprehensive learning strategies complemented a multicultural environment.

Despite the rationale presented above, the order in which the cases are presented is somewhat arbitrary. All ten institutions were chosen because of their track records for graduating students from underrepresented groups. All furnished positive environments for minority achievement. The order of presentation was selected primarily to assist in communicating how the model functions rather than as an exercise in hairsplitting to overemphasize modest differences in institutional approaches. All the universities studied make important contributions to knowledge of how institutions adapt to improve the environments they provide for minority achievement without sacrificing appropriate concerns for maintaining quality.

The data presented in tables 3.1 and 3.2 suggest that there is more reason for optimism about improving outcomes for Hispanics than for African-Americans, a view that was shared by some of the state policy leaders with whom we talked. Five of the six institutions serving African-American student populations of 10 percent or more in 1980 experienced declining participation by 1986. The lone exception, Memphis State, maintained its proportional representation during the period. Graduation equity scores declined significantly at Memphis State and in three of the other five institutions enrolling more than 10 percent African-Americans in 1986.

The case-study institutions are by no means exceptions to the national experience during the past decade, as suggested by the aggregate data for the study states presented in chapter 2. The decline in African-American participation rates in predominantly Anglo institutions has not resulted in improved graduation rates for the ones who remain. Among institutions enrolling 5 percent or more African-Americans, only at highly selective UCLA and Brooklyn College did graduation rates stay the same or improve. And only at these institutions were African-Americans even 75 percent as likely to graduate as their Anglo counterparts. While we have shown data for UNM and UTEP, the graduation scores must be interpreted with caution because of the small numbers.

The situation for Hispanics is very different. Their presence in seven of the study states increased by at least 1 percent between 1980 and 1986. In five of these states, increases in representation in the case study institutions matched or exceeded increases in the state population figures. None of the case-study institutions lost Hispanic participation.

Even more impressive, graduation rates were at parity in six of the ten institutions by 1986. The rate declined significantly in only one institution, Wayne State, where this result must be attributed in part to small numbers. Hispanic participation, unlike that of African-Americans, is increasing, dramatically so in some institutions. And in most institutions, increased participation translates into improved graduation rates as well. Again, these results are consistent with those reported for all public institutions in the study states in the preceding chapter. The results for American Indians living in states with large reservations are very similar to those for African-Americans.

The difference in equity patterns suggests that the changes in organizational culture required to achieve optimal results with American Indians and African-Americans may differ in emphasis from those most effective with Hispanics. Put somewhat differently, institutions that achieved good results with African-American students also achieved good results with Hispanics, although the reverse was not necessarily true, as evidenced by Florida State and Florida International.

INTERVENTIONS: VISIBLE EVIDENCE
OF ORGANIZATIONAL CULTURE

Administrators adopt interventions to preserve an equilibrium between the results their institutions produce and the outcomes those who provide resources expect. In terms of often conflicting pressures for access and quality, an organizational culture is "in equilibrium" when the emphasis placed on student diversity is matched by the emphasis on student achievement. Cultures in a state of equilibrium produce acceptable results for the racial and ethnic groups they serve because their learning environments are a reasonable match for the students they admit. Institutions may achieve or maintain equilibrium by developing interventions to help diverse student populations achieve, as in the case of CSUDH and UTEP. Alternatively, more selective institutions maintain equilibrium with low minority participation levels by excluding students whose opportunity orientations and preparation are not a good match for their environments.

When institutions are pressured by internal commitment, location, or influences from the state and federal policy environment to admit students for whom their environments are not a good fit, equilibrium is adversely affected. Graduation rates for African-Americans are low at many selective institutions because admission requirements and recruiting strategies have increased student diversity without compensatory changes in the environments provided for student achievement. Administrative interventions to increase diversity must be balanced by interventions to maintain or improve achievement to prevent graduation rates from declining.

The experiences of the case-study institutions suggested the three stages of the model described in chapter 1. In the first, or *reactive*, stage, the emphasis is on increasing participation rates through interventions related to recruiting, financial aid, and admissions and scheduling. Stage 1 interventions are typically adopted as discrete responses to pressures for greater participation by minority students without any systematic planning effort. Little consideration is given to the characteristics of the available pool in relation to the environment the institution provides for student achievement. While stage 1 interventions create or magnify differences in achievement rates by attracting minority students whose characteristics are a mismatch for institutional cultures, they also increase the expectations of previously excluded groups by encouraging them to attend. When expectations are frustrated by hostile environments or unyielding academic practices, students and their supporters turn to the political process. The resultant conflict and adverse publicity signal to institutional leaders the need to give higher priority to minority achievement to restore the equilibrium essential to continuing support from political leaders.

The second, or *strategic*, stage of institutional adaptation, is characterized by more comprehensive and better-coordinated interventions than those adopted in stage 1. Colleges and universities shift attention from activities designed to increase the institution's share of the existing pool of minority students to longer-term outreach and collaboration strategies aimed at expanding the pool of minority high school graduates who have the preparation and opportunity orientations needed for college success. In addition to efforts aimed at expanding the pool, institutions develop transition programs designed to accomplish two things: first, to help those who do not meet regular admission requirements overcome preparation deficiencies, and second, to reduce the shock of academic and cultural expectations that differ from those in the schools which many minority students have previously attended.

During stage 2, mentoring and advising help students make the link between course work and careers, and encourage staff to identify academic problems early so that they can intervene before problems threaten persistence. There are also systematic efforts to help minority students to feel comfortable in the social environment through publications, cultural programs, and designated gathering spaces. Institutions with residence halls use them to support their minority programming efforts.

Stage 2 interventions serve two primary objectives. The first is to change students so that they become a better match for the institutional environment. The second is to change the environment, or to buffer elements that cannot easily be changed, to make the institution less difficult to negotiate for students who differ in preparation, objectives, or skin color from those traditionally served.

Stage 2 leadership comes largely from student affairs administrators as was true in stage 1. Stage 2 contributes to adaptation of organizational culture by helping leaders to recognize the need to change academic practices as well as student preparation. Stage 2 also contributes a core of minority professionals who are recruited to staff the achievement interventions and to reduce the dissatisfaction of groups that feel culturally isolated by the absence of appropriate role models among faculty members and the administration. Beyond lending the program expertise for which they were hired, minority professionals raise legitimate student concerns and aspirations in internal decision-making forums in ways that cannot easily be ignored. Perhaps even more important, they serve as linkages to the external political culture. By providing accurate information about the gaps between current and desirable practices, they contribute to external pressures for higher minority enrollments and more graduates.

Institutions enter a third, or *adaptive,* stage, when leaders recognize that the efforts of student affairs professionals must be augmented by faculty involvement and changes in academic practices if an institution is to achieve the balance between diversity and achievement essential to comparable graduation rates for all students. During stage 3, institutions identify differences in the preparation of entering students and establish appropriate expectations for progress to the upper division and graduation. Comprehensive learning assistance programs and services become a part of the institutional commitment to all students rather than an intervention to accommodate a special clientele. The curriculum is revised to ensure that appropriate emphasis is placed on the contributions of minority cultures to American life. All students are encouraged or required to develop sensitivity to the minority experience.

The attention focused on providing programs and services according to student need rather than race or ethnicity is a distinguishing characteristic of stage 3 strategies, as is the attempt to mainstream successful interventions. Institutions that achieve stage 3 outcomes have made sufficient progress toward meeting equity goals to turn their attention to maintenance of the new equilibrium they have established between student diversity and student achievement. Stage 3 interventions require intensive faculty involvement, signaling fundamental shifts in organizational culture.

Stage 3 institutions are predominantly multicultural in their composition and outlook. They value their multicultural status as a strength rather than seeing diversity as a threat to quality. Multicultural case-study institutions, such as the University of Texas at El Paso and California State University, Dominguez Hills, have achieved success with African-American, Hispanic, and American Indian students partly because they have already confronted the reality that many other four-year institutions will face during the next quarter-century. These institutions cannot succeed and survive unless their students, many of whom are minority, also succeed and survive.

Relatively few institutions have reached stage 3 of the adaptation process, and most of those few are located near population centers for the groups they serve. More teaching-oriented four-year institutions have made progress toward a new equilibrium than research universities or community colleges because there is less distance between the core values of such institutions and the blend of achievement and diversity strategies necessary for institutions to have both quality and access.

MANAGING ORGANIZATIONAL CULTURE

Moving institutions through the three stages requires leaders to manage organizational culture. Movement is not automatic, nor is it irreversible. Institutions can stay in stage 1 or stage 2 long after the problems of these stages should have been recognized and addressed. Cyert (1985) identifies the most promising strategies for counteracting faculty preferences for historic continuity as goal setting, attention focus, rewards, and information flow. These general strategies for managing culture do not vary regardless of the nature of the goal. The first requirement for improving minority participation and graduation rates is its definition as one of a small number of top institutional priorities. Few public institutions have the resources to pursue with observable results more than two or three priorities simultaneously. Institutional leaders can be aided in establishing equity concerns as an institutional priority by external incentives or accountability measures.

Achieving priorities requires strategic planning, as well as allocation of scarce discretionary dollars. When institutional leaders are serious about improving equity outcomes, both of these activities are in evidence. Availability and use of information is another important indicator of administrative commitment to managing culture to improve equity outcomes. Institutions that lack or conceal information about current status and past trends for the minority students they serve are unlikely candidates for changing the conventions of past practice. Institutional leaders keep track of the information they consider important to attainment of their priorities. Those committed to improving equity outcomes are familiar with the indicators of minority participation and achievement for their institutions.

Systematic efforts to alter culture to better support minority achievement require coordination, as do those directed toward strengthening research activity or reforming the undergraduate curriculum. Fragmented activities operating under competing jurisdictions are often found in stage 1 institutions. During stage 2, activities designed to enhance minority persistence are frequently coordinated by a single administrator. In stage 3, the need for improved coordination may lead institutions to mainstream successful interventions to better integrate them with the regular academic program. An important part of coordination, however implemented, involves establishing accountability procedures to assess progress toward objectives, and to reward success and punish failure.

Goal setting, information, resource allocation, and evaluation of outcomes are key elements of any strategic plan to make organizational culture more responsive to student diversity. In more successful institutions, planning activities are enhanced by activities aimed at capturing the attention focus of current staff. It is clearly important to modify the reward system to place greater emphasis on teaching and mentoring, but as Cyert (1985, 302) notes, it is difficult to tie the reward system as closely as desired to behavior. Administrators can set an example by including senior minority leaders among their own ranks. They can also adopt policies to increase the pool of potential minority faculty members and enhance the number who are hired and tenured. Finally, administrators can use publications, speeches, and workshops to increase faculty awareness of the issues and alternatives.

The process through which institutions change to improve equity outcomes is, of course, not as neat as the preceding discussion suggests. The stages and management strategies were described as tools for helping institutions understand the factors that contribute to their outcomes for minority students, as well as the interventions they can consider in efforts to improve. The stages represent intermediate points in a journey rather than discrete classifications. Some institutions, by virtue of their mission and location, have further to go than others. Not all interventions are appropriate for all institutions.

Nevertheless, in any journey it is useful to have a road map that provides information about present location and the immediate actions required to reach an ultimate objective without unnecessary side excursions. The current location of any institution in terms of its equity outcomes is a function of the nature and intensity of the interventions it has designed to improve minority participation and achievement as well as the length of time those interventions have been in effect. Interventions mirror efforts by institutional leaders to manage organizational culture.

With assistance from the Office of Educational Research and Improvement (OERI) of the U.S. Department of Education, we are currently involved in collecting information about the management strategies and interventions in use among 143 different public colleges and universities in ten states. We plan to develop normative data about distribution among the stages and to test empirically the proposition that progress through these stages is positively related to strategies for managing culture and improvements in outcomes. In chapter 14 we draw upon the surveys developed for this current study with extensive input from state and institutional cooperating researchers to profile the case-study institutions and to suggest a process through which institutions can assess their environments, as well as the characteristics of the strategies they are using to manage them.

INTERPRETING THE CASE STUDIES

The case studies presented in this book illustrate two polar approaches for promoting comparable achievement among students who begin from significantly different starting points. In the first, special access programs provide a parallel track for the first year or so of the college experience for students who are admitted on the basis of differential admissions criteria. While such programs typically use such descriptors as "low income" and "first-generation college student," in addition to race and ethnicity, to select program participants, the primary intent of such efforts is clearly to expand racial and ethnic diversity. Specially employed staff members provide the quality of instruction and academic support necessary to students' success while they are in the program. The federally funded Special Programs For Students From Disadvantaged Backgrounds (Trio programs) and their state-funded equal opportunity equivalents provide examples of this approach.

Clearly, no state has the resources to construct parallel programs in every discipline and specialization. Most institutions that rely heavily on this approach provide the equivalent of a maximum of two years of transitional assistance and catch-up after which students are expected to cope with the regular demands of the academic and social environment with minimal additional support. The records for special programs are generally excellent. Often the retention rates for underrepresented minority students for the time they participate in the programs is better than the retention of regularly qualified majority admittees for the same time periods. But when the completers of special programs are turned over to the mainstream academic program and experience faculty members who have low expectations for identifiable minority students, partly because of their disproportionate representation in institutional programs for the underprepared, many of the good effects of the special programs are undermined.

The alternative to special programs is to alter organizational culture as it contributes to attitudes about diversity and the design of learning environments. This is a more difficult and time-consuming proposition, but it has the great virtue of enlisting all the resources of an institution in equity strategies rather than relying on special staff who can retain, but who are powerless to graduate. The regular three-credit-hour English class offered at UCLA in optional format, with added hours of classroom instruction, is one example of the second approach. So are the discipline-based learning laboratories at Memphis State and Treisman's math laboratory at the University of California, Berkeley (1985). Unlike the first and more expensive alternative, the second approach relies on changes in the values and practices of existing faculty members. Changing the values that govern faculty behavior, in a scenario in which standards are maintained, minority students achieve, and costs remain reasonable, requires management of organizational culture to create an environment in which an increased emphasis on diversity is matched by more comprehensive and systematic strategies to help students achieve.

Examples of both approaches abound among the cases reported in the next ten chapters—partly because of funding regulations, partly as an artifact of each institution's unique history, and partly because both approaches are needed to provide acceptable progress toward proportional representation and comparable achievement until institutions are able to recruit faculty and administrators more representative of their changing student clientele. The institutions with the best results are those that have made the most progress in adapting their cultures so that they value diversity for the strength it adds to colleges and universities serving a pluralistic society.

PART TWO

Case Studies in Equity

In the first part of this book we provided a framework for understanding the variables that contribute to African-American, Hispanic, and American Indian success in predominantly Anglo colleges and universities. Our conceptual model was based in large measure on in-depth study of ten institutions chosen because of their above-average contributions to the ranks of college-educated minority citizens. The model considers historical context, institutional mission, state influences, leadership, organizational culture, and outcomes. In the model we argue that progress toward proportional enrollments and comparable graduation rates (as distinct from the absolute figures which may be a function of historical context) results from changes in organizational culture that improve the balance between emphasis on diversity and emphasis on achievement.

In this second part we present the edited case studies, each of which was authored by a senior member of the research team working with the assistance of one or two cooperating researchers who were at the time of the study members of the institution's staff. Each case begins with a brief introduction outlining mission and institutional characteristics. The introduction is followed by a discussion of state influences and the community setting, with special attention to coordinating board influences, the public schools, and community colleges. The case then examines student characteristics as a means of setting the context for institutional behaviors and reported outcomes. Each case then discusses university environment and academic environment. Under university environment attention is given to administrative leadership, admissions and recruitment, early intervention, community college articulation, student financial aid, and residence life, in roughly that order. The discussion of academic environment includes sections on faculty characteristics, the academic program, and academic support services.

In a concluding section entitled "summary," each case is linked to the model and the results used to explain outcomes. The model should be understood as a set of propositions that represent the best explanation of the observed linkages between policies, practices, and outcomes among the case-study institutions. The intent is to perform analytic generalization, that is, to develop and generalize theory; and not to create statistical generalization, that is, not to imply that these institutions are representative of all institutions or even of all public institutions (Yin 1988).

The usefulness of the theory elaborated through the ten case-study institutions can only be determined through its application in other institutional settings. To this end we provide in chapter 14 a process through which institutions may assess their outcomes and environments, and use the results to manage their cultures for improved success with underrepresented groups.

4

UNIVERSITY OF NEW MEXICO

GORDON VAN DE WATER
MARY FLANIGAN
with the assistance of RICHARD CADY

The University of New Mexico, created in 1889, twenty-three years before New Mexico became a state, has grown from its original 20-acre site east of Albuquerque to 600 acres surrounded by the city. In 1987 the Albuquerque campus consisted of fourteen schools and colleges offering over 4,000 courses in more than 125 fields of study to approximately 24,000 students.

The university's mission is similar to that of other comprehensive research universities. Among the dozen goals the university has set for itself, two (as stated in the university catalog for 1985–1987) are particularly important to attainment of access with quality: first, "recruiting, admitting, and retaining students from elements of the state's populations now underrepresented in its programs, especially at the graduate level" and, second, "taking advantage of the unique opportunities offered by the state's rich history, multi-cultural society, geographic setting, and natural resources to shape its programs."

THE STATE ENVIRONMENT

Historically, the principal approaches to providing access to higher education within New Mexico have been: widely dispersed two-year campuses of three of the state's four-year institutions, four community colleges, and a policy of low tuition. Aside from these fragmented structural arrangements, providing opportunities for American Indians and

Gordon Van de Water is a partner in Augenblick, Van de Water, & Associates, Denver Colorado. Mary Flanigan was a policy analyst with Augenblick, Van de Water & Associates at the time of the study. Richard Cady is director of the Office of Planning and Policy Studies at the University of New Mexico, Albuquerque.

Hispanics, the state's largest minority populations, has been the responsibility of individual institutions. The decision to create a community college in Albuquerque out of an existing technical institute occurred late in the study. The state legislature has periodically urged increases in admission standards for four-year institutions, but did not consider the impact of such changes on minority participation until 1987.

The most recent example of state-level concern is House Memorial 28 (what is called a "memorial" in New Mexico is called a "resolution" in other states) which was approved by the legislature in 1984. House Memorial 28 requested the Board of Educational Finance (now the Commission on Higher Education) to hold public hearings and study the issues and state role in native American higher education. Testimony was gathered and a report submitted to the legislature. The report produced a program to waive out-of-state tuition for Navajo students residing in Arizona. In addition, the Board of Regents of UNM appointed its own task force to report on conditions for American Indian students at the university.

The state's modest attention to higher education for American Indians has a historical basis. New Mexico tribes, especially the predominant Navajo, view themselves as nations within a nation rather than as subdivisions of a state. The Navajo have their own government and court system and look to the federal government through its Bureau of Indian Affairs for the structure and funding of their schools and community college. While education on the reservations has become increasingly tribally controlled, the principal source of funding remains the federal government. There are few American Indians in the state legislature and none on the staff of the Commission on Higher Education. Relations between the American Indian tribal leaders and the state government are not strongly developed.

Because the Commission on Higher Education is a relatively weak coordinating board, institutions of higher education experience substantial autonomy. The only constraints that operate in the search for opportunities to expand mission or programs and services are funding limitations and the complicated requirements for approval that operate at the university branches. Four-year institutions are supported through an enrollment-driven funding formula in use since 1977–1978. The formula has been criticized for no longer reflecting actual costs of providing educational services, being unresponsive to enrollment changes, and not providing funds for equipment or start-up costs of new programs.

At the time of the study, the funding mechanism contained no provisions for enhancement of quality.

During the period 1985–1987 three interim legislative committees were active in an attempt to stimulate higher education reforms. Conservatives on these committees sought higher freshman admission standards, the abolition of remediation, reduction in state support for the two-year sector, and reduction in the number of university employees other than faculty. None of these efforts had come to fruition by the end of the study.

Financial Assistance

Because of reliance on low tuition to promote access, state funding for student financial assistance has been limited. As of 1987–1988, the state provided only $3 million of need-based undergraduate student aid through the State Supplemental Incentive Grants (SSIG) program. New Mexico has a substantial state loan program and developed one of the first state-sponsored work-study programs. The Bureau of Indian Affairs funds financial aid through the American Indian self-governing pueblos and tribes.

COMMUNITY INFLUENCES

Albuquerque, New Mexico's only large urban area, has grown from approximately 35,000 in the 1940s to roughly half a million today. The population is approximately 33 percent Hispanic, 2 percent American Indian, 2 percent black, and 1 percent Asian-American. While the economy of the rest of the state has been fairly stable or declining, Albuquerque has experienced rapid growth.

As compared to other large urban areas, race relations in Albuquerque are good. The underlying philosophy has been one of accommodation rather than absorption into the dominant Anglo society. There are many Hispanic-owned or -operated businesses, and political leadership typically includes a number of prominent Hispanics. The American Indian and black populations are not well represented among the business and political leadership.

The large Hispanic community in Albuquerque is increasingly concerned about improving the educational status of its members, as evidenced by the Stay in School program of the Hispano Chamber of Commerce. Part of the program includes increasing parental awareness of the importance of education and the opportunities available to Hispanic youth. Several businesses participate in mentoring programs for students such as those operated through UNM's College of Engineering.

Hispanic students also receive support from such external sources as the League of United Latin American Citizens (LULAC), which sponsors the Talent Search program to recruit disadvantaged high school students by providing workshops and individual help for students and their parents. Among the most requested services are assistance in completing financial aid and admission forms and assistance in preparing for the American College Testing (ACT) examination. Approximately

75 percent of the students in the Talent Search program enroll at the University of New Mexico.

At the inception of the study, Albuquerque remained the only large metropolitan area within the country that had no formal arrangements for community college services. Past efforts to establish a community college had been frustrated by resistance from existing institutions. The UNM was committed to providing access to baccalaureate education through its general college. The Albuquerque Technical Vocational Institute did not want to add a transfer function, and a private institution, the University of Albuquerque, was concerned about the impact of a community college on its enrollment. The absence of a comprehensive community college in Albuquerque made it difficult for students who chose vocational or technical education after high school to subsequently change their minds and pursue a baccalaureate degree. These arrangements also kept admission standards at UNM low and served as a rationale for the relatively high attrition rates experienced by all students.

STUDENTS

Characteristics of 1981 and 1987 regularly admitted freshmen by race or ethnicity appear in table 4.1.

Hispanics attended UNM in proportions close to their representation in the 20 to 29 age group of the state population in 1981, but by 1987 their proportional representation had declined significantly, partly as a consequence of increasing admission standards in the absence of offsetting interventions. American Indians attended in 1981 at a rate 50 percent below their representation in the population. Their proportional representation had further declined by 1987.

TABLE 4.1. Characteristics of UNM Entering Students, Fall 1981 and Fall 1987

	ANGLO		AMERICAN INDIAN		HISPANIC	
	1981	1987	1981	1987	1981	1987
Percentage of enrollment	61	67	4	3	31	26
ACT composite	20.1	21.1	15.1	17.4	17.7	19.2
High school GPA	2.9	3.0	2.9	2.9	2.9	3.0
First-semester GPA	2.1	2.4	1.7	1.8	2.0	2.2
Percentage female	50	52	50	61	52	58
Percentage needing basic skills in:						
English	41	15	77	51	55	24
Math	6	13	22	23	11	17
Social sciences	22	18	59	47	36	27
Natural sciences	19	12	45	25	34	22

Source: Office of Planning and Policy Studies, University of New Mexico, 1987.

The college-going population of Hispanics and Anglos was fairly similar in 1981 on such characteristics as family income, community size, and grade-point averages (GPAs). American Indians, however, tended to come from smaller communities, had lower family incomes, scored lower on the ACT examination, had a slightly lower high school GPA, demonstrated a much higher need for basic skills assistance (based on subscores of the ACT exam), and achieved significantly lower GPAs. As a result of raising admissions standards in 1983, the freshman class entering in fall 1987 had higher high school grade-point averages and higher standardized examination scores, required significantly less remedial work, and had higher first-semester grade-point averages. While all three groups improved, the relative performance of Anglos, Hispanics, and American Indians, as indicated by first-semester grade-point averages, did not change.

More than 60 percent of regular undergraduates attending UNM come from Albuquerque and surrounding Bernalillo County. All but 14 percent of the remainder are from other counties in New Mexico. Regular undergraduates are young (average age is 24) and enter as freshmen within a year after graduation from high school (81 percent).

Table 4.2 reports the retention and graduation data for the cohort that entered in 1981.

The performance of Hispanics was quite similar to that of their Anglo colleagues in terms of credit hours attempted and completed, stop-out rates, and graduation rates. In fact, given the significant differences in ACT scores and the percentages in need of basic skills courses at

TABLE 4.2. UNM Student Progression, 1981–1986

	ANGLO	AMERICAN INDIAN	HISPANIC
First semester:			
GPA	2.11	1.69	2.03
Credit hours	12.74	12.87	12.90
Second semester:			
GPA	2.15	1.78	1.94
Credit hours	10.52	9.28	10.87
Eighth-semester cumulative:			
GPA	2.04	1.55	1.88
Credit hours	60.24	43.56	59.06
Cohort stop-out percentage rate:			
Second semester	22	33	21
Third semester	40	48	40
Tenth semester	72	85	70
Percentage graduated in:			
Four years	5	1	4
Five years	19	1	14

Source: Office of Planning and Policy Studies, University of New Mexico.

TABLE 4.3. Rates of Reenrollment in UNM after Three Semesters, 1981 and 1986 Cohorts

	REENROLLMENT RATES		
COHORT	Anglo	American Indian	Hispanic
Fall 1981	60	52	60
Fall 1986	69	54	69

Source: Office of Planning and Policy Studies, University of New Mexico.

the time of entry, it could be argued that Hispanics performed as well as better-prepared Anglo students. Hispanics' initial need for improvement in basic skills, however, extended the period required for graduation. American Indians, by contrast, accumulated significantly fewer credit hours over an eight-semester period, and had significantly lower grade-point averages and higher attrition rates at every stage of the process.

The retention rates of freshmen entering after admissions standards were increased in 1983 (see table 4.3) show significant improvement. University officials consider the improved preparation of students entering under the new standards to be a key factor in improvement of retention rates. Improved preparation has also resulted in a substantial decrease in the number of credit hours of remedial instruction generated. Five years ago, just before admission standards were raised, 13,000 credit hours of remedial work were reported. By 1987 the number had shrunk to 5,000.

The increase in admission standards and the closure of the General College into which students in need of remediation were previously admitted has meant that many applicants, including a substantial number of minorities, are being denied admission. The 1988 legislative session recognized this problem and authorized approximately $300,000 to fund remedial education at the community colleges. The governor vetoed this item, thus creating confusion about the state's willingness to support remedial work for students who do not meet the new university standards.

The American Indian graduates interviewed shared a number of characteristics, besides exhibiting some striking differences. Most had completed their degrees either in health-related fields or in the social sciences. For many, attending college meant separation from their families, a sacrifice that was particularly difficult for women with small children. The graduates had previously attended a wide range of public, reservation, and boarding schools. Several mentioned that the UNM two-year branch at Gallup (located near a large American Indian population) had particularly helped them in making the transition between high school and the much larger and more impersonal UNM main campus.

The most important personal influences on successful completion of a baccalaureate degree identified by the American Indian graduates were family relationships (psychological and financial support from parents, grandparents, and siblings), personal motivation and dedication, friends (typically fellow students in the same academic discipline but not necessarily other American Indians), high school teachers or counselors (typically supplying confidence and specific goals), and individuals on campus (key professors or counselors who helped students focus on a particular academic area, shored up low confidence levels through counseling, or directed students to needed tutoring services).

American Indian students frequently cited the following stumbling blocks: poor preparation for college (especially in math, English, and writing), inadequate financial resources and lack of knowledge of the financial aid system, missing or poor advice about academic requirements and career possibilities, and cultural differences (mostly centered on making the adjustment from the rural, reservation culture to the urban, university culture and on the American Indian's lack of Anglo aggressiveness and assertiveness).

Hispanic graduates, like their American Indian counterparts, came from a wide range of public New Mexico high schools. With rare exceptions, Hispanic graduates reported that English was the primary language spoken in the home. The most popular majors for Hispanic graduates were business, arts, and humanities. Hispanic and American Indian graduates uniformly reported an absence of any feeling of racial tension or discrimination while attending UNM. Many commented on the wide diversity of the student body and said their friendships tended to be based on living location or academic discipline rather than race or ethnic group.

Among Hispanics, the factors consistently cited as positive influences were individual dedication, discipline, and motivation; family support; having a clear set of goals; and support and encouragement from a key educator (either a high school teacher or counselor or a college professor). Major stumbling blocks were lack of or poor academic advisement and poor high school preparation.

American Indians received 3 percent of UNM degrees awarded in 1982–1983, over half of which were in education. Hispanics received 21 percent of degrees distributed in fields similar to those for Anglos. Interestingly, the pattern of degree achievement reverses the relationships between achievement by Hispanics and American Indians noted in the previous tables. For the period studied, American Indians earned degrees at rates closer to their representation in the undergraduate population than did Hispanics. These are composite figures rather than the results of studying a specific cohort as in table 4.3. They suggest that while American Indians start with more deficiencies and take longer to finish school, they earn degrees at rates similar to their representation in the undergraduate student population. (These results are also consistent with the study's analysis of the 1984 HEGIS data.)

THE UNIVERSITY ENVIRONMENT

UNM, as a multicultural institution, has encouraged enrollment of American Indians and Hispanics through its willingness to take risks on academically underprepared students—providing remediation services where necessary, advising them carefully, and guiding them into the mainstream of the university by the time they reach the upper division. However, programs and services based on ethnicity, age, or gender are rare. Except for students entering the colleges of engineering and education, American Indian and Hispanic students receive no special treatment at the upper division level. The university's Native American Task Force identified specific problems and formulated recommendations in the areas of curriculum and testing, financial aid, student services, affirmative action policy, and on-site and community outreach.

For Hispanics the campus environment is comfortable because there are so many of them. The experience of American Indians is somewhat different. While they too reported an absence of discrimination, American Indians compared themselves with African-Americans as minority students and reported the lack of understanding of their culture as a concern. From the American Indian perspective, Hispanics are part of the majority at UNM, a view shared by many Hispanics as well.

Many faculty and staff members were surprised to learn that the University of New Mexico had been chosen as a site for a study of American Indian and Hispanic success in achieving the baccalaureate. They saw the university efforts directed toward American Indians as ineffective. It was much easier for them to discuss shortcomings and problems than to identify achievements. Respondents tended to attribute institutional success with American Indians or Hispanics to demographics and the multicultural setting rather than to specific interventions by the state or the university.

Staff members who provided special assistance to American Indian students were American Indians themselves, and the same was generally true for Hispanics. These individuals, particularly the American Indians, felt overwhelmed by the magnitude of the job and described a need for a much larger effort. Special programs such as those formerly offered by the College of Education and currently available in the College of Engineering have been externally funded either by the federal government or by private sources. In the minds of those most closely associated with minority initiatives, these funding arrangements indicate an absence of ongoing commitment to the programs from either the state or the university.

TABLE 4.4. Distribution of UNM Administrators by Salary, 1986

	ANGLO		AMERICAN INDIAN		HISPANIC	
SALARY LEVEL	N	%	N	%	N	%
Below $16,000	33	49.2	3	4.5	29	43.3
$16,000–29,999	169	73.5	5	2.8	48	20.9
$30,000 and above	138	78.9	0	—	33	19.0
Total	340	72.2	8	1.7	110	23.4

Source: University of New Mexico, EEO-6 Report, 1986.

UNM had visible Hispanic leadership, including the vice-president for academic affairs and the dean of students. Nineteen percent of administrators who earned over $30,000 were Hispanic. There were no American Indians with major administrative responsibilities as reflected by salary levels. Administrative commitment to minority access and achievement stemmed largely from a general awareness of the multicultural setting. Their prevailing philosophy was one of running a good university for the benefit of all citizens and assisting students equally. The distribution of administrators by salary level for 1986 appears in table 4.4.

Hispanics and American Indians were concentrated at the lower salary levels. Hispanics and American Indian administrators exceed the representation of their groups within the student body only in the "Below $16,000" category.

Admissions and Recruitment

Prior to 1987 the University of New Mexico maintained relatively open admissions. Less qualified students were required to enroll in the General College (modeled on the General College of the University of Minnesota), where they were given an opportunity to qualify for admission to the college of their choice. They received instruction in smaller classes, individual counseling, and course work in academic skills to provide the preparation necessary for success in regular university courses. The General College was abolished in spring 1987, however, and all students are now enrolled in University College for lower-division work. Under current policy, when students are ready to declare a major, they must meet all requirements of the school or college offering the major.

There are currently three methods of entering the university: (1) presenting a high school grade-point average of 2.0 or better (on a 4.0 scale) in a curriculum consisting of a minimum of 13 specified units; (2) meeting a formula requirement that combines high school class rank with performance on a standardized college entrance examination, either ACT or the Scholastic Aptitude Test (SAT); or (3) petitioning for special admission based on particular talents or circumstances (the number entering under this method is limited to 5 percent of the previous year's total freshman class.

The university has separate offices for recruiting and admitting students. The Office of School Relations handles most of the freshman recruiting. The college enrichment program recruits disadvantaged students, mostly Hispanic, from rural settings. Recruiting strategies are similar for all portions of the target population. The Office of School Relations visits high schools, prepares and distributes literature (including special publications on native American and Hispanic student services, and native American and Chicano studies programs), conducts career fairs, uses current students to contact prospective students, and each fall conducts the "senior day," which includes special segments for American Indians and Hispanics.

The Office of School Relations has three Hispanics and two American Indians on its staff. It also uses staff from the Native American Student Services (NASS) office in its recruiting. NASS staff participate in high school visits to schools with substantial American Indian populations and attend career fairs. Current American Indian students are used to contact prospective students, matched by tribe and location wherever possible.

Early Intervention Programs

In fall 1986, UNM initiated a project called "Improving Academic Preparation for College," in cooperation with the State Department of Education, the commission on Higher Education, and the College Board. The College Board's "green book" and "rainbow books" were used by committees of high school and college faculty to define the competencies that students should master in high school in order to succeed academically in college. The State Board of Education is expected to make the teaching of these competencies a requirement. Minority students are expected to achieve the greatest gains under this curricular reform.

Paving the Way, another new program, was started in fall 1987. This program is aimed at helping middle school students and their parents plan for college both academically and financially. The need for the program stems from the university's higher admissions standards and the increasing costs of attending college. Student role models are used to explain the admissions and financial aid processes to students and their parents and to inform students about the courses they will need in high school to make a smooth transition into college. Currently focused on the Albuquerque metropolitan area, the program is designed for low-income students who will be the first in their families to attend college.

Upward Bound, a federally funded supplementary college preparation program, provides high school students who meet two of three criteria (low income, first-generation college student, and physically handicapped) with orientation, information, and exposure to postsecondary education. Participants come to the university campus for classes in English, math, science, and humanities. Tutors are provided for those who need extra help.

The Hispanic Engineering Organization (HEO) is a student chapter of the Mexican American Engineering Society and the Society of Hispanic Professional Engineers. Formed to provide networking support and role models, HEO students serve high school students through the UNM chapter of Math, Engineering, and Science Achievement (MESA). MESA is designed to increase the number of underrepresented minorities in the professions related to mathematics, engineering, and the physical sciences. Tutors in math and science are assigned to each participating high school, field trips are conducted, and financial support is provided to students who perform well in their classes. Though enrollment in MESA is open to any minority student, 84 percent of those participating in 1985–1986 were Hispanic. During 1986–1987 there were 604 students involved in the program, and 72 graduates. Ninety-five percent of the graduates were accepted to their first-choice college, and two-thirds declared engineering as their major. In fall 1987 a pilot program aimed at middle school students was started in Albuquerque.

Advisement and Counseling

A number of special services have been designed to help American Indians and Hispanics negotiate the requirements of campus life. The Native American Student Services office provides outreach, counseling, and tutoring; serves as a gathering place for Indian students; and disseminates information on scholarships, grants, and employment. Student organizations, such as the Kiva Club, provide opportunities for students to organize and run programs of special interest, as well as meeting to discuss campus life.

Hispanic Student Services aids Hispanic students and anyone else who needs assistance in all aspects of university life. Services include advisement, counseling, referrals, and advocacy in such areas as admissions, employment, and financial aid. Because of its large constituency (approximately 5,900 Hispanic students on the main campus), Hispanic Student Services confines its work to dealing with crises and individual referrals or walk-in cases. The staff often take the lead in organizing cultural events and fiestas on campus and sponsor three student organizations: the National Chicano Health Organization, Estudiantes por la Cultura, and Movimiento Estudiantil Chicano de Aztlan (MECHA). These student organizations and others, like the Chicano Business Club, provide an opportunity for students with similar interests to meet, socialize, and coordinate programs.

Student Financial Aid

Most American Indians and many Hispanics receive student financial aid. The Office of Student Financial Aid provides counseling services for all students but reports that American Indian students need more assistance to successfully complete school. In addition to standard financial aid applications and processing, American Indian applicants require two additional steps: (1) notification of the appropriate tribal agency to coordinate campus and tribal financial support and (2) adjustment of the financial aid package based on the amount and type of financial aid provided by the tribe. Typically, the tribe substitutes grant money for loan or work study funds available through the campus.

The Office of Student Financial Aid has 21 Hispanics on its full-time staff, and six of ten peer counselors are Hispanic. There is one full-time American Indian on staff and two of the peer counselors are American Indians. The full-time staff has recently begun to provide special services to American Indians through the Office of Native American Student Services. Difficulties in the financial aid process tend to revolve around language barriers (especially with parents) and the slowness of students to respond to requests for additional information necessary to the verification process.

ACADEMIC ENVIRONMENT

The faculty has learned through experience that American Indian students retain strong ties to their home base and may disappear for a period of time to participate in tribal ceremonies or assist in crop harvest. Successful American Indian students learn to operate within the university structure, notifying professors when they will be away from campus and making arrangements to keep up with their academic work while they are gone or to catchup when they return. The strong presence of Hispanic students, along with the similarities they share with their Anglo colleagues, supports the university philosophy of providing services based on student needs rather than by race or ethnicity.

Faculty and Staff

Table 4.5 displays the percentage of American Indians and Hispanics among the faculty and professional staff at the University of New Mexico. Most of the American Indian faculty and professionals are clustered at the lower salary levels. While the salaries of Hispanic faculty are competitive with those of Anglo counterparts, most nonfaculty Hispanics are also clustered at the lower salary levels. Both Hispanics and American Indians are seriously underrepresented among both faculty and professional staff. Only at the lowest salary levels does their pres-

TABLE 4.5. Distribution of UNM Faculty and Professional Staff by Salary, 1986

	ANGLO		AMERICAN INDIAN		HISPANIC	
SALARY LEVEL	N	%	N	%	N	%
Faculty:						
Below $16,000	7	70.0		–	2	20.0
$16,000–29,999	396	88.8	7	1.2	30	6.7
$30,000 and above	713	89.2	4	0.5	54	6.80
Total	1116	88.9	11	0.9	86	6.9
Professional, nonfaculty:						
Below $16,000	100	65.4	6	3.9	38	24.8
$16,000–29,999	707	74.6	13	1.4	189	19.9
$30,000 and above	151	88.3	1	0.6	14	8.2
Total	958	75.3	20	1.6	241	18.9

Source: University of New Mexico, EEO-6 Report, 1986.

ence approach Hispanic and American Indian representation in the student body. Anglos make up 89 percent of the total faculty, Hispanics 7 percent, Asians 3 percent, American Indians 0.9 percent, and African-Americans 0.5 percent.

According to UNM faculty and administrators, research is the most highly rewarded activity, and teaching is clearly important. Advising students, however, appears to be neglected. Student interviews frequently elicited comments about poor advising and the necessity of relying on one's own initiative and research to sort out graduation requirements and career options.

Academic Programs

The Native American Studies program provides academic advisement, conducts research, and offers course work through various departments, although no degree program or major is available. Chicano Studies is the academic component of the Southwest Research Institute. This program offers courses on New Mexico and the Southwest through such departments as anthropology, political science, history, sociology, and English.

The Native American Program in the College of Engineering (NAP-COE) was established in 1975 to increase the number of American Indians earning degrees in engineering. The program supports approximately a hundred students (seventy-five in the lower division and twenty-five in the upper division) with tutoring in math, science, computing, and English; personal counseling and advising; and job placement. NAPCOE also sponsors a local chapter of the American Indian Science and Engineering Society (AISES), through which professionals in the community provide mentoring and American Indian students tutor their peers. Many of these professionals are themselves alumni of the program. A summer program for high school graduates planning to matriculate at the university is also offered by NAPCOE. While American Indian students take longer to finish than other students and generally earn lower GPAs, as noted earlier, the program has been successful in increasing the number who graduate. NAPCOE is funded primarily through private donations from commerce and industry. The program coordinator's salary is provided by the university.

MESA provides many of the same services for Hispanic students that NAPCOE provides for American Indians. Most MESA students join the Hispanic Engineering Organization (or NAPCOE). Both HEO and MESA are reviewed by a faculty advisory committee, which recommends program improvements to the dean. The MESA program is totally funded through corporate and foundation contributions.

The College of Education in the past offered a number of programs designed to increase the number of American Indian teachers available to schools on or near reservations. All these programs were supported by federal funds and have been closed in recent years as federal support was withdrawn. The loss of these programs, along with the use of the National Teacher Examination as a screening device for new teachers, has reduced the number of new American Indian and Hispanic teachers being produced. Only two American Indian students entered the teacher certification program in 1987. The College of Education has recently added a half-time American Indian adviser (a Navajo doctoral student) whose responsibilities include recruiting and advising students, and providing faculty with information about teaching American Indian students.

Academic Support Services

The universitywide Skills Center serves over 5,000 students each year either on a walk-in (75 percent) or a referral (25 percent) basis. Referrals are typically made by departmental instructors, especially English composition faculty. Center services include tutoring and study groups. Tutoring is provided in major subject areas—math, science, social science, natural science, and Spanish. A separate writing laboratory also uses the tutorial approach. Study groups provide small group discussion for each of the subject areas. The most important services provided to American Indian and Hispanic students are in the area of basic language skills. American Indian students require writing laboratory services more frequently than other groups. There is a full-time American Indian staff member (with a master's degree in English as a second language), and two of the ten student tutors are American Indians. Twenty-two of forty-five students who work at the Skills Center are Hispanic. The center is currently engaged in a follow-up analysis of how well students do after using its services.

The College Enrichment Program (CEP) offers special support services to students who have low incomes, are underprepared, or are first-generation college students. About 70 percent of those it serves are Hispanic and 13 percent are American Indians. CEP staff provide special orientation sessions and counseling services; monitor academic progress, offer tutoring on an individual basis; and assist with job placement. They also take part in recruiting, especially in rural, low-income areas. The program seeks to create an intimate supportive environment within a large university. CEP participants have a 44 percent graduation rate after seven years, well above the general university rate. CEP graduates include twelve lawyers, six medical doctors, and two Ph.D.'s.

SUMMARY

The University of New Mexico does not target many of its academic support services by race or ethnicity. For the most part, American Indian and Hispanic students are treated exactly like everyone else. Important to the success of this approach in the UNM setting is an organizational culture developed in response to a mission that has emphasized both diversity and achievement. UNM was for many years the open-access institution for baccalaureate study in the Albuquerque area. As did the staff of the General College of the University of Minnesota, UMN's General College staff developed considerable expertise in working with underprepared students and preparing them for upper-division success. The experience of the university in providing access influenced the development of support services for all students. Learning laboratories and tutorial services form a major dimension of the academic experience.

UNM admission policies also help to make the practice of treating everyone the same (known as "mainstreaming" in some institutions) work. The two-year campuses practice open admissions as did the General College during its existence. Under current policy, UNM remains relatively nonselective. Because admission requirements are quite flexible, it is unnecessary to rely extensively on waivers to enroll minority students. Students who attend exhibit greater diversity of preparation than in more selective institutions, but diversity is a fact of life for all students, not exclusively for Hispanics and American Indians.

Race- and ethnicity-specific programs are offered in engineering and through special components of student affairs, but such programs are relatively small and rely for the most part on external funding. The university also devotes some attention to early intervention through a combination of federally funded programs and the cultivation of business and professional support. The results achieved by the federally funded

College Enrichment Program are particularly interesting because they suggest the potential for at-risk students when they are provided with systematic and comprehensive support.

Clearly important to student success at UNM are demographics, state history, and a supportive multicultural environment. Hispanics attend the university in large numbers and graduate at rates not too different from those of their Anglo colleagues, despite differences in standardized test scores. Many business and community leaders and government officials are Hispanic and serve, along with Hispanic faculty and staff, as role models for Hispanic students. In addition, the state's proud multicultural heritage is reflected in the university. Hispanics report feeling comfortable on campus.

Demographics and the multicultural environment also contribute to baccalaureate success among American Indians. While many university representatives did not consider the American Indian experience to be a success story because of their significantly lower rates of progression and graduation within cohort survival studies, our analysis of HEGIS data suggests that even though American Indians take longer to earn degrees, they may ultimately earn them at rates closer to those of the Anglo population than do Hispanics. Any assessment that American Indians who succeed at UNM do so exclusively because of their own initiative, family support, and the dedicated efforts of a small, overextended group of American Indian faculty and staff must be tempered by the obvious commitment the university has undertaken to provide support to diversely prepared learners of all races and ethnicities.

While the American Indian presence is not large enough to make institutional life as comfortable for individual American Indians as it is for individual Hispanics, the absence of discrimination and the respect for diverse cultures evidenced by the provision of space and organizations to celebrate differences as well as commonalities makes UNM's multicultural environment more hospitable than that provided by most large research universities. Also important to American Indian success is the role of the two-year campuses operated by the university. Sixty percent of students on the Gallup campus in 1986 were American Indian. Several graduates in our survey credited that campus with helping them make the transition between a reservation school and the Albuquerque setting.

5

FLORIDA INTERNATIONAL UNIVERSITY

LOUIS W. BENDER
with the assistance of NORMA M. GOONEN

Florida International University (FIU) is a predominantly commuter institution offering programs on two campuses in Dade County: University Park in the west-central part of the county and North Miami in the northeast. FIU was one of six universities created by the state legislature during the 1960s in response to the state's rapid population growth and the political demands of urban areas for public universities. The legislative delegation from Dade County was instrumental in gaining legislative authorization for FIU and has since promoted its interests vigorously. When FIU opened its doors in 1972, it offered upper-division baccalaureate and masters programs. The lower division was added in 1981. In 1984 FIU was authorized to offer limited doctoral programs.

Programming priorities at FIU support the goals of the greater Miami area to become an international center of trade, finance, and commerce. While the university has strong ties to its region, it is also involved in cooperative activities with institutions, agencies, and governments throughout the Western hemisphere. The university has openly declared its ambition to become the flagship institution in Florida, despite the historic and contemporary prominence of the University of Florida and Florida State University. Such an ambition may not be unrealistic, given the university's strategic location, the central role it enjoys in the Miami community, and its resultant political base in the legislature.

STATE INFLUENCES

Responsibility for all public education in Florida is constitutionally assigned to the State Board of Education, composed of the elected state

Louis W. Bender is professor of higher education and director of the State and Regional Higher Education Center, Florida State University. Norma Goonen at the time of the study was acting associate dean of undergraduate studies at Florida International University.

cabinet officers and the governor. The Postsecondary Education Planning Commission (PEPC) provides planning and recommendations to the legislature and the State Board of Education. The PEPC 1982 master plan, along with its 1984 supplement and 1988 update, specifically addresses the participation of minority and disadvantaged students. Under the plan, Florida's community colleges have primary responsibility for achieving state access goals.

Florida's public system of higher education includes nine state universities, governed by the Board of Regents, and twenty-eight community colleges, governed by local boards and coordinated by the State Board of Community Colleges. The nine university presidents report to a chancellor who in turn reports to the board of regents. Legislative intent in Florida calls for 60 percent of all baccalaureate-bound students to begin in a community college. To achieve that intent, enrollment caps are maintained on all universities.

The Florida Constitution of 1885 declared "... white and colored children shall not be taught in the same school, but impartial provision shall be for both." Until 1957 all public education was segregated. African-Americans were served by Florida Agricultural and Mechanical University (FAMU) and twelve segregated junior colleges, eleven of which were established after the 1954 Supreme Court ruling that separate systems of public education were unconstitutional. While the system of separate junior colleges was ended in 1966, it was not until 1974, in response to *Adams v. Richardson,* that Florida developed specific plans for equalizing educational opportunity in both state universities and community colleges. The 1974 plan, as revised in 1977, stressed three broad areas: (1) mission and enhancement of FAMU; (2) enrollment and progression of African-American students from first registration through graduate and professional schools; and (3) representation by African-Americans on governing boards and on the faculties and staffs of universities.

In 1984, the year before the federal court ruling expired, the legislature enacted the Florida Educational Equity Act which charged public institutions with responsibilities for increasing the participation of groups traditionally underrepresented in programs or courses because of race, national origin, sex, handicap, or marital status. Under this act, institutions were required to have an office for equal opportunity, the functions of which were to coordinate an institutional plan for ensuring equitable participation and to monitor results. Both the state university system and the institutional plans call for special initiatives to identify, recruit, and admit minority students as well as for appropriate academic and support services after entry.

A unit record system for state university students provides the tracking capabilities essential to monitoring institutional progress in achieving outcomes specified by the plans. The success of the system has motivated legislators to require community colleges to develop a comparable and compatible system. It is also a legislative requirement that universities provide regular feedback on transfers to community colleges to alert them to academic problems. The information has been used to improve curriculum and instruction and to identify and correct problems related to minority student progression.

Minority Initiatives

The Florida Educational Equity Act of 1984 requires proactive planning and programming to increase minority participation and achievement in institutions where minorities are underrepresented. In annual reviews and updates, systems and the institutions they supervise must identify reasons for unachieved milestones together with projected corrective action. On-site reviews may be carried out by the Board of Regents' equal opportunity office.

The state-funded College Reach-Out Program supports community college and university initiatives to motivate minority and low-income high school students to prepare for entrance to college. The nine universities compete for state funds to carry out school and campus visitations, workshops and summer programs, counseling and tutoring support, and providing role models for secondary school students. The Florida Institute of Education Pre-Collegiate Programs support similar initiatives through a combination of state and private support. Cooperative Trust Fund Grants encourage joint articulation projects between universities and community colleges or high schools.

Universities may waive admissions criteria to improve minority participation based on a sliding scale of SAT scores, high school grades, or approved alternative programs, provided that they outline their exception policy and provisions for student support in a plan submitted to the state university system. All nine universities participate in a state-supported retention program to assist African-American students in overcoming academic deficiencies at both undergraduate and graduate levels.

Financial Assistance

The Florida Student Assistance Grant Program provides need-based assistance to students attending public or private institutions. In addition, State Board of Education rules require universities to set aside a part of their student fees as designated student financial aid. Many universities use these funds as financial incentives to recruit minority students. The McKnight Programs in Higher Education, which are partially supported by state funds, provide scholarships for both undergraduate and graduate minority students.

Articulation

Tough articulation policies support legislative intent that 60 percent of the students with baccalaureate goals will begin in community colleges. A comprehensive and dynamic articulation agreement between the state university and community college systems is monitored, reviewed, and amended by a state articulation coordinating committee. The committee also hears student grievances about the transfer process. Both systems follow semester calendars. A common course designation and numbering system simplifies program planning for students and reduces uncertainties about course equivalencies. Each university must have an articulation officer, who typically carries out ombudsman duties in addition to providing support for the transfer function. Universities must also provide community colleges annually with an academic advising manual to assist them in guiding potential transfers and to codify the requirements for majors. An on-line advisement and articulation system provides computerized support for academic advising.

Quality Initiatives

Several legislative actions during the 1980s have addressed the issue of quality. Minimum admissions standards for the university system were implemented in phases early in the decade, to provide school districts with time to make the necessary changes to their programs. Entry as a freshman now requires the completion of a specified distribution of high school courses, a C+ (2.5) grade-point average and a combined score of 900 on the SAT or 19 on the ACT. Universities are authorized to establish higher requirements locally and may, with Board of Regents approval, use differential criteria for high-demand or oversubscribed programs.

A diagnostic testing program identifies the academic deficiencies of students admitted to a university. Remediation is mandatory with responsibility assigned to community colleges. Under the legislation creating the college preparatory program, funding for remedial courses was denied to universities. Most now contract with community colleges for remedial services through the college preparatory program. Baccalaureate or associate degree candidates pursuing this program qualify for an additional year of state financial aid. Universities supplement the subcollegiate work provided under contract by community colleges with academic support laboratories, tutoring, and other enhancements.

All community college and university students are required to pass the College Level Academic Skills Test (CLAST) to be eligible for junior status. The Gordon Rule, passed by the state legislature, requires all associate and baccalaureate degree candidates to complete a minimum of six credits at mathematics at or above the level of college algebra, as well as twelve credits in English with required compositions of at least 24,000 words over four terms.

COMMUNITY INFLUENCES

At the time of the 1959 Cuban revolution, the population of Cuba was one of the most culturally and economically advanced in the Western hemisphere. Middle- and upper-class Cubans prized education and favored private schools. Many sent their children to be educated in other countries. While Castro's political and economic policies resulted in virtually total loss of wealth and physical possessions, exiles to the United States brought with them their education, skills, and ambitions.

The half-million Cubans currently residing in Miami and the Dade County area came in three distinct waves of immigration. The initial wave, made up primarily of professionals, business people, and exiled political leaders, arrived between 1959 and 1962 prior to the "missile crisis" which severed diplomatic relations between the United States and Cuba. During the "freedom flight" wave between 1965 and 1973, an additional 270,000 immigrants arrived. As was true for their predecessors, this wave included many professionals and business people. FIU was established in time to assist many of these immigrants with recertification, language enhancement, and career training. Through such services the university earned the reciprocal support it has since enjoyed from the Cuban community. Municipio organizations (reflecting immigrants' cities of origin) administer scholarships for Cuban students and participate in FIU fund-raising activity.

The third immigrant wave came in the 1980 boat lift of more than 150,000 political refugees from Mariel, Cuba. More heterogeneous than the first two groups, the "Mariels" included more blacks and many rural and urban poor. The differences between the Mariels and earlier immigrants initially provoked hostilities. Relationships have improved over time, and the Mariels have been able to gain an economic base within the community. The U.S. Immigration and Naturalization Service projects the arrival of 300,000 more Cubans during the next fifteen years. Hispanics are also arriving from throughout Central America, South America, and the Caribbean.

The Metro-Dade County Planning Department study (1986) describes the positive results of the immigration. "The resulting bicultural, bilingual community is largely responsible for South Florida's present and future economic prosperity." But the demographic changes taking place are not without problems. Referendums to require English as the official language for all local and state governmental agencies have been proposed in Dade County, leading to predictions that friction over language and culture will produce problems similar to those experienced by the French Canadians in Quebec.

The progress of Cubans within the economic, social, political, and cultural life of the Metro-Dade area has also caused concern among African-Americans, who increasingly believe that they occupy a third rung in the community hierarchy, a perception that is shared by many Anglos and Hispanics. The 1985 Dade County population of 1.8 million was 43 percent Hispanic, 37 percent Anglo, and 21 percent African-American. By the year 2000, the Hispanic population is expected to increase to almost half the total county population while Anglos decline to less than a third. African-Americans will probably continue to represent about a fifth of the total.

A study of Hispanic households in the Miami area revealed that 78 percent were headed by persons of Cuban origin, 9 percent by persons from countries in Central America, 8 percent by persons from countries in South America, and 3 percent by persons of Puerto Rican descent. The designation "African-American" includes those born in the United States as well as immigrants from such Caribbean nations as Jamaica and Haiti and some countries in Africa. The out-migration of Anglos in Dade County between 1981 and 1985 exceeded their in-migration.

Public Schools

The Dade County Public School System received national recognition for meeting the Herculean challenge of absorbing the various exile waves, particularly the Mariels. The multilingual, multicultural composition of the student body can be seen in the district's comprehensive multilingual program, which includes classes in English for speakers of other languages, home language arts instruction in native languages, bilingual curriculum content in Spanish and ten other languages, and Spanish as a second language for English-speaking children.

The school system is also the most segregated in Florida and one of the most segregated in the South. From 1976 to 1986 African-American enrollment increased by 17 percent, Hispanic enrollment by nearly 30 percent. In the same period Anglo enrollment decreased by 41 percent. The number of all-African-American schools has more than doubled since 1970. In the words of the *Miami Herald* (April 20, 1987), such schools "are at an academic disadvantage, in part because of the social class and economic status of their students" who are significantly more likely to drop out than their Hispanic and Anglo counterparts. One-fifth of all Dade schools are at least 80 percent Hispanic, but several of these "... enjoy the advantages of suburban schools: a broad curriculum [and] a core of advanced students who set high standards."

Predominantly African-American schools have fewer resources and less experienced teachers, and offer less advanced course work. Not surprisingly, their graduates are less likely to attend college. The school system's three predominantly African-American high schools contributed a total of 8 students to FIU's fall 1986 freshman class. In contrast, the three predominantly Hispanic high schools produced 59 FIU freshmen, while the three predominantly Anglo high schools contributed 56.

Private schools play an important role in the Miami area, as in other urban settings. Six of the top ten contributors to the 1985 FIU entering freshman class were private schools. Together they produced 162 freshmen, compared to the 90 entering from the top four public high schools, Thirty-seven percent of the 1985 entering first-time freshmen came from private schools. Nearly 17 percent of K-12 enrollment in Dade County can be found in private schools, which enroll few African-Americans.

Community Colleges

Miami-Dade Community College annually transfers about 1,000 students to FIU. Historically, Miami-Dade faculty and administrators have perceived FIU as a hostile transfer environment, particularly for African-American students. Returning transfer students have reported hearing faculty members in FIU classrooms make disparaging remarks about them and about Miami-Dade as a collegiate institution. Partly in response Miami-Dade has negotiated special articulation agreements with selected colleges and universities throughout the nation to provide alternatives for their African-American transfers. More recently FIU and Miami-Dade have been cooperating in the Ford Foundation–sponsored Transfer Opportunity Program providing for follow-up study on community college transfer students as well as special collaborative efforts to improve the transfer process for minorities.

STUDENTS

In 1987 FIU enrolled almost 55 percent of all Hispanic students in the state university system. The comparable percentages for Anglos and African-Americans were respectively 7 and 11. FIU's contribution to the education of minority students within the state university system is placed in sharper perspective when one considers that the eight predominantly white institutions within the system educate about 62 percent of African-American students. (FAMU accounts for the rest.) Eighteen percent of all African-American students in the state university system and not at FAMU attend FIU.

The different patterns of admission and progression at FIU as a function of race and ethnicity are revealed by table 5.1, which also provides information about public high school graduation in Dade County.

Hispanics apply, are accepted, and enroll in proportions that exceed all other groups. Only about one in three of those African-Americans who are admitted as freshmen actually enroll, a yield far below the percentages for other groups. Clearly, FIU is very dependent on community college transfers for achieving its affirmative action results. The graduation proportions are not time-lagged here (as was the informa-

TABLE 5.1. Public High School Graduation in Dade County Compared with FIU Access and Graduation, 1987

	ANGLO (%)	AFRICAN-AMERICAN (%)	HISPANIC (%)
Dade County public high school graduation	33.2	28.1	37.2
FTIC applications	41.9	10.8	43.9
FTIC admissions	40.8	8.9	46.3
FTIC enrollments	35.9	3.4	56.2
CCAD admissions	37.5	10.9	50.0
CCAD enrollments	35.4	9.8	53.6
Total enrollments	46.5	9.0	42.0
Baccalaureate degrees	50.0	6.1	41.4

Source: State University System, "Three-Year Trend Analysis of Minority Enrollment and Degrees Conferred in State University System," Board of Regents, Tallahassee, Florida, 1988.

Note: FTIC = first time in college. CCAD = community college associate's degree recipients.

tion presented in chapter 3), but they nonetheless suggest a lower rate of graduation for African-Americans. The lower proportion of Hispanics graduating is more a function of the rapid growth in Hispanic enrollments than a differential rate of achievement.

The international character of the institution is illustrated by the number of foreign nonresident students (6.3 percent in 1986) and the number of resident alien undergraduates who have established permanent residency in the United States (18 percent). Approximately two-thirds of all students attend part-time, although full-time students outnumber part-time students in the freshman and sophomore classes.

Retention

Retention rates at FIU are similar to those for other units in the state university system. One year after entry, first-time-in-college (FTIC) African-American students persist at a rate that lags the system average by approximately 5 percent, a significant improvement from the 10 percent lag that was characteristic in earlier years. Anglo students persist at slightly higher rates, while Hispanics continue at rates substantially above the other two groups. For the cohort entering in 1983–1984, retention rates after two years for African-American students was 65 percent. The comparable rate for Anglo was 69 percent, and for Hispanics, 82 percent. Among upper-division transfer students entering in 1983–1984, the retention rate for African-Americans was 55 percent; for Anglos, 68 percent; and for Hispanics, 72 percent.

Sixteen percent of the graduates who responded to our survey were of traditional age, a statistic that is low in comparison with other case-study institutions. However, 31 percent reported completing degrees within four years, a midrange figure; CSUDH, UNM, Memphis State, and UTEP all had lower proportions. FIU had the highest proportion of graduates (94 percent) who had transferred from other postsecondary institutions. FIU also had the highest proportion of graduates (65 percent) reporting that their primary language was not English. A relatively low proportion (25 percent) reported they were first-generation college-goers. Among Hispanic graduates only 27 percent were first-generation, in contrast to 47 percent of Hispanics at UNM and 56 percent at UTEP.

Degrees Conferred

FIU conferred 2,237 baccalaureate degrees during its first ten years. Table 5.2 provides the ten-year average by race and ethnicity, as well as the yearly patterns for 1981 through 1985. The number and proportion of degrees earned by African-Americans has declined slightly. The number and proportion of degrees earned by Anglos has steadily declined, while Hispanics have steadily increased their share. These outcomes generally reflect the enrollment patterns and the tendency for African-Americans to earn degrees at rates substantially lower than other racial or ethnic groups.

TABLE 5.2. FIU Baccalaureate Degrees Conferred as of September 1985

Year	Total	African-American	Hispanic	Anglo	Nonresident Alien
Ten-year total	23,337	1,548 (6.7)	4,536 (19.4)	15,098 (64.7)	1,120 (4.8)
1980–1981	2,188	128 (5.9)	485 (22.16)	1,275 (58.3)	195 (8.9)
1981–1982	1,876	95 (5.1)	517 (27.6)	1,025 (54.5)	173 (9.2)
1982–1983	1,910	108 (5.7)	583 (30.5)	956 (50.05)	188 (9)
1983–1984	1,884	120 (6.36)	542 (28.8)	907 (48.1)	239 (12.7)
1984–1985	1,934	114 (5.9)	646 (33.4)	897 (46.3)	232 (12)

Source: Office of Institutional Research, Florida International University.

Note: Figures in parentheses are percentages for the adjacent base numbers.

UNIVERSITY ENVIRONMENT

Internal minority initiatives`at FIU are largely limited to recruitment, admission, and retention of African-American students. FIU does not have affirmative action initiatives addressed to Hispanic or Asian-American students, other than categorical financial aid and incentives intended to attract students of high scholastic potential as measured by previous academic achievement and scores on admission exams.

The responsibility for support services, particularly those focusing on African-American students, is organizationally decentralized. The state-funded college Reach-Out and Partners in Progress (PIP) programs are supervised by the office of undergraduate studies, while recruitment is shared between admissions (which reports to student affairs) and faculty members within individual colleges. Responsibility for retention is assigned to the office of student development under student affairs, but support systems are widely dispersed.

Until 1987, institutional research at FIU focused on system and federal reporting requirements, giving little attention to retention, outcomes, or related programmatic assessment. While faculty members and administrators have discussed the importance of analyzing data so that information about students is disaggregated by race and ethnicity, no such analyses were available during the study. Most of the data reported for this case, even for problem areas identified by the institution, came from the state university system data base and reports.

FIU has the highest representation of Hispanics among its administrative staff of any unit in the state university system. African-Americans are also well represented. Among the eight historically Anglo institutions, FIU employed one of every five African-Americans in executive, administrative, and managerial positions in 1984–1985. Table 5.3 compares system averages (excluding FAMU) with the FIU statistics for 1984–1985.

Hispanics were better represented than African-Americans both among executives, administrators, and managers and in the more restrictive professional, nonfaculty category. While increases in Hispanic representation among university administrators have not kept pace with their representation among undergraduates, the figures show steady growth since 1982–1983, when they represented 9.9 percent of the larger category, less than the 13.9 representation for African-Americans in the same year. The strong representation of African-American administrators is in part a function of the number who direct minority programming supported by federal or state categorical funds.

The current FIU president, the fourth since the institution was established, is the first Cuban-born chief executive officer of a four-year university in the United States. Important to his choice were the academic credentials he had earned from Ivy League institutions and his

TABLE 5.3. Comparison of FIU and Florida State University System Work Force Distribution, 1984–1985

	African-American (%)	Hispanic (%)
FIU:		
Executive and administrative Managerial	11.6	14.4
Professional, nonfaculty	8.2	23.6
Florida State University system (except FAMU):		
Executive and administrative Managerial	6.6	2.5
Professional, nonfaculty	6.1	2.7

Source: Florida International University, EEO-6 Report, 1984.

previous experience in the private sector. An official was quoted in a university publication: "We were looking for a leader who could represent the University in a multi-ethnic, multi-cultural community and who could build closer relationships between the university and the community" (Regents Appoint Modesto Maidique to Fill Presidency," *Vistas* 7:10, October 1986, p. 1). To a considerable degree, the priorities of his administration have embraced multiethnic and multicultural goals.

Admissions and Recruitment

FIU's admissions requirements for first-time freshmen are the highest of any university in the state system, partly because of the lower division enrollment limit. Candidates must have completed seventeen academic units in college preparatory courses with an overall B average, and must have earned a minimum score of 1,000 on the SAT or 23 on the ACT. As part of the Board of Regents "exception rule" for improving equity, FIU is authorized to waive its admissions criteria for up to 20 percent of the students admitted in any year, as long as follow-up and academic support services are provided.

FIU admissions and recruitment officers direct their primary attention to high school graduates as potential first-time freshmen. Many faculty members and administrators stated that native students outperformed transfer students, although there had been no systematic institutional research conducted to test the accuracy of this assertion. Ninety-six percent of native FIU freshmen pass the College Level Academic Skills Test (CLAST). This rate substantially exceeds the 78 percent posted by all other students at FIU, a group which includes transfer students as well as those from out of state and from other four-year institutions.

As the study ended, a new vice-president for student affairs had initiated a strong programmatic effort to recruit larger numbers of African-American Students. Also a part of the initiative was the improvement of services for those in residence.

Early Intervention

FIU carries out a number of special initiatives directed toward identifying, recruiting, and retaining African-American students. The absence of comparable initiatives directed toward Hispanic students reflects their high performance as well as the prevailing staff view that such students come to the university highly motivated and with strong support from their families.

Several programs respond to federal or state initiatives, but there are also internal programs. The largest and most successful initiative identifies promising secondary school students, motivates them to attend college, and assists them in strengthening their preparation. Supported fiscally by FIU, the Dade County Public School System, and State Reach-Out funds, the program is carried out by the office of undergraduate studies in cooperation with the Dade County Public School System. The program, known as Partners in Progress I and II, involves university-sponsored seminars during the regular academic year and a six-week summer program on the FIU campus for high school sophomores and juniors. Activities encompass academic, social, and cultural dimensions of college life. In 1986–1987 over 550 qualified applicants sought the opportunity to participate in PIP I, but available resources limited actual participation to 200. A follow-up study of early program participants revealed that 80 percent had subsequently been admitted to baccalaureate institutions after high school graduation, although fewer than one-fifth enrolled at FIU.

PIP II is a program for students who have already participated in PIP I. In the summer between their junior and senior years of high school, students receive scholarships covering costs of tuition, books, and fees for two courses involving 3 to 6 hours of college credit. In addition to special counseling and skills development, participants also receive assistance during the summer in such areas as test taking and study skills. Those who complete both PIP programs and are subsequently admitted to FIU receive an invitational scholarship of $500 a semester which remains in effect as long as the student maintains a satisfactory GPA. The PIP program was designated in 1986 by the Florida Board of Regents as a pilot program to encourage replication of the system in other locations and for other target groups.

The PIP program began in 1982 with 5 participating schools and 41 students as a part of the state incentive grants program. By 1987 the program had grown to 14 schools with 175 students in PIP I and 105 students in PIP II. Participants in PIP were 84 percent African-American and 12.6 percent Hispanic. The comparable figures for PIP II were 90 percent and 6.6 percent.

University Housing

By Board of Regents regulation, residential housing is limited to 10 percent of the undergraduate population and does not play a prominent part in the programming of the institution. Approximately 365 units at the University Park campus opened in 1986 with potential capacity of 725 beds (2 per apartment); the North Miami campus (opened in 1985) has 375 units which could serve about 550 students. While no organized programming initiatives were carried out in the university housing during the time of our study, the University Master Plan calls for increases in the number of residence halls and the number of rooms in the years ahead.

Student Organizations and Activities

An array of social, cultural, and educational clubs contribute to the multicultural environment of the university. Weeks during the year are dedicated to the celebration of specific cultures, and events are coordinated to produce a year-long program celebrating the international and multilingual nature of the campus. The program culminates in the International Festival, during which the many cultures represented in the student body exhibit customs, beliefs, foods, dance, clothing, and related highlights.

Latino nations and groups are represented by clubs formed by students from Central America, South America, the Caribbean, Spain, and Cuba. These clubs champion the political as well as the educational and social interests of their members. The Federation of Cuban American Students keeps alive the hope of the ultimate liberation of Cuba for the early exile and freedom flight waves. The Cabildo Casa de la Cultura Cubana works to help the more recent Mariels succeed. The Colombian Students Club has actively tried to counter the negative publicity associated with Colombia and the drug trade. Iranian and Korean clubs have also worked to promote a more positive image of their nation's people.

African-Americans are not as visibly active in clubs, nor do they have as many clubs as their Hispanic counterparts. Black History Week is the major focus of their involvement. The staff perception is that African-Americans tend to get lost in the Spanish-speaking cultures which predominate among the clubs and during the International Festival.

ACADEMIC ENVIRONMENT

Hispanic students constitute an important part of the dominant culture at FIU. Faculty members were surprised to learn that the university had been selected for study because of the graduation rates of Hispanic students. Even Anglo faculty members thought it presumptuous to view Hispanic students as a minority for whom special interventions were required. The same could not be said for African-Americans, who were widely perceived to be at disadvantage. Several African-American students described campus life as inhospitable. One noted: "Blacks can't see themselves in the university environment." FIU obviously does not provide the same level of comfort for African-Americans as it does for Hispanics.

Initiatives designed to assist African-American students can be easily misunderstood in such an environment. Under one initiative the records of African-American students encountering academic difficulty or admitted by waiver of admissions criteria were flagged to ensure that they saw a counselor before registering for a subsequent semester. The policy, while intended as special assistance, was perceived as a harassment intended to embarrass African-Americans. With the benefit of hindsight the university broadened the policy to flag all students who met these criteria, but because of the way the program was initiated it is still viewed with hostility by African-Americans.

Faculty Characteristics

In 1986–1987, 14 percent of FIU full-time faculty members were Hispanic, 7 percent Asian, and 6 percent African-American. Among tenured faculty members 11 percent were Hispanic, 5 percent African-American. While Hispanics are significantly underrepresented in relation to their presence among undergraduate students, the degree of underrepresentation for African-Americans is substantially less than in most other historically Anglo institutions serving the proportion of African-American undergraduates that attend FIU. Of course, this observation must be tempered by the significant underrepresentation of African-American students at FIU in relation to their presence among high school graduates in the Miami-Dade area.

In 1985-1986 FIU set a goal to fill at least 35 percent of all faculty openings in business administration, engineering and applied sciences, and selected disciplines in arts and sciences with African-Americans, Hispanics, and/or women. While the university actually filled 42 percent of these openings from the specified groups, most of the new hires were women. The university carries out a conscientious search for qualified minorities, but administrators feel disadvantaged because of the size of the applicant pool and the fiscal resources available to compete for available candidates.

Academic Programs

The international emphasis of the campus is reflected in the variety of teaching and service programs directed toward improving understanding among the people of the Americas as well as the challenges of the urban area in which the institution is located. Grants and contracts projects frequently reflect multilingual and multicultural perspectives. The College of Education received federal funds to investigate indigenous cognitive styles and cultural values as they influence achievement and behavior in school. A second federal project provides training to school personnel in affective multicultural understanding and community understanding to help them promote greater Hispanic parental involvement in the education of their children. A third federally funded program provides multidisciplinary training in Haitian culture and bilingual special education for classroom teachers and paraprofessionals.

The School of Nursing conducts research into cultural sensitivity to patient or client needs as well as race and culturally specific gerontological studies. Students receive clinical experience at a health education center located in rural Dade County, where they provide health care for indigents and migrants. Hispanic students are particularly helpful in this activity because they also serve as role models to encourage migrant Hispanics to think of higher education and nursing as possibilities for them.

The departments of biological sciences, chemistry, medical laboratory sciences, and physics participate in a federally funded minority biomedical research program. The College of Business Administration works with neighborhood groups in the greater Miami area offering workshops for African-American and Hispanic entrepreneurs and other small business owners. The school has also established an incubator–development center bordering an African-American neighborhood to encourage new industry. The College of Engineering and Applied Sciences emphasizes bilingualism and international trade.

The baccalaureate degree requirements for the schools and colleges also give evidence of the international emphasis. The College of Education has infused multicultural and bilingual competencies into its teacher education and administrator training curricula. The School of Nursing places heavy emphasis on enhancing the cultural sensitivity of nurses to patient needs in both the preservice baccalaureate degree program and the continuing education program offered to community professionals. All graduates take course work that directly or indirectly relates to international and multicultural understanding. This emphasis permeates the institution, making FIU a unique environment for students from all cultures.

Academic Support

As noted previously, academic support services are widely dispersed. The Office of Undergraduate Studies has the responsibility for supervising program activities which span more than one academic unit. The office also serves as an ombudsman for undergraduate and nondegree-seeking students, and coordinates or participates in such diverse functions as readmission applications, dismissal appeals, advising un-decided upper-division students, certification for associate of arts de-grees, financial aid consortium agreements, and academic counseling for prospective students. It has jurisdiction over the student testing and assessment center, a writing laboratory, and an advisement center.

SUMMARY

The most important influences on Hispanic baccalaureate achievement in this case clearly appear to be external to the university. In the Cuban community, unusual support networks such as the Municipio organi-zations, the media, and grassroots support help to maintain already existing cultural values that emphasize the work ethic, education and credentialing, and optimism about the future.

FIU contributes to baccalaureate achievement by its Hispanic and international students through emphasis on multilingual and multi-cultural programming. This emphasis permeates every aspect of the institution, as seen in the diverse cultures of the students admitted; the courses and related academic studies focused upon cultures and worldwide understanding; and the student activities of the institu-tion, which are clearly oriented toward appreciation and understanding of diverse cultures. Students gain support from working in an envi-ronment in which their language and customs are respected and re-flected in the classrooms and in the related services and activities of the university.

While Hispanics may be a minority in American political and social life, they are already a majority in the political and educational life of the area served by FIU. They do not think of themselves as "minorities" in the sense that this term has been used in this study, to describe groups of students who may be at special risk in majority colleges and universities. Neither are they thought of in this way by the Anglo faculty members and administrators who still dominate the FIU staff rosters, as they do elsewhere—although there is clear evidence that even this fact of academic life is undergoing change at FIU.

Certainly the importance of location cannot be overemphasized in explaining FIU's success. But to location FIU adds a mission emphasis well attuned to the strengths and interests of the dominant Hispanic population it serves and a level of selectivity that consistently produces well-prepared second- or third-generation Hispanic college-goers. Be-cause of its location, mission, and selectivity, the university succeeds in recording impressive outcomes without extensive special effort or the dedication of institutional resources through a strategic planning process.

However, the approach that has produced positive outcomes for an immigrant Hispanic population does not work nearly as well for an indigenous African-American population just a quarter-century away from segregation and legalized discrimination. African-Americans do not find the university environment comfortable, as evidenced by the small numbers who actually attend in relation to the numbers admitted as freshmen, as well as in the comments of recent graduates. Those who attend do not graduate at significantly higher levels than elsewhere in Florida, or for that matter in other institutions where minority achievement is largely taken for granted. Clearly there are also important differences in preparation between African-Americans who attend FIU and their Anglo and Hispanic counterparts.

The initiatives established to improve African-American participation and achievement appear to be relatively limited and discrete, and largely externally funded. At the time of the study there was no central coordination of these strategies beyond that provided by the Office of Undergraduate studies which had many responsibilities in addition to its charge to coordinate educational opportunities for underrepresented groups. Information about student achievement by race and ethnicity across majors was conspicuous by its absence, creating barriers to the use of planning or accountability strategies to identify or improve the performance of lagging academic units. Under the new president, the rejuvenated and renamed Office of Institutional Research has begun to study retention issues.

Florida International University is a particularly interesting case because it illustrates so many of the variables both positive and negative that contribute to the outcomes an institution achieves in working with minority students. The university is rightfully proud of the record it has achieved with the Cuban Hispanic population. Institution spokespersons are the first to admit, however, that their institution has a distance to travel before it can take equal pride in the opportunities provided for African-Americans.

6

TEMPLE UNIVERSITY

HOWARD L. SIMMONS
with the assistance of **VALAIDA S. WALKER**

Temple College was founded in 1884 in Philadelphia by Russell H. Conwell, to provide the urban poor with the opportunity to advance their position through education. Today, as one of four state-related universities in Pennsylvania, Temple University still embraces a populist and democratic mission. In its recently adopted academic plan, references are made to the Conwell tradition, reaching out to those who can least afford higher education while at the same time maintaining a commitment to excellence.

Temple offers 241 degrees with almost 400 specializations and sub-specializations at the baccalaureate, masters, preprofessional, and doctoral levels. Among the diverse fields included are allied health professions, arts and sciences, business administration, communications and theater, dentistry, engineering and architecture, education, horticulture and landscape design, health, physical education, recreation and dance, law, medicine, music, pharmacy, social administration, and art. While the Philadelphia metropolitan area is the primary source of students, the university draws significant numbers from the rest of Pennsylvania, other states, and foreign countries. In addition to its main complex along Broad Street, Temple also has campuses in the center city and Elkins Park neighborhoods of Philadelphia; in suburban Ambler; in Harrisburg; and overseas in Tokyo and Rome.

STATE INFLUENCES

Public higher education in Pennsylvania includes four state-related universities (Temple, Lincoln University, Pennsylvania State University, and the University of Pittsburgh), each with its own board; fourteen state-owned universities governed by a central governing board; and thirteen

Howard L. Simmons is executive director of the Middle States Association of Colleges and Schools, Commission on Higher Education, Philadelphia, Pennsylvania. Valaida Walker is associate provost at Temple University.

community colleges. Penn State and Pitt also operate their own systems of branch campuses.

The State Board of Education, operating through a council of basic education and a council of higher education, provides coordination for the review and processing of the budgets of the three sectors. The board also exercises a planning function. Through its master plan the board has reaffirmed its commitment to equal educational opportunity by recommending that institutions encourage increased entry of women and minorities into higher education and by expressing its support for transition courses and programs that help disadvantaged and handicapped students develop their potential.

Temple University became a state-related university in 1965. While essentially public, it retains some of the characteristics of the independent status it previously held. In the 1986–1987 academic year Temple received more than $110 million from the state, or roughly 25 percent of its total revenue and approximately 50 percent of its educational and general expenditures. As one of the states subject to Title VI regulation by *Adams v. Richardson* and successor litigation, Pennsylvania was required to submit an equal opportunity plan (for desegregation), but the participation objectives in the plan had little impact on Temple since the university already enrolled a substantial proportion of African-American students. More relevant to Temple were the plan's priorities for improving retention and the attainment of baccalaureate degrees.

In 1984–1985, 12.9 percent of children enrolled in Pennsylvania's public and nonpublic elementary and secondary schools were African-American, 2 percent were Hispanics, and less than 1 percent were American Indian. Only 8.1 percent of high school graduates were African-American. A recent study by the Pennsylvania Association of Colleges and Universities revealed that participation rates for Pennsylvania's high school graduates were significantly lower than those of contiguous states. While in recent years a number of commissions have been appointed by the governor to study issues related to equity, this particular study's importance was its emphasis on recruitment of minorities. The study suggested that the best way to increase participation rates was to devote much greater attention to students' career and educational decisions at the elementary level. Financial support for this nongovernmental effort was provided by the State Board of Education.

State-Sponsored Student Support Services

Pennsylvania has developed the ACT 101 program as its initiative to improve higher education opportunities for underrepresented groups. The program, initiated by a Philadelphia legislator serving as speaker of the house, was authorized in 1971 to provide support for learning and special counseling services for undergraduate students. In 1985–1986 the program provided $5.7 million for tutoring, counseling, and cultural activities in 74 institutions including Temple. Of the more than 11,000 students served by the program, about 41 percent were African-American. More than half the students in the program were Anglo.

The State Board of Education annually calls for reports of progress on ACT 101. A recent study by the Department of Education concluded that the achievement, persistence, and attitude of ACT 101 participants was much higher than would otherwise have been expected for this group of students. The study did note that mathematics, natural sciences, and engineering had not been popular majors for ACT 101 students. While students who entered ACT 101 programs in four-year institutions in the 1970s were significantly below the U.S. average in achievement and aptitude, they managed to graduate in proportions higher than the national average for four-year colleges. Noted in the study as a matter for concern was the general decrease over the years in the numbers of African-Americans and Hispanics entering ACT 101 programs, while the numbers of Anglos, Asian-Americans, and American Indians increased.

State Financial Aid Initiatives

The Pennsylvania Higher Education Assistance Agency (PHEAA), a quasi-governmental agency, coordinates the flow of financial assistance guaranteeing private loans, issuing state higher education grants, making alternative loans, and administering work-study programs and a program of institutional assistance grants. Using funds appropriated by the general assembly, PHEAA determines grant awards based on demonstrated financial need. PHEAA has simplified the applications process by developing a common application on which students can request both state grants and assistance under various federal student financial aid programs. Guided by a recommendation in the recent participation study described above, PHEAA now sends financial aid information and the common application forms directly to parents, in addition to sending them to high schools and to individual students who request information.

While PHEAA does not maintain records on the race or ethnicity of the recipients of grants and loans, it does maintain data on grants made to institutions. Under the state grant program, 5,566 students at Temple University received about $5.7 million in 1986–1987, with an average award of $1,066. The total available to PHEAA for grants in 1986–1987 was $96 million, the fourth largest state financial aid program in the country. The state meets one-third of a student's calculated need for tuition and fees; the 1986 ceiling was $1,750. Through a lease arrangement, PHEAA permits Temple to have direct access to loan information about its students.

Pennsylvania also administers the Commonwealth Scholarship Fund through which the state between 1983 and 1988 provided about

$3.3 million intended to aid minority students primarily from historically black Cheyney University and Lincoln University to complete graduate study at Temple, Pittsburgh, and Penn State. In 1986–1987, 59 students attended Temple University under this program, enrolling in such fields as social administration, education, law, medicine, and theatre arts.

Other State Influences

Other strategies to improve the participation rate of minorities in higher education are directed at elementary and secondary schools. The Department of Education has designed a program to increase parental involvement in raising student aspirations. A diagnostic testing program in grades 3, 5, and 8 uncovers serious deficiencies in basic skills, general education, and cultural awareness. A preliminary review of the program indicates that it has been relatively successful in schools with few minority students, but there are questions about its utility for students in urban settings like Philadelphia.

While hearings on minority opportunities in higher education have been sponsored by the legislature, there have been no recent new legislative initiatives. There are some concerns as well that the programs already in existence may not be sufficiently well coordinated to produce optimum results.

Education officials in Harrisburg attribute much of the success attained with minority students at urban institutions like Temple University and the University of Pittsburgh to location. While state officials commend institutional efforts to provide developmental work in reading, writing, and math, they see a need for greater attention to retention strategies and to programs for social and cultural adjustment. Higher education policy officials in Pennsylvania believe that preparation in basic education is the single most important barrier to minority success in achieving the baccalaureate degree.

COMMUNITY SETTING

Philadelphia, affectionately called the "City of Brotherly Love," is the fifth largest city in the nation. Even though the city has lost population and industry to its suburbs and the Sunbelt during the last two decades, there are many signs that its economy is reviving, including the establishment of a high-tech corridor in the metropolitan area, the revitalization of the central core of the city, and improvements in mass transit. Because of its strategic location and because the cost of living is lower than that of its New York and Baltimore/Washington neighbors, Philadelphia is attracting new businesses and new residents.

From the earliest times the city has been populated by a broad spectrum of ethnic and racial groups. According to the 1980 census, 52 percent of the 1.7 million city residents were African-American and 6 percent were Hispanic. While relations among ethnic and racial groups have generally been good, struggles between African-Americans and newly arrived Asian-American refugees as well as attacks on African-Americans and interracial couples who have moved into previously all-white neighborhoods in recent years have permanently shattered the city's sedate atmosphere.

African-Americans have become a vital part of the city and its large labor force and growing service-oriented economy. A wide range of postsecondary educational opportunities contributes to expanded career opportunities for minorities. African-Americans have been elected to high political offices including mayor, president of the city council, city managing director, and superintendent of schools.

A number of strong African-American organizations promote educational opportunities. Churches and religious organizations provide scholarship assistance, tutorials, counseling services, and programs to increase student aspirations. The American Foundation for Negro Affairs has an extensive program for expanding minority students' awareness of career possibilities and providing academic intervention. The program assigns preceptors to work with students in such learning situations as laboratories, hospitals, law firms, courts, banks, and accounting houses. Students enter the program after completing the tenth grade of high school and are immediately enrolled in special academic programs designed to assist them in overcoming basic skills deficiencies in science, mathematics, and communications. The program, targeted for minorities from lower socioeconomic levels, is provided at no cost to the students or their parents. Funding comes from a variety of community agencies and groups, including the city of Philadelphia. Dropout and dismissal rates for the program have been consistently under 10 percent.

Unlike some major universities set in high-density urban environments, Temple has experienced little friction with its neighbors. The positive relationships between the university and the African-American community have developed over a long period, beginning with the time of the founding of the university. Many university activities involve minority residents in areas adjacent to the campus, and the community has access to university facilities and services.

Public Schools

The school district of Philadelphia had slightly more than 200,000 students in 1986–1987, making it the fifth largest in the nation. Sixty-four percent of the students were African-American, and 24 percent were Anglo, 9 percent Hispanic, and 3 percent Asian-American. The residential patterns and exodus of many middle-class Anglo families from the city have left the public school system essentially segregated.

When the local human relations commission filed suit to compel integration through a massive program of busing, a newly appointed African-American superintendent was able to persuade the school board that desegregation and improved quality could be achieved through a "modified plan" involving some busing but concentrating more heavily on the use of "magnet" schools created along such specialized lines as fine and performing arts, science and technology, and business. While it is too early to tell whether this approach will achieve integration, the new school administration has been successful in getting community groups and business leaders more involved in the schools.

In recent years, public schools in the city of Philadelphia have gained citizen support as the result of increases in student achievement and more efficient management. An instructional improvement effort has established a standardized curriculum, a citywide testing program, and a new promotion policy. In addition, high school graduation requirements have been raised and new remediation programs implemented. In order to deal with the preparation problem at the most critical stages, the public schools have fortified already successful early childhood education programs, and have initiated a comprehensive K-12 guidance and counseling program which focuses on career development, career awareness, and close cooperation between the counselor and the classroom teacher.

The school district has excellent relations with Temple University. Many of its employees received undergraduate or graduate degrees there, and many are currently active members of the Temple University alumni association. One high-ranking district administrator summed up the relationship: "Temple University is a very positive environment for our high school graduates and for our staff; there are minority role models and the University has always been very cooperative in assisting in the improvement of the schools."

Parochial Schools

Of the fifteen top feeder high schools for Temple, seven are part of the Catholic Archdiocese of Philadelphia. The Office of Catholic Education of the Archdiocese of Philadelphia oversees elementary, secondary, and special education schools in Philadelphia and the four adjacent counties. In 1986 the elementary schools enrolled a total of 98,635 students, and the high school student population totaled 35,607.

Affected by white flight, Catholic schools are enrolling an increasing proportion of minorities, who now make up approximately 23 percent of the elementary enrollment and 16 percent of the high school enrollment. School officials believe they are able to attract minority families because of a perception that Catholic schools provide strict but equitable discipline; a strong academic program; and close monitoring of student academic progress, including the provision of personal counseling and career guidance. The Office of Catholic Education has established a standing committee on recruitment and retention to improve outreach to minority and disadvantaged youth and to work closely with the parishes and with parents to reduce attrition, improve students' study habits, and create a comfortable environment.

Postsecondary Institutions

Temple University receives a large number of transfers from two-year institutions and experiences a net gain in transfers at the sophomore and junior levels from other state-related universities in the commonwealth and from private universities in the Philadelphia region. In fall 1987 transfers accounted for 40 percent of all entering students, with 37 percent of the transfers from area community colleges, especially the Community College of Philadelphia (CCP). Two historically black colleges—Lincoln University and Cheyney University of Pennsylvania— are in close proximity to Temple. Although they compete for African-American students, both also have cooperative programs with Temple.

STUDENTS

Temple enrolled 31,492 students in 1986, about two-thirds of whom attended full-time. More than 80 percent worked at least part-time, and an estimated 20 to 30 percent were employed full-time. Fourteen percent were African-American, 6 percent Asian-American or Pacific Islander, and 2 percent Hispanic. The rate of participation for African-Americans at Temple, while well below their representation in the city, was sufficiently high that Temple was not assigned enrollment goals in the equal opportunity plan for Pennsylvania.

While the largest numbers of African-Americans are enrolled in the arts and sciences, education, and social administration, their participation in other fields is reasonably proportional to their representation in the university, as revealed in table 6.1.

Enrollments within colleges, however, reveal uneven distribution across program areas. The largest number of African-American, Hispanic, and Asian-American students in the College of Allied Health Professions were enrolled in nursing. Most African-Americans choosing majors in engineering, computer science, and architecture were enrolled in engineering technology as opposed to engineering science.

The progress Temple has made in enrolling minority students has not been matched by similar progress in retaining and graduating them. Tables 6.2, 6.3, and 6.4 reveal that graduation rates for African-American and Hispanic students who entered in 1980 were lower than the rates for Anglos and Asian-Americans who entered in the same admission categories. Forty-two percent of all African-Americans were special ad-

TABLE 6.1. Temple University Fall 1986 Enrollments by College or School and Ethnicity

College or School	Total N	Asian-American (%)	African-American (%)	Hispanic (%)	Minority Total (%)
Allied Health Professions	597	3.2	11.9	1.7	16.8
Arts and Sciences	7,236	9.5	17.0	3.1	29.6
Business and Management	6,554	4.4	14.2	1.3	19.9
Communications and Theatre	2,522	1.4	14.0	1.2	16.6
Education	2,759	2.5	14.2	2.0	18.7
Engineering, Computer Science, and Architecture	1,741	12.6	10.3	1.8	24.7
Social Administration	624	2.1	41.5	3.0	46.6

Source: Temple University Office of Academic Planning.

missions, contrasted with less than 6 percent of Anglos. Clearly there are significant preparation differences among students entering Temple, as a secondary function of race and ethnicity. Interestingly, the differences in retention and graduation were least noticeable among transfers.

The survey made for this study revealed a relatively high proportion of graduates (36 percent) in the traditional age range and a high proportion (48 percent) completing degrees in four years or less. Only 12 percent reported taking more than six years to graduate. Thirty-nine percent of the graduates were first-generation college-goers, with

TABLE 6.2. Temple University Retention and Graduation Rates, 1980 Entry Cohort

Regular Freshman Admissions by Race or Ethnicity

Race or Ethnicity	Total	Percent Fall 1984		Percent Fall 1985	
		Retained	Graduated	Retained	Graduated
Anglo	100.0	56.3	29.9	55.6	46.9
	(1,767)	(995)	(529)	(983)	(829)
African-American	100.0	42.0	16.6	37.8	28.5
	(193)	(83)	(32)	(73)	(55)
Hispanic	100.0	30.8	15.4	30.8	23.1
	(13)	(4)	(2)	(4)	(3)
Asian-American	100.0	54.3	20.0	57.1	40.0
	(35)	(19)	(7)	(20)	(14)

Source: Temple University, Office of Academic Planning.

Note: Figures in parentheses are base numbers for the adjacent percentages.

TABLE 6.3. Temple University Retention and Graduation Rates, 1980 Entry Cohort
Transfer Admissions by Race or Ethnicity

Race or Ethnicity	Total	Percent Fall 1984		Percent Fall 1985	
		Retained	*Graduated*	*Retained*	*Graduated*
Anglo	100.0	61.4	52.8	61.4	56.2
	(1,634)	(1,003)	(862)	(1,003)	(920)
African-American	100.0	46.9	33.8	43.4	39.0
	(367)	(172)	(124)	(163)	(143)
Hispanic	100.0	33.4	29.2	33.4	29.2
	(24)	(8)	(7)	(8)	(7)
Asian-American	100.0	65.9	47.7	61.3	56.8
	(44)	(29)	(21)	(27)	(25)

Source: Temple University Office of Academic Planning.

Note: Figures in parentheses are base numbers for the adjacent percentages.

African-American and Hispanic graduates more likely to be in the first generation than Anglos. Only 17 percent reported that their father or mother had not completed high school, a lower proportion than in other urban universities like Wayne State or CSUDH.

TABLE 6.4. Temple University Retention and Graduation Rates, 1980 Entry Cohort
Special Admissions by Race or Ethnicity

Race or Ethnicity	Total	Percent Fall 1984		Percent Fall 1985	
		Retained	*Graduated*	*Retained*	*Graduated*
Anglo	100.0	47.2	21.5	44.4	34.7
	(144)	(68)	(31)	(64)	(50)
African-American	100.0	29.8	5.8	24.6	12.0
	(309)	(92)	(18)	(76)	(37)
Hispanic	100.0	22.6	0.0	19.4	12.9
	(31)	(7)	(0)	(6)	(4)
Asian-American	100.0	50.0	0.0	33.3	33.3
	(6)	(3)	(0)	(2)	(2)

Source: Temple University Office of Academic Planning.

Note: Figures in parentheses are base numbers for the adjacent percentages.

THE UNIVERSITY ENVIRONMENT

Because of its history and location, Temple has from its inception served minority students, especially African-Americans. There has been a commitment to building an administration devoted to the concept of diversity and pluralism. The university's archives document that African-Americans enrolled in and graduated from undergraduate and professional programs such as law and medicine even before Temple College was merged with Philadelphia Dental College in 1907 to form a university. In its more recent history, Temple has developed special programs to respond to the working adults and ethnic minorities of the community.

At the same time there is little evidence that the university has ever developed a broad-based, coordinated approach to the education of minority students, primarily because its position has always been that minority students should be mainstreamed. Temple works to establish an atmosphere conducive to achievement for all students.

The university's commitment to the minority student is underscored in its recently adopted Academic Plan: "We must attract more minority undergraduate students interested in science, engineering and the arts, and encourage them to go on to graduate and professional school." This commitment is reflected in the progress made in expanding cultural diversity among senior administrative personnel. Among deans and above, three (14 percent) are African-American. In the more inclusive executive, administrative, and managerial group the number is 153 (about 21 percent). Hispanics are not represented at the level of deans and above, and are significantly underrepresented in the more inclusive category. Minority persons are in highly visible directorships, particularly in student support areas such as admissions, financial aid, and counseling.

Table 6.5 shows that only historically black Lincoln University exceeds Temple among state-related institutions in the number of African-Americans on the Board of Trustees. The board has taken a strong po-

TABLE 6.5. African-American Trustee Representation at State-Related Universities in Pennsylvania, 1986

	Total number of of trustees	Number of African-American trustees	Percentage of total
Lincoln University	31	23	74.2
Penn State	32	02	06.2
Temple	34	07	20.6
University of Pittsburgh	42	02	04.8

Source: Pennsylvania Department of Education, *The Commonwealth of Pennsylvania Fourth Annual Desegregation Progress Report for the Period of July 1, 1986 - June 30, 1987.* Adaptation of Table H.

sition on minority and equity issues. African-American members are influential in the board's decision-making process and have contributed to the board's strong position on affirmative action and nondiscrimination. Even though Temple has been relatively free of overt racism, the board has used a special ad hoc committee to investigate the campus environment. The committee decided that over the years Temple's record with minorities had been "far superior to other institutions."

Admissions and Recruitment

Recruitment receives a high priority at Temple, and the admissions office and recruiting staff are very multicultural. The university uses a variety of recruitment approaches with local high schools, community agencies, and other colleges. It actively seeks out minority candidates and also relies upon its visibility in the community as a recruiting device. A strong marketing campaign includes endorsements from African-American celebrities such as Bill Cosby. The university has found that use of African-American and Hispanic students to recruit other minority students is extremely effective.

Undergraduate admissions policies at Temple specify that students must be graduates of accredited high schools with at least a 2.0 grade-point average, and must have taken a designated distribution of courses. In addition, the university requires that entering students, with the exception of older applicants (age 26 and up) and special admissions, submit standardized test scores. For admission, students must normally have a minimum score of 900 on the SAT or 19 on the ACT.

Temple has traditionally sought a comprehensive mix of students. The Temple Opportunity Program was developed more than fifteen years ago. Its successor, the Special Recruitment and Admissions Program (SRAP), maintains a yearly enrollment of about 600 students. SRAP students are predominantly African-American, but there are also sizable numbers of Anglos, Hispanics, and Asian-Americans. While students admitted under this program are not required to have SAT scores, a special admissions test (for which norms have been computed by the Educational Testing Service) is administered. The students enrolled in SRAP participate in an orientation program and receive academic support services. Temple has also developed alternative admissions and academic support programs in its School of Law and School of Medicine. Both of these schools have above-average enrollments of African-Americans.

Admission to the university does not automatically admit a student to the various colleges and schools. The College of Allied Health Professions, as an example, has stringent prerequisites for entering students and no special admissions programs. This college has recently implemented New Career Ladders in Social Welfare to address what is clearly a serious preparation problem.

Financial Aid

As a state-related university with a mission to serve underrepresented groups, Temple has tried to maintain reasonable tuition rates and to provide students with help in finding the necessary funds to attend college. Financial aid includes scholarships and grants, educational loans, and employment opportunities. The factors in determining eligibility for financial aid at Temple University are academic promise and need.

Students enrolled in the academic support programs of the Russell Conwell Services Center, about half of whom are minority, are eligible to receive a financial aid package that contains more grant and work-study monies than loans. The admissions and financial aid offices try to assure that students in the SRAP program get the maximum financial aid allowed. In extraordinary circumstances, they also work closely with the housing office to assure suitable housing accommodations.

Early Intervention

Philadelphia Regional Introduction for Minorities to Engineering (PRIME), Incorporated, founded originally in 1973 with significant financial support from business, industrial, and philanthropic organizations, serves as the university's major thrust for increasing the number of minorities in engineering, mathematics and computer science, pharmacy and allied health sciences, and actuarial science. The four-year program, involving students in grades 8 to 11, includes a month-long summer program in the final year. This residential component is organized around a curriculum that includes instruction in science and mathematics, communication skills, computers, and special career introduction courses. Of the 159 PRIME seniors who graduated in 1987, 96 percent enrolled in a mathematics- or science-based college program.

Temple's ACT 101 program is organized as a comprehensive effort to provide counseling, tutoring, and precollege instruction for 250 students. The program offers two components, a six-week precollege summer bridge program and an academic year program. Each component provides students with intensive study and guidance to strengthen their academic and personal skills. Temple's own Educational Services Component also offers the extensive Summer Bridge Program and provides a six-week seminar for high school students to prepare them for college. An educational services program for adults extends similar opportunities in a different format to the residents of Philadelphia's center city, including a large number of minority persons. The key components are community outreach, academic counseling, and workshops on preadmissions information. Most of these services are free.

College Articulation

The Mellon Foundation and the Ford Foundation have provided grants to assist the Community College of Philadelphia and Temple in exploring ways to improve the transfer experience. The results of these efforts are documented in a recent report entitled Transfer Experiences of Former CCP Students at Temple University" (by Jane Grosset and Tom Hawk, "Institutional Research Report No. 40, Temple University). The report found that students were least likely to make satisfactory progress in allied health programs. Minority graduates, particularly in nursing, reported inequitable treatment and the absence of necessary academic support. In response, the college has applied for and received a grant for $86,000 over a three-year period to initiate a retention program that will include a course in the basic sciences, mathematics, and study skills, and an orientation to the health professions. Students also will be able to obtain clinical experiences during summers.

Articulation arrangements between Temple and historically black Lincoln University and Cheyney University provide additional opportunities for African-American students. These include, with Cheyney, a doctoral program in educational administration and a three-plus-two Engineering Program designed so that students spend three years at Cheyney taking any necessary remedial work, along with basic academic and engineering courses. The students then transfer to Temple for two years of advanced engineering courses. With Lincoln University, Temple has developed a joint baccalaureate program in English and journalism. The English component is pursued primarily at Lincoln, the journalism at Temple; the degree is granted by Lincoln.

Advisement and Counseling

Universitywide academic, career, and personal counseling programs are open to students of all races and ethnicities. The guiding policy has focused on making services available to all students rather than isolating and possibly stigmatizing minority students by singling them out for special treatment. Even such programs as New Career Ladders in Social Welfare in the School of Social Sciences and the Health Career Opportunity Program in the College of Allied Health Professions, while directed toward minorities, were open to all. At the time of the study the university had only recently hired a director of minority affairs and created a special center for minority students to use when they were not in class.

ACADEMIC ENVIRONMENT

While still feeling the effects of a difficult strike at the time of the study, faculty members were generally very positive and responsive to questions concerning their role with minority students. One of the major priorities of the recently adopted academic plan is recruitment of more African-American and Hispanic faculty in order to reach a goal of 15 percent. As of fall 1986, full-time tenured and nontenured faculty numbered 1,662, with 12 percent being members of ethnic minority groups. About 3 percent were African-American, the majority of whom were concentrated in a small number of programs. The numbers and percentages of minority faculty across schools and colleges are presented in table 6.6.

Faculty in the School of Social Administration, (SSA) and the College of Allied Health Professions reflect the composition of the student body; in all other academic divisions, African-American and Hispanic faculty members constitute fewer than a third of the number required for a faculty reflecting the demographics of student majors. The School of Business and Management reported no tenured African-American faculty members and only one nontenured. The high number of Asian faculty members in this school is the result of a fully operational campus in Japan.

Academic Programs

The School of Social Administration, where African-American faculty are well-represented, offers the New Careers Ladder Program. This program primarily reaches African-American and Hispanic students who are already working in social service agencies. The university's Center for Social Policy and Community Development, staffed in part by SSA faculty members, offers a complex of outreach programs focusing on career development and job training. These programs have served approximately 750 students, many of them Temple students, and virtually all minorities. The center's literacy program primarily serves community members, both African-American and Hispanic.

The College of Arts and Sciences has a highly visible department of African and African-American studies which, in addition to it academic function, serves as a center where African-American students can congregate, learn about culture, discuss contemporary problems in the minority experience, and air any grievances they may be harboring. The department has close ties with the Philadelphia community and is recognized nationally for the quality of faculty and programs.

To increase opportunities for African-American students to interact with scholar role models and to create a more comfortable environment, the college recently established the Center for the Study of Black History and Culture as a place for study with particular emphasis on the African-American experience in the Philadelphia region. The center was also designed as a way of bringing additional African-American scholars to Temple to do archival work and other research, and to interact with students.

The School of Business and Management was awarded a grant by the American Economic Association for the purpose of conducting a summer program to increase the number of minority graduate students in economics. Focused on minority undergraduates, the program is de-

TABLE 6.6. Temple University Full-Time Faculty, Tenured and Nontenured, by College and Ethnicity, Fall 1986

COLLEGE OR SCHOOL	AMERICAN INDIAN	AFRICAN-AMERICAN	ASIAN-AMERICAN	HISPANIC	TOTAL MINORITY	TOTAL NUMBER
Allied Health						
Professions: Tenured	-0-	3 (16.7)	1 (5.5)	-0-	4 (22.2)	18
Nontenured	-0-	-0-	-0-	-0-	-0-	29
Arts and Sciences:						
Tenured	1 (.03)	13 (3.6)	12 (3.3)	5 (1.4)	31 (8.5)	365
Nontenured	-0-	6 (7.7)	7 (9.0)	2 (2.6)	15 (19.2)	78
Business Adminis-						
tration: Tenured	-0-	-0-	12 (11.1)	-0-	12 (11.1)	108
Nontenured	-0-	1 (1.9)	8 (14.8)	1 (1.9)	10 (18.5)	54
Communications and Theatre:						
Tenured	-0-	1 (1.8)	1 (1.8)	1 (1.8)	3 (5.4)	56
Nontenured	-0-	4 (18.2)	-0-	1 (4.5)	5 (22.7)	22
Education:						
Tenured	-0-	4 (4.8)	1 (1.2)	-0-	5 (5.9)	84
Nontenured	-0-	1 (16.7)	-0-	1 (16.7)	2 (33.4)	6
Engineering, Computer Science, and						
Architecture: Tenured	-0-	1 (2.6)	1 (2.6)	-0-	2 (5.3)	38
Nontenured	-0-	1 (2.7)	4 (10.8)	1 (2.7)	6 (16.2)	37
Social Administration:						
Tenured	-0-	12 (34.3)	1 (2.9)	1 (2.9)	14 (40.0)	35
Nontenured	-0-	1 (33.3)	-0-	-0-	1 (33.3)	3

Source: Temple University Office of Academic Planning.

Note: Figures in parentheses are percentages for the adjacent base numbers.

signed for students who have the ability and interest to pursue a Ph.D. degree. Students receive a stipend in addition to having subsistence and tuition costs paid.

The College of Engineering, Computer Science, and Architecture makes extensive visits to schools in the Philadelphia region that have large African-American and Hispanic student bodies. Students from the High School of Engineering and Science, located near the university campus, can complete their final year of high school at Temple, partially subsidized by the school district of Philadelphia. Students from the program are highly regarded and about 25 percent are African-American. The college also sponsors a minority students engineering association.

Academic Enrichment Programs and Services

Temple has a variety of programs and services that provide enrichment; most have significant African-American enrollments. While the programs have distinctive objectives, they all have the common goal of providing academic support to students whose prior preparation was inadequate. Students admitted through the SRAP program (previously described) experience developmental work in English and math, and receive special tutoring, academic advising, and other support services. A science course for university credit is offered to SRAP students through the College of Education. During enrollment in the SRAP program, students usually complete sixteen to eighteen university credits in addition to courses that do not count toward graduation.

Students must remain in the program until they earn thirty-two credits. Placement and exit tests are used to measure results. During the 1985–1986 academic year, 74 percent of participants exited from the program with the thirty-two credits set by the program's objectives. The retention rate among new students enrolled for the second year is 80 to 83 percent, well in excess of the rate for regular admissions during the same time period.

The Russell Conwell Services Center provides learning skill development seminars and workshops, individual and group tutorial services, and supplemental academic assistance. There is significant emphasis on time management; test taking; assertiveness in the classroom; and critical reading, library and research skills. Special modules are also available in computer applications; career exploration; and supplemental academic assistance in mathematics, communication skills, social sciences, science, engineering, business, and other areas. Students who participate in these programs improve their grade-point averages when they move into regular undergraduate courses. The programs are funded by a combination of external grants and university appropriations.

Qualitative Enrichment Studies at Temple (QUEST) provides a non-credit course for students whose scores are below average in arithmetic and a similar course for students who need work in basic algebraic concepts before moving into finite mathematics. The courses are self-paced and guided by workbooks although there is an instructor present to grade papers, give exams, explain results, and answer questions. The support system for QUEST includes forty-five hours of tutoring and a hot line operating three hours a week for students who can't get to campus. Approximately 30 percent of students enrolled in QUEST are minorities. Between 1984 and 1986, 65 to 71 percent of students attempting the mathematics course and 60 percent attempting the algebra course successfully completed their course work.

The English Language Enrichment Center at Temple (ELECT) is a universitywide program to assist students in improving their communication skills. The program is mandatory for students scoring below a prescribed level on a screening exam. It includes writing, speech, reading, and English for nonnative speakers. All courses in ELECT are remedial and do not carry college credit. Students who participate in ELECT have the same success rates as non-ELECT students in the university-required composition course.

Special academic enrichment programs and services are also offered through educational services for adults and special services for disadvantaged students.

SUMMARY

Temple University as a case study of minority degree achievement is distinctive in several ways. Its tradition of serving first-generation college students is important to the outcomes it achieves, as is its location in a predominantly African-American, urban environment. Pennsylvania's experience as an *Adams v. Richardson* state has contributed the influences of planning to improve recruitment and retention, special initiatives embodied in the ACT 101 program and set-aside funding for scholarships. Pennsylvania also has one of the most comprehensive student financial assistance programs of any state in the nation and has developed special initiatives for helping minority students get information and apply for aid.

The many educational, social, and cultural resources available in Philadelphia are a significant asset for Temple. The role African-Americans play in civic, business, and political arenas is also important. In 1987, the leading African-American business journal *Black Enterprise* concluded that Philadelphia was one of five top metropolitan areas for black professionals: "Probably the most significant development is that Blacks [in Philadelphia, Atlanta, Chicago, Los Angeles, and Washington, D.C.] have a sense of pride that can not be easily found in other municipalities. [Students] know that Blacks are leaders in the political and economic development of their city."

Other variables from the model are less positive. The intensity of state influences on Temple is moderated by the institution's historic success in attracting enough minorities to exceed the requirements of the affirmative action plan and by the absence, except for the Equal Opportunity Plan, of state governance arrangements for developing and monitoring accountability measures. Although the university has implemented targeted student support programs with the assistance of external grants, the primary emphasis has been on mainstreaming minorities.

While faculty members are sympathetic to minority participation, as evidenced by the reasonably proportional enrollments across majors, Temple is a research university which affects both its learning environment and the values that guide faculty recruitment. The number of African-American students and the composition of the adjacent community produce a comfortable social environment and make acts of overt racism rare. But the positive elements of the social environment are not duplicated in the academic environment, where the representation of African-American faculty in all but a few programs is minimal.

The Philadelphia public schools have taken important steps recently to improve student performance by standardizing the curriculum and devoting more resources to preventing attrition at the lower grades. However, they still have a long way to go in addressing student preparation problems, as evidenced by the increased numbers of African-Americans enrolling in the Catholic schools and by the fact that some of Temple's larger feeder schools are in the Archdiocese of Philadelphia.

Overall the university has made significant progress in stimulating minority participation, but its record for graduating African-Americans and Hispanics is less impressive.

In general the African-American and Hispanic students who attend Temple are less well prepared than their Anglo and Asian-American counterparts. Temple's philosophy of treating everyone the same, even though students inevitably differ in preparation as a function of their race and ethnicity, may work to the disadvantage of less well prepared minorities. Lack of finances and personal hardships also play a role. The differences might be greater if it were not for the special programs and the excellent support services that Temple provides to all students as a result of long experience with first-generation college-goers.

7

WAYNE STATE UNIVERSITY

A. WADE SMITH
with the assistance of RUTH C. PANAGOS and
HAROLD E. CRUGER

Wayne University was created in 1933 when the Detroit Board of Education combined four of the colleges under its jurisdiction, including the former Detroit Junior College, into a single unit. The first doctoral programs were established following World War II as the institution began its evolution to research university status. In 1956 Wayne was transferred to state control, with the new name Wayne State University, in recognition of the need for Michigan to provide a university to serve the population concentrated in its southeastern region. In 1986 Wayne State enrolled slightly fewer than 29,000 students in twelve colleges and schools. Nearly all students commute; there are no residence halls, but the university does have 700 apartments, leased mainly to graduate students.

Historically Wayne has defined its mission to include educational programs for those financially unable to leave home, those who want to continue their educations while employed, and those who seek general cultural enrichment or who want to follow particular personal interests. The university has also concerned itself with students whose educational backgrounds would not normally have gained them admission to college, and is proud of its tradition of service to the public school system.

THE STATE ENVIRONMENT

Michigan is the eighth largest state and one of the most urbanized, with 71 percent of its population residing in medium to large cities. Between 1980 and 1985 the state lost over a half-million people as a result

A. Wade Smith is associate professor of sociology at Arizona State University. Ruth Panagos is assistant director of special student development, University Counseling Services, at Wayne State University. Harold E. Cruger is assistant vice-president for student support services at Wayne State University.

of out-migration stimulated by high rates of unemployment. African-Americans constituted less than 13 percent of the total Michigan population in 1985, but because there was less African-American out-migration than Anglo, African-Americans made up almost 20 percent of 18- to 25-year-olds, and more than a quarter of those under 18.

Despite its economic woes, or perhaps because of them, the state has increased its commitment to educating its labor force. By mid-decade, Michigan was spending $1.16 billion per year on higher education—the fifth highest state expenditure for higher education in the nation. In the 1986–1987 academic year, more than 520,000 students were enrolled in ninety-two postsecondary institutions. About 9 percent were African-American. Among the three major state universities, only Wayne State, with about 22 percent, enrolled more than 6 percent African-Americans. While total enrollments declined only 3.5 percent between 1980 and 1985, the impact was felt most heavily among first-time and full-time students. Overall, the state system lost 17,000 students between 1980 and 1984. Wayne State absorbed over 23 percent of the total decrease.

In Michigan there is no single governmental agency responsible for the overall coordination of higher education. The community college systems each have their own boards, appointed by county supervisors. The boards of the ten regional universities are appointed by the governor. The University of Michigan, Michigan State University, and Wayne State University each have independent boards whose members are elected in statewide general elections. The autonomy provided by these arrangements has left Wayne State largely free to determine its own direction and development, subject primarily to the constraints of available resources.

At the time of this study, the most important attempt to influence the course of higher education within the state by the executive branch involved the 1984 report of the Governor's Commission on the Future of Higher Education. The commission described a state higher education system in severe distress and advanced seventy-eight recommendations to help address immediate and long-term needs. Many of the commission's recommendations in such areas as access, transfer of community college credits, and programming for nontraditional students have since been enacted. Adoption of a tuition prepayment plan is a recent example of state concern with access.

The State Board of Education has little power to intervene in the operations of the state universities, acting mostly as a clearinghouse for information. In its *Better Education for Michigan Citizens: A Blueprint for Action* (1984), scarcely 4 percent of the plan addresses higher education, and then only to make "recommendations" and to "develop plans."

Michigan's major statewide initiative for minorities, the King-Chavez-Parks program, has provided $2.5 million annually since 1986–

1987, divided among the fifteen state colleges and universities. The program provides funding for three separate programs: (1) visiting professorships to increase the number of minority instructors in postsecondary institutions; (2) fellowships, to increase the number of minority students pursuing doctoral degrees; and (3) outreach to the schools, to encourage students to complete high school and begin postsecondary education.

COMMUNITY SETTING

Detroit is the sixth largest Standard Metropolitan Statistical Area (SMSA) in the United States. In 1985 the population was 20 percent African-American and less than 2 percent Hispanic. The population of the city of Detroit was 1.5 million in 1980, of whom 44 percent were African-American. Between 1980 and 1986 the city's population declined by 9.7 percent, with the decrease disproportionately Anglo.

The economic outlook for African-Americans and other minorities is improving. In 1985 Detroit ranked sixth in the nation in the percentage of minority-owned businesses. Despite the high failure rate for minority businesses, the number of establishments headed by an African-American with at least five employees increased by 4.2 percent from 1980 to 1985. And in 1985 there was a 138 percent increase in federal contracts granted to minority-owned businesses, compared to a 20 percent increase nationwide.

While manufacturing wages have continued to rise in the 1980s, there are 12 percent fewer jobs generating those wages. To counter this fact of life, the state and city are cooperating in development of a "robotics corridor" geared toward research and the mechanization of production. As the demand increases for engineers, managers, and their support personnel, Wayne State's reemphasis on academic research and productivity should help to forge new relations with this developing component of the Michigan economy.

The Public Schools

The most severe barrier to Wayne State's ability to increase participation and graduation rates for African-Americans is the condition of the Detroit public schools. With the exception of two schools with competitive admissions (Cass High School and Renaissance), Detroit-area high schools were frequently described during the study as terribly deficient. Wayne State's African-American faculty, administrators, and staff (some of whom were previously employed by the Detroit public schools) lamented social promotions, lack of discipline, union influence, drugs, and lack of home training as inherent problems in the public schools. Both African-Americans and Anglos saw the problems with the public

schools as systemwide, with elementary and junior high schools need-
ing as much, if not more, help than the high schools. Given Wayne
State's dependence on the products of these schools, the outlook for
any immediate change for the better in the preparation of the students
Wayne State serves seems remote.

Community Colleges

Wayne State has had close working relationships with the eight community colleges serving southeastern Michigan within easy driving distance, two of which are predominantly African-American. Recently,
however, growth in the Detroit suburbs and improvements in the quality of community college instruction has increased competition for their
graduates. In particular, two regional universities, Central Michigan
University in Mount Pleasant and Eastern Michigan University in Up-
silanti, have aggressively marketed themselves to nearby community
colleges, cutting into Wayne State's territory. Oakland Community College in Bloomfield Hills attracts Anglo suburbanites away from Wayne
State because of its modern campus and state-of-the-art instructional
facilities, a curriculum much like Wayne State's general studies requirement, easy access, and a cost per credit hour about 25 percent less than
Wayne's.

The community colleges were able to upgrade themselves during
the 1980s because increasing standards at the state universities forced
many students to begin their baccalaureate pursuits at community colleges, while the economic downturns of the 1970s and 1980s increased
the attractiveness of low-cost, part-time study. But the two predominantly African-American community colleges closest to Wayne State
University did not benefit from these developments to the same degree
as their suburban counterparts. These schools currently have higher stu-
dent/faculty ratios and a smaller range of courses than other community
colleges close to Wayne State.

Demographic trends indicate that the traditional university-aged
population will increasingly be found in areas more distant from Wayne
State where competing institutions are located. At the same time, Wayne
State has experienced stabilizing state financial support and continuing
increases in costs. As Wayne State faces the prospect of increasing dependence on less well-prepared students from Detroit-area schools, it
may well have fewer resources to devote to the interventions necessary
to serve them effectively.

STUDENT CHARACTERISTICS AND ACHIEVEMENT

Describing the characteristics and progress of students at Wayne State
posed a formidable challenge. The provost accurately described the uni-

versity's system of student record keeping as "still pretty much a quill and paper operation." Although the university has internally reallocated $2.4 million to update its information systems in admissions, registration, records, financial aid, and student accounts receivable, during the study there was no central, unified system for maintaining academic records. The information reported here was developed using estimates of institutional staff, small sample studies, existing reports, and national data bases.

As an urban school, Wayne State is geared toward working students with family responsibilities. Twenty-five percent of the total curriculum and 30 percent of undergraduate courses are offered after four p.m. Only about half of all students attend full-time. Our survey supported the picture of a nontraditional student body. Only 15 percent of the graduates responding were of traditional age, and only 21 percent completed a degree within four years. A relatively high proportion (42 percent) were first-generation college-goers. Only Brooklyn College reported a higher proportion (45 percent) of first-generation college graduates.

The distribution of African-Americans, Hispanics, and American Indians attending Wayne State in 1980 and 1986 appears in table 7.1. The loss of African-American students during this period involved both absolute numbers and proportion of the total student body. However, the proportion enrolled in 1986 was comparable to their representation in the tricounty area from which Wayne State draws most of its students (31 percent were residents of Detroit, 20 percent suburban Wayne County, 20 percent Oakland County, and 16 percent Macomb County).

While many students enter as freshmen and continue to graduation, there are three other common patterns of attendance. First, Wayne State is a destination school for community college transfers who come as juniors with completed general education requirements, ready to declare a major. Second, many students view a good performance at Wayne State as a mechanism for entering other state universities for which they could not qualify directly out of high school. So Wayne State is also a donor school for students who leave without a degree, but presumably finish elsewhere. Finally, there are students who matriculate

TABLE 7.1. Ethnic Distribution of Students at Wayne State, 1980 and 1986

Ethnic Group	1980 (%)	1986 (%)
African-American	23.7	21.9
Hispanic	1.7	1.7
American Indian	1.1	1.0

Source: Wayne State Report to U.S. Office of Management and Budget, 1986.

at either Michigan State University in East Lansing or the University of Michigan in Ann Arbor and transfer to Wayne State for academic, financial, or personal reasons.

For a number of reasons, these attendance patterns do not affect African-Americans and Anglos in the same way. African-Americans take longer to graduate and are underrepresented among completers in comparison with their representation in the undergraduate student body. They work more hours per week and change majors more frequently. Anglo transfer students are more likely than African-Americans to have A.A. degrees, which facilitate timely graduation. An Anglo who begins at Wayne State is more likely to transfer to a community college to obtain an A.A. degree and then to return to Wayne than is an African-American colleague who began at the same time. Wayne State also accepts fewer credit hours from the predominantly African-American community colleges.

Besides taking longer to graduate than Anglos, African-Americans are also more likely to drop out. Table 7.2 reports the results of a recently completed study of first-time-in-any-college students (FTIAC). The FTIAC study was based on the total population of entering students in spring, summer, and fall 1979, tracked through January 1985. After the first year, 23 percent of all African-American FTIACs were no longer enrolled at Wayne. By January 1985 the percentage of African-American FTIACs who were no longer enrolled and who had not graduated was 57 percent, the highest attrition figures for any of the four groups. The figures for Hispanics were not much better. While Wayne State does not know whether these students dropped out, temporarily stopped out, or transferred to other institutions, *The Transfer Migration Report* (Michigan Association of Collegiate Registrars and Admissions Officers 1987) indicates that Wayne State gained far more African-American students through transfer than it lost during each of the preceding three years.

Wayne State may be losing some of its better-performing African-American students, according to the FTIAC study. As college GPAs increase for Anglos, attrition consistently decreases to approximately 20

TABLE 7.2. FTIAC Retention Study of 1979 Entering Students at Wayne State

Ethnic Group	Continuing January 1980 (%)	Graduated or Continuing, January 1985 (%)
African-American	77	43
Hispanic	76	50
Asian-American	94	77
Anglo	84	62

Source: FTIAC Study, Office of Institutional Research, Wayne State University.

percent for those with GPAs of 3.25 or higher. In contrast, when the college GPAs of African-Americans reach approximately 3.0, attrition rates rise to almost 50 percent and remain at that level for those with higher GPAs.

Because they take longer to graduate and are more likely to leave the institution before graduating, African-Americans have constituted only 12 percent of the last three graduating classes, in comparison with 24 percent of the undergraduate population as a whole. Historically committed to diversity, Wayne State officials are concerned about the low rate of African-American completions. In addition, they are now under legislative pressure to explain and remedy race-related discrepancies in graduation rates. At the same time, the level of preparation of many of the minority students who seek admission to Wayne State inhibits efforts to increase both participation and graduation rates without compromising standards.

THE UNIVERSITY ENVIRONMENT

From its beginning the university has attracted students with widely varying levels of preparation and aptitude for college work. Trial admissions, begun at Detroit Junior College, were continued after admissions standards were raised in 1927. Trial students, together with many students in the evening program not working toward degrees, made up the nonmatriculated category that, in the 1930s, regularly constituted about 35 percent of the student body. Many students won transfers to regular, matriculated status after establishing satisfactory records as nonmatriculants. To the present day, similar programs have kept the door open to ambitious but underprepared adults.

Despite a statewide mission, Wayne State is captive to the demographic, political, and economic realities of the Detroit SMSA. Fully 89 percent of the total student enrollment, and 69 percent of Wayne State graduates, reside in the tricounty area. The university has to work to attract students from outside the city. According to a May 1987 university report, Anglo suburbanites may be fearful of Wayne State's African-American image, may desire a residential environment for their children, or may perceive Oakland Community College as a better educational value. Middle-class African-Americans, like middle-class Anglos, desire a residential environment for their children. And the city location conjures up for many the images of crime and other urban ills. Nevertheless, the university maintains a student body that is approximately 70 percent Anglo.

In the early 1980s the physical plant suffered because adequate funds were not available for maintenance. In 1983 the situation changed as Michigan emerged from recession and increased its sup-

WAYNE STATE UNIVERSITY 107

port to public universities. Concurrently, Wayne State's leadership began to emphasize the maintenance and enhancement of buildings and grounds, and the rebuilding of the campus became a major budget priority in the middle years of the decade. At the time of the study, however, the condition of the physical plant remained a factor in the lack of attractiveness of the university to suburbanites, out-of staters, and some of the area's more academically competitive African-American students.

Through both good and bad economic conditions, the university has continued to play a major educational role in southeastern Michigan; 1 out of every 3.5 college-educated persons in the Detroit metropolitan area has a degree from Wayne. While a substantial majority of alumni in the metropolitan area are Anglo, almost every prominent African-American in every sector of the economy—in elected political office, in public education at all levels, in the print and broadcast media, and in the arts—has studied at the university. African-American students at Wayne State University have more contacts with potential role models than is possible in most other institutions of higher education in this country.

The university administration has supported both special admissions programs and remediation. At the time of this study, there were sizable and visible cadres of African-American administrators throughout the university, including a vice-president for community relations and a vice-president for administration and finance. The deans of the College of Liberal Arts, College of Nursing, College of Lifelong Learning, School of Social Work, and College of Education were all African-American. Fourteen others served as associate deans and in similar administrative positions.

Admissions and Recruitment

Regular admission to Wayne State requires a 2.75 high school grade-point average. The overwhelming majority of all students, including many minority students, are admitted on this criterion. In a second avenue of regular admission, students with a general equivalency diploma (GED) or a high school diploma may take courses either in the community colleges or in Wayne State's division of continuing education, an educational outreach program within the College of Lifelong Learning. The Division of Community Education has an open-admissions policy and a schedule of credit-bearing courses, most of which meet one night per week. The completion of twenty-four credit hours within the division with a B average, or thirty hours with a C average, entitles students to transfer into other colleges within the university.

Wayne State is one of only two schools in the country to administer all five of the federally funded Trio programs. Project 350, one of the Trio programs, is designed to provide marginally prepared students with a chance for academic success through skills instruction and tutorial assistance. The first 250 positions in the program each year are reserved for students with GPAs of 2.4 or better. Although their high school GPAs may fall below 2.4, students from selected private schools and from the two competitive-entry public schools (Cass High School and Renaissance) who have pursued a rigorous college preparatory curriculum are considered for the first 250 positions if their GPAs are 2.0 or higher. The remaining 100 positions go to high school graduates whose GPAs are below 2.4. Students at the lower end of the scale are admitted on the basis of a combination of factors, including counselors' recommendations, standardized test scores, upward trend in grades, personal interviews, and college preparatory courses completed.

Project 350 students are very high risk. Nevertheless, 90 percent of Project 350 students return after the first year and 70 percent after the second. When students complete their involvement with the program by the end of the second year, many return as counselors. University staff estimate that 30 to 40 percent of Project 350 students ultimately graduate from a postsecondary institution, though not necessarily from Wayne State. Project staff have found that the problems encountered by those admitted to the program on the low end of the GPA scale are similar to the problems encountered by students whose better high school performance qualifies them for one of the first 250 positions. For both groups, the major barriers to success involve deficiencies in verbal, computational, and writing skills.

Student Financial Aid

Wayne State participates in the same financial aid programs typically found at other Michigan colleges and universities. Pell grants are the foundation for other need-based awards. Board of Governors incentive grants are combined with Pell grants for Project 350 students to discourage them from assuming debt or work loads that might interfere with academic pursuits during the first year. After the first year the aid office combines grant funds with self-help. Board of Governors scholarship and grant funds are also available to low-income students who do not participate in Project 350. In addition, there are several private scholarship programs specifically designated for minority students.

Early Intervention

A survey administered by the office of the provost identified forty-eight outreach activities undertaken in collaboration with eighteen different school districts within the Detroit metropolitan area. Practically every academic unit is involved in some type of formal or informal arrangement, ranging from an alternative high school for troubled students to dual enrollment for high school students with very high SATs. In aggregate, the programs address a wide range of students with emphasis on expanding the pool of college-prepared students through such strategies as mentoring, motivational enhancement, special recruitment, and academic support. Complementing the programs designed to enhance the qualifications students bring to the university, are other linkages to the community in such areas as nutrition, health, AIDS education, and library outreach.

The Detroit Area Pre-College Engineering Program provides enrichment courses in physics, precalculus, calculus, chemical engineering, computer science, communication, study skills, and self-paced mathematics for qualified minority students in grades 9 to 12. The Research Apprenticeship Program, co-sponsored with the Detroit Public Schools (DPS), uses a minimum-wage stipend to attract minority high school juniors to research in biology, chemistry, and engineering. Project SEED, sponsored by the American Chemical Society, provides a ten-week career development program for economically disadvantaged high school students. Tutorial assistance in reading and mathematics for grades 3 to 12 is provided for a fee through the student Achievement Center.

Midwest Talent Search focuses on minority youth in the eighth or ninth grade who score at least 1000 on the Preliminary Scholastic Aptitude Test (PSAT). To broaden exposure to the program, Wayne State selects at least one student from every Detroit high school, lowering the minimum acceptance score when necessary. Participants are offered a selection of exploratory and enrichment courses given on the campus and taught by Wayne State faculty. Through this and related programs, talented area youth are invited to presentations by university faculty, given weekend and summer tutorial assistance, sometimes allowed to take courses for college credit, and advised to enroll in additional high school math and science courses, with their grades reported to the university.

Orientation and Advising

Students admitted through Project 350 are required to attend a summer bridge program. In addition to academic enrichment through tutorials, reading and study skills, English, mathematics, and speech, the program has a mandatory counseling component. This program is highly regarded by participants. Some minority students seek to attend the program even though they plan to enroll at the University of Michigan or Michigan State.

Minority students participate in the same universitywide collegiate and departmental advising activities as those offered to the general student body. The university advising center offers a voluntary summer and fall freshman orientation that includes academic advising and registration. About 75 percent of new students take advantage of these sessions. Further advising for new students occurs in the advising center through individual conferences, in the collegiate student services units, or, in the case of engineering, in the departmental units. Once students declare a major in liberal arts or are accepted into a professional school such as business or education, they are assigned to faculty advisers.

Transfer students are invited to attend an informational orientation during the summer or fall and again prior to the winter term. Several collegiate units offer group orientation or advising sessions. A 1987 committee report, while endorsing current orientation and advising activities, noted that these activities were not sufficiently coordinated to eliminate noticeable differences in the quality of advising across academic units. The report recommended centralizing outreach staffs, funds, and activities, and suggested that the program relied too heavily on support staff in the absence of faculty involvement.

ACADEMIC ENVIRONMENT

Wayne State has traditionally been a union campus, as Detroit has been a union town. The academic staff, including counselors and advisers, extension program coordinators, and librarians and archivists, were organized as a faculty collective bargaining unit in 1972. Administrative staff were also organized at about the same time. The number and diversity of positions covered by the university's collective bargaining agreements limit administrative discretion to direct resources to new initiatives at the expense of existing programs.

Faculty

In 1986–1987 there was a significant minority presence among the faculty of Wayne (see table 7.3). Seven percent were African-American, which is slightly less than a third of their representation in the student body but fairly impressive when compared with the national average of 2.7 percent or with the numbers at most of the other case-study institutions. Asians, with 10 percent, outnumbered African-Americans and significantly exceeded their 3 percent representation in the student population. Hispanic and American Indian faculty representation closely matched their shares of the student population. As in other universities, African-Americans were clustered in the lower ranks, but representation among professors and department heads is increasing.

Wayne State has African-American faculty in every school or college unit, as indicated in table 7.4. Education, Liberal Arts, and Medicine have the largest numbers, with 29, 22, and 17, respectively. The pro-

TABLE 7.3. Full-Time Faculty at Wayne State, 1986–1987

	Anglo		African-American		Asian-American		Hispanic		American Indian	
	N	%	N	%	N	%	N	%	N	%
Lecturer	74	76	16	16	7	7	1	1	0	0
Instructor	37	73	3	6	9	18	2	3	0	0
Assistant professor	284	76	38	10	43	11	8	2	2	1
Associate professor	342	82	26	6	39	9	10	3	1	0
Professor	318	86	14	4	32	8	7	2	1	0
Chair or head	70	91	3	4	4	5	0	0	0	0
Athletic coach	5	71	2	29	0	0	0	0	0	0
Total	1130	81	102	7	134	10	27	2	4	0

Source: 1986–87 Classification and Salary Listing, Wayne State University.

portion of African-American faculty members exceeded this group's representation in the general student body in Library Science, Social Work, and Education. Nursing and Lifelong Learning also reported very substantial representation, as did Health and Physical Education. As a proportion of total faculty, representation is most problematic in Engineering, Business Administration, and Liberal Arts among the undergraduate colleges. Of the three, only Business Administration failed to record a gain between 1983 and 1987.

TABLE 7.4. Full-Time African-American Faculty at Wayne State, 1983 and 1987

	Total Faculty, 1987 (N)	African-American 1983 (%)	African-American 1987 (%)	Goal, 1987 (%)
Division, School, or College				
Business Administration	59	5.1	5.1	9.8
Education	123	19.2	23.6	21.3
Engineering	61	0.0	3.3	15.0
Health and Physical Education	26	16.0	19.2	15.0
Law	33	4.9	9.1	7.0
Liberal Arts[a]	373	4.1	5.9	6.0
Library Science	8	0.0	37.5	33.3
Lifelong Learning	26	13.8	15.4	18.8
Medicine	481	3.4	3.5	5.6
Nursing	57	15.5	17.5	17.5
Pharmacy and Allied Health	40	9.3	10.0	12.0
Social Work	24	25.0	25.0	29.6
Total	1367	6.4	8.5	

Source: Affirmative Action Data Survey from Deans and Directors, Wayne State University.

[a] Weighted average.

Overall the institution was very close to meeting its affirmative action goals for 1987, with the exceptions of the College of Engineering and the School of Business Administration. Several academic units had proportions of African-American faculty in excess of the national average for their disciplines. However, the data also suggests that African-Americans remain disproportionately concentrated outside the tenure stream, serving mostly as lecturers, instructors, and athletic personnel, despite some progress over the past several years.

Academic Program

Business and engineering, program areas known within the university for graduating high proportions of the African-Americans entering their degree programs, have strong undergraduate and graduate programs. The departments providing preprofessional training for these programs at the undergraduate level have active African-American student organizations and aggressive advisement policies. All students are required to see an adviser every semester, and advisers are required to document reasonable progress.

There are several other programs which attract minority students to Wayne State and support their achievement. The Journalism Institute for Minorities recruits and trains talented and scholastically achieving minority students for mass communications careers through a four-year program. The institute is unique because Detroit's media professionals are involved in providing special training. Only students with outstanding potential are considered for the program. Many receive full tuition scholarships and internships.

The federally funded Minority Access to Research Careers provides an honors program for juniors and seniors from minority groups that are underrepresented in the sciences. Participants must have a minimum 3.0 GPA and a biomedical major. Also federally funded is the Minority Biomedical Research Support Program, which combines scholarship and research incentives in a program to increase the number of students from underrepresented groups majoring in the biomedical sciences and health professions. Wayne State is the only institution in Michigan to offer either program.

The Labor Studies Center provides educational programs for workers from the greater Detroit area. Minority workers are targeted through the Union Minorities/Women Leadership Training Project, a six-university cooperative that takes courses and seminars to the sites where minority workers are employed.

Academic Support Programs

Students admitted in high-risk categories through such programs as Project 350 receive effective academic support through required coursework and tutoring at the Reading and Study Skills/Achievement Center (RSS/AC). The center is also Wayne State's major vehicle for tutoring in basic math, reading, and English, but it is dependent on walk-ins. The absence of campuswide assessment programs makes it difficult to identify students in academic need. The Educational Opportunity Center (EOC) conducts tutorials and remedial courses in the summer and works with students (other than those in Project 350) to try to head off academic problems. The inadequacy of the university's record-keeping system has precluded effective tracking and follow-up of students.

SUMMARY

Wayne State has achieved excellent participation rates as a function of its location, historic links with the public schools, and long-standing commitment to providing educational opportunities to a diverse student body. But prior to 1986, Wayne State did not place the same degree of emphasis on achievement as it did on access, as evidenced by the fairly significant and growing disparities in graduation rates related to race and ethnicity, and the tendency for attrition rates among high-performing African-Americans to remain at higher levels than those among their Anglo colleagues.

In addition to institutional practices, the growing difference in attrition rates can be traced to at least two factors over which the institution was able to exercise only limited control. The rate of part-time attendance has increased much more rapidly among African-Americans than among Anglos, stretching out the time they require to graduate. And the competition from residential colleges for academically prepared African-American students has increasingly left the university with a pool of students whose academic attainments in high school are not equivalent to those who attended previously.

Wayne State faces two important challenges in recruiting the students it needs to remain educationally and fiscally viable. The first is to retain its share of the talented African-Americans graduating from suburban schools and from the more rigorous city schools. Several of the special programs Wayne State provides are focused on this group. Only the federally funded Trio programs target students of less than proven academic potential. To attract top minority scholars, Wayne State must go head-to-head with University of Michigan and Michigan State, without the advantages of the residence halls and athletic visibility which the other two institutions enjoy. There is evidence that Wayne State is faring less well in this competition than previously.

The second challenge involves attracting enough able Anglo students to avoid the image of a predominantly minority institution. Of the two challenges, it seems to be the latter that has caused the most concern among institutional representatives who emphasized that the institution has always been at least 70 percent Anglo despite a national and outstate image as a minority-dominant institution. It is difficult to argue with this line of reasoning. A dominant feature of the tricounty area from which Wayne State University draws most of its students is the fifth largest school district in the nation with an enrollment in 1984 of 86 percent African-American. The university is located in the middle of an area with a substantial African-American and an increasingly Hispanic population. African-American alumni role models saturate the political, financial, educational, and cultural infrastructure of Detroit and dominate the public schools. The admissions policies of the university, its aggressive recruiting practices in the Detroit Public Schools, and financial assistance from special minority scholarships would seem to guarantee continuing high levels of participation from the African-American population.

The key to achieving university objectives as a research university, however, is to attract enough able students of any race or ethnicity to maintain or improve the quality of existing academic programs. The condition of Detroit Public Schools makes them an unlikely source of additional well-qualified students, especially given the increasing competition for the most able graduates. The university must attract talented students from the Anglo-dominant suburban school systems to avoid increased reliance on underprepared students or further enrollment losses. The relatively limited size and scope of special programs designed to increase enrollments from the Detroit public schools may stem from two conclusions: that the university is already doing its share to extend opportunity to disadvantaged populations; and that to assume a greater burden in light of the relatively modest contributions of University of Michigan and Michigan State would jeopardize other important goals, and might also jeopardize the quality of education experienced by the better-qualified African-Americans who currently attend.

The issue for Wayne State thus centers more on achievement than on access, a reality that institutional leaders clearly recognize. The estimate provided by the FTIAC study, as well as our own analysis of HEGIS data, indicates that an African-American student who entered in 1979–1980 was about 70 percent as likely as an Anglo to graduate or continue to attend after a six-year period. Our analysis of HEGIS data further indicates that graduation equity scores for African-Americans declined by nearly 15 percentage points between 1980 and 1986.

There are many aspects of Wayne State that promote minority achievement. African-American faculty members are present in greater numbers than in most other predominantly Anglo institutions, and many of them serve as mentors for African-American students. The substantial minority enrollment and the surrounding community contribute to a comfortable social environment. The university's tradition of providing opportunities for less well prepared students affords an experiential base for understanding the needs of a diverse clientele. At the same time, the absence of systematic assessment practices and an inadequate student information system leaves university staff with insufficient information about preparation deficiencies that interfere with academic success.

During the study the university recognized the need to strengthen and more systematically coordinate undergraduate student retention efforts. In a request to the legislature that was subsequently funded for the 1987–1988 academic year, the university asked for funds to enhance learning support activities, including comprehensive assessment, advising, counseling, faculty mentoring, and learning skills instruction. Important steps were also taken to improve the student information system, and the university began the process of developing a comprehensive strategic plan for improving student retention.

Unlike many of the other case-study institutions, Wayne State was not pressured by its state policy environment to increase student diversity. In fact, the proportion of minority students enrolled during the study was lower than it had been a decade earlier. In the absence of external pressures for change, until 1986 the university relied primarily on its environment and location to attract and retain African-American students. Most special interventions aimed at either recruitment or retention were externally funded, and there was no central coordination of retention initiatives.

Since 1986 the university has used internal evidence of problems created by a changing external environment to move rapidly toward becoming more strategic and more proactive in its approach to outreach and retention. In one sense, the absence of compelling external reasons for change and acceptable outcomes, as far as anyone could determine them, protected Wayne State from more than cosmetic changes in long-term practices for the first half of the decade. The development of a new student information system, the opportunity to replace retiring faculty, and the ambition to become a better institution are now causing Wayne State to reexamine and alter past practices in the direction suggested by the model.

8

MEMPHIS STATE UNIVERSITY

RICHARD C. RICHARDSON, JR.
with the assistance of JOHN DILL

Founded in 1912 as the West Tennessee State Normal School, Memphis State University (MSU) has undergone many changes in its 75-year history. Currently it is one of two comprehensive graduate and research public universities in the state of Tennessee and is second only to the University of Tennessee at Knoxville in the size and scope of its programs and activities. The university is composed of a graduate school; a school of law; a university college; a school of nursing; and five colleges in arts and sciences, business and economics, communication and fine arts, education, and engineering. The rapidity of the university's evolution is reflected in the tension between a new emphasis on research and the traditional emphasis on teaching.

THE STATE CONTEXT

Public higher education in Tennessee is provided through two major systems, each with its own governing board. The University of Tennessee operates four major campuses and provides statewide outreach for public service and agricultural extension and research. The State Board of Regents (SBR) governs six universities, fourteen community colleges and technical institutes, and twenty-seven area vocational technical schools. Memphis State University is the largest and most comprehensive institution in the system governed by the State Board of Regents.

Higher education is coordinated by the Tennessee Higher Education Commission (THEC). THEC is a strong coordinating board with broad powers, including: master planning; approval of all new academic programs, new departments, and new organizational units; review of operating budgets for all public higher education institutions; development of funding formulas used to allocate public funds among public institu-

John Dill is associate vice-president for academic affairs at Memphis State University.

tions; and maintenance of a data base and conduct of analytical studies on higher education. Through these functions the commission serves as a major source of information and professional advice on higher education for the governor and the legislature. The commission has strong credibility, and its recommendations for funding are typically supported by the governor and legislature in substance, if not in total appropriation.

The consent decree approved in September 1984 to end a sixteen-year statewide desegregation lawsuit, *Geier v. Alexander*, is an important influence on higher education for minority students. The agreement established goals for each of the institutions. Progress in implementing the consent decree is overseen by a desegregation monitoring committee composed of representatives appointed by the two systems and by THEC.

Section 97 of the Comprehensive Education Reform Act also had far-reaching influence on minority participation by establishing the 1983–1984 academic year as a bench mark and requiring presentation to the legislature by 1985 of goals for improving education in such areas as: (1) an increase in the percentage of students who enter baccalaureate programs and subsequently earn degrees, (2) an improvement in average scores on the national teacher's examination, (3) an increase in scores on the ACT and SAT for public university entering students, (4) an improvement in the scores of public university graduating seniors on a standardized examination, and (5) an end to the practice of providing credit toward graduation for remedial courses at public universities.

The act also required that the competencies spelled out by the College Entrance Examination Board (CEEB) in its Educational Equality Project be used in measuring outcomes of any improvement in high schools during the following five years. Colleges and universities in turn were expected to peg admission requirements to the level 1 competencies of the College Board Project. The consent decree that settled *Geier v. Alexander* requires an impact study whenever admission or retention standards are changed. If the study shows that the change will cause a reduction in the number of minority students, institutions must report how they will compensate to prevent any overall reduction.

Both the general funding formula and a performance funding program have been used in careful but limited ways to encourage institutions to support statewide affirmative action objectives. A performance funding program as a strategy for influencing institutional behavior predated both the Reform Act and the consent degree. Initially up to 2 percent of the annual budget was made available in the form of additional funds distributed on the basis of institutional performance. Currently the amount equals 5 percent, and over the five years the program has been in effect the legislature has appropriated $50 million.

State Board of Regents

SBR staff use strategic planning, resource allocation, cooperative projects, and evaluation to pursue statewide priorities related to access and quality. During the 1985–1986 academic year the focus was on strengthening general education requirements and mandatory assessment and placement of underprepared students in remedial or developmental courses not granting credit toward degree requirements.

The SBR system receives approximately $3 million annually in special funds to implement the desegregation stipulation. Among the initiatives funded by this special allocation are incentive scholarships, graduate scholarships, improvement of minority faculty recruitment efforts, released time to enable new minority faculty members to achieve doctorates, access to graduate assistants, and computer time.

As a part of regular funding procedures, retention ratios are examined with the expectation that institutions will be within 5 percent of the system average. The relationship between retention and funding encourages institutions to give careful attention to keeping students enrolled. SBR funding policies also encourage community colleges to strengthen remedial or developmental courses by reimbursing them at a higher rate than general transfer courses.

Through cooperative programs with state agencies, the University of Tennessee system, and the public schools, SBR has carried out three major initiatives aimed at entry-level freshman. The first focused on the basic academic competencies constituting adequate preparation for college. The second addressed the basic academic subjects regarded as standard for college entry. The third was aimed at strengthening the college-level curriculum. High school course requirements have been established for admission to all SBR institutions.

The Tennessee Collaborative for Educational Excellence helped high school students to meet competency requirements for college admission by convening high school teachers and college faculty members to improve articulation and teaching strategies in their subject matter areas. Funds were also provided to support collaborative projects implementing the strategies. High school graduates who score below a prescribed level on the ACT must complete a series of tests which measure performance in writing, reading, logical relationships, and mathematics. The results of these assessment tests are sent to the high schools. Efforts to reform the high school curriculum and to assess the performance of graduates were closely tied to a review of the courses without prerequisite for freshmen to ensure that both high school and college work reflected the Educational Equality Project competencies.

SBR staff planning for mandatory assessment and placement predicted that 40 percent of entering freshmen would be judged deficient in at least one area and would require an average of twenty-four credit hours to develop entry-level skills for college work. The cost of im-

plementing a remedial or developmental program on this scale was calculated at $11 to $12 million. To persuade the legislature to provide
these funds and to achieve reasonably uniform results across the system, the program design specified a requirement for a program director,
the number of hours of instruction to be available, the qualifications of
faculty, and the requirement for demonstrated proficiency at exit.

Student Financial Assistance

The Tennessee Student Assistance Corporation administers four need-
based student programs of grants and loans. In addition, the consent
decree in *Geier v. Alexander* requires a study of tuition discounts, loans,
scholarships, and other incentives for the purpose of achieving desegregation. For the first time in fall 1986, there was a set-aside of scholarship
funds for minority students at Memphis State University, administered
according to a different set of guidelines than those that had previously
prevailed.

COMMUNITY INFLUENCES

Memphis, like many urban areas, is a city with an economic problem.
The assassination of Dr. Martin Luther King is frequently described by
African-Americans and whites alike as an event that badly split the community. An Anglo university leader described Memphis as "years behind other communities in the area of race relations but making progress
while other communities are regressing." African-American professionals noted that support for public schools was dependent upon political
leaders who did not have children in the schools, while concurrently
acknowledging a limited tax base and unlimited competition for resources.

In Memphis, as in the rest of the South, jobs take priority over
education. According to an editorial in a local newspaper (*The Commercial Appeal*, May 26, 1987), 20 percent of the community lives below the poverty level, and a large percentage of the urban poor
are African-American. There are not enough jobs for college-educated
African-Americans who want to remain in Memphis. In our survey of
graduates, 13 percent of African-Americans, compared to 1 percent of
Anglos, were unemployed six months after graduating, and 23 percent
were employed in a field unrelated to their field of study in college. While the city has its liabilities, it also has many assets. Memphis,
though a metropolitan area with more than 800,000 residents, is still
regarded by many as a small town. Memphis State is a community university. Most of its students reside in Shelby County. There are many opportunities for them to work in the city to help support their education.
Sometimes the jobs are closely related to their educational experience.

Local business and industry support African-American academic achievement. The Memphis Partners Program, founded with leadership from the Holiday Corporation, provides a meaningful employment and educational experience to middle-range students selected on the basis of interest, attitudes and previous performance in the schools. Area colleges provide remedial training and ACT preparatory classes during the summer between the student's junior and senior year of high school. The primary emphasis of the program is on job development and remediation. Other facets include career counseling, use of mentors, incentives for outstanding teachers and counselors, financial incentives for students, and tutoring. The long-range vision of the program is to serve as a catalyst to bring all elements of the community together in a strategy for developing human resources.

The Urban League has operated a program called Youth Employment Success since 1982. The program provides summer internships to African-American high school graduating seniors who are college-bound and who rank in the top 10 percent of their high school graduating class. Participants, with their parents, receive an orientation and are placed in summer internships which require productivity, while providing insights into the corporate demands of the business environment. During the internships students participate in rap sessions on aspects of job readiness such as attitudes, dress, and work habits. When students complete their postsecondary education, the Urban League provides job assistance to those seeking employment.

Memphis Public Schools

Following desegregation, a substantial number of white students enrolled in private schools. One estimate suggested that 20,000 students were lost overnight to schools that "fear built." Beyond "white flight," middle-class African-American students and the teachers who taught them were dispersed to achieve desegregation guidelines, disrupting patterns of strong academic achievement in a number of previously segregated high schools. The effort to achieve racial balance within systems that had lost or dispersed many of their more talented students limited opportunities for talented children who remained. The response to this dilemma, as in big cities elsewhere, was development of magnet schools, called "optional schools" in Memphis.

In addition to optional schools, to encourage the development of children with a variety of talents, the Memphis public schools embarked upon an aggressive marketing campaign under the leadership of a widely respected African-American superintendent. The philosophy of recognizing a variety of talents and encouraging their development is recreating centers of academic achievement within the public schools.

Shelby County, outside the city of Memphis, is served by a separate public school system. The administrative offices of the two districts are housed in the same building, and staffs share a common cafeteria. Cooperative efforts are limited, however. During the study, county high schools were overcrowded, while city schools had vacant classrooms. According to the 1980 census there were about 8,000 more Anglo high school students than African-American high school students in Shelby County. However, about one in four Anglo students attended private high schools, compared with less than 2 percent of African-Americans.

Relationships between the Memphis public schools and Memphis State are largely informal and occur primarily through the College of Education. Some senior school district administrators are visiting faculty members at the university. Staff members from Memphis State also work with public school officials through such programs as Memphis Partners and the Memphis Urban Math Collaborative, but the leadership in these programs comes from organizations other than Memphis State.

Shelby State Community College

Community colleges are a recent development in Tennessee. Shelby State, the community college serving Memphis, was founded in 1972. A technical institute located on the outskirts of Memphis dates only to 1967. Because there were no two-year institutions in Memphis during desegregation, Memphis State became the access institution. Even today the two-year sector in Memphis is not a very large one, totaling only about 11,000 full- and part-time students.

Shelby State serves Memphis from its major midtown campus and several outreach sites. Under the state's desegregation plan the college has an enrollment goal for African-American students of just under 42 percent, very close to the Memphis State University goal of 40.3 percent. The actual enrollment of African-Americans at Shelby State exceeds 60 percent and appears to be inching upward. African-Americans are much more strongly represented at Shelby State among administrators (42 percent), professional staff (37.5 percent), and faculty (36 percent) than at Memphis State.

New assessment and remediation requirements of the State Board of Regents classify 80 percent of the students entering Shelby State as requiring remediation. In one or more basic skills areas, 30 to 40 percent place at the lowest levels. All students have problems with math.

Shelby State has had consistently good relationships with Memphis State. The founding president was a former senior administrator at Memphis State and the university provided technical assistance in curriculum and staff development. Shelby State continues to follow the Memphis State catalog closely in the design of its transfer offerings. Ninety-six percent of the 100 to 125 students who graduate from Shelby State each year with an A.A. or A.S. degree transfer to Memphis State. While SBR policy requires that associate degree graduates be placed as juniors, the policy does not address the issue of elective versus credit in the major. So students admitted as juniors may still require three years to finish a baccalaureate degree.

STUDENT CHARACTERISTICS

In fall 1985 Memphis State University enrolled slightly over 16,000 undergraduate students. Two-thirds of the students attended full-time, although most worked at the same time. Of the undergraduate population, about 1,800 were first-time freshmen. Transfer students at all levels and from all sources numbered only about 1,300, of whom 222 came from the two-year colleges serving Shelby County. Overall, 81 percent of the undergraduate students came from Shelby County.

On our survey Memphis State had the second lowest proportion of graduates (9 percent) at a traditional age. Only CSUDH, where 4 percent of respondents reported that they were 22 years of age or younger at the time of graduation, had a lower proportion. Memphis State also had a relatively low proportion (21 percent) of graduates who completed a degree within four years.

Memphis State was integrated in 1959 and graduated its first African-American in 1964. By the spring of 1986, one in five students was African-American. Table 8.1 provides demographic information on ethnic proportions for Tennessee, the Memphis area, and the university.

Enrollment of African-American students across academic units was reasonably proportional to their presence among undergraduate students. As in other universities, engineering had the lowest proportion, but even there African-American students constituted 16 percent of the total enrollment. Memphis State has generally been able to maintain the proportions of African-American students enrolled, while noting an improvement in average ACT score from 14 several years ago to 17+ at the time of the study.

The success Memphis State has experienced in retaining and graduating African-Americans has to be evaluated within the context of the relatively low graduation rates overall, due in part to the incidence of part-time study combined with employment. From a low of 16 percent part-time study for the freshman class in 1986, the figures rise steadily year by year until they reach 42 percent for the seniors. The results of

TABLE 8.1. Tennessee Ethnic Proportions, 1985

| | High School Graduates | | Memphis State |
Group	Tennessee	Shelby County	Freshmen
African-American	17.4	40.3	17.7
Other	82.6	60.0	82.3

Source: Desegregation Monitoring Committee, Sept. 9, 1986.

TABLE 8.2. Retention Rates for Entering Freshmen at Memphis State, 1977 to Spring 1983

	ADMISSIONS IN FALL 1977		
GROUP	Number	Graduated	Continuing
African-American	463	22.7	14.2
Anglo	1514	26.8	11.7

Source: Institutional Research Report, Memphis State University, 1985.

a recent long-term study of retention and graduation rates appear in table 8.2.

For first-time freshmen who entered in 1977 the average time to completion of a degree was six years. Only 9 percent of students attained a degree in four years, and 20 percent in five years. The retention figures for the first two years for the class of 1977 revealed better persistence for African-Americans than for Anglos.

The university is also studying the cohort that entered in 1980. After five years 18 percent of African-Americans had graduated, compared with 26 percent of the Anglos. A comparison of cohorts for the classes of 1976, 1977, and 1980 appear to show a falling graduation rate for African-Americans, along with a rising rate for Anglos. However, after comparing the five-year rates for the class of 1980 with the additional three years available for the classes in 1976 and 1977, an institutional research report speculates, "The blacks are not so much failing to graduate as taking longer to graduate than their white counterparts." Given the differences in entering qualifications, the extra time to graduation would appear to be a normal expectation.

The graduation rates for African-Americans seem to hold up across majors. In 1985–1986, 18 percent of graduates from the College of Business and Economics were African-American. For the same year, the College of Engineering reported about 13 percent, a figure that must be interpreted in light of a 12 percent enrollment in the college in 1980. Engineering enrollments are increasing more rapidly than graduation rates (enrollments grew from 12 percent in 1980 to 18 percent in 1985), but the results are still extremely impressive when compared with those reported by most other engineering schools. Another view of African-American achievement appears in table 8.3. It is clear from the data that Memphis State retains higher proportions of its African-American freshmen than do other universities in its own system or in the University of Tennessee system.

In 1986 about 9 percent of total first-time freshmen were admitted in the remedial or developmental category, with scores between 6 and 15 on the ACT. Sixty-five percent of these, or about one out of every three African-American students admitted, had to enroll in the remedial or developmental program. The comparable figure for Anglos was 4 out of

TABLE 8.3. Retention Rates for Memphis State, State Board of Regents, and University of Tennessee Systems, 1982–1985

| | No. of Fall 1982 Freshmen | | Percentage Retained as | | | | | |
| | | | 1983 Sophomores | | 1984 Juniors | | 1985 Seniors | |
	African-American	Anglo	African-American	Anglo	African-American	Anglo	African-American	Anglo
Memphis State	346	1,863	48	50	26	28	17	22
SBR University[a]	786	7,366	39	44	20	26	14	22
University of Tennessee system	551	4,401	23	36	9	25	7	24

Source: Desegregation Progress Report, table 13, 1986.

[a] Excluding historically black TSU.

100. While the entry qualifications of all students have improved, poor preparation remains a problem and more African-American than Anglo students were underprepared.

THE UNIVERSITY ENVIRONMENT

The emphasis of the university on minority issues has been low-profile. As one administrator noted:

> We don't single out the minority issue as a separate agenda item. We have tried quietly to achieve our objectives without causing adverse effect. We have not been too vocal about what we were doing and instead have concentrated on avoiding resentment and building acceptance.

The official position of the university was that African-American students were treated exactly like everyone else. A faculty member said, "Our objective is to get everyone out. We don't see students in terms of race. We treat all of them the same." Another added, "The education of minorities does not seem to be a priority. We do not treat blacks any different from anyone else." The emphasis on avoiding special programs causes African-American faculty members and administrators to conclude that the university is not doing nearly as much as it could. But all agree there has been a shift in campus from tolerance ("They're here") to acceptance ("Let's work with it").

The city of Memphis is frequently mentioned as a major advantage to the university. An African-American administrator elaborated:

> This is an unusual place. Because of the presence of blacks on campus, because of the city and its size and the ratio of blacks within the city, blacks bring their culture to the college in a way that does not happen on other campuses. At Memphis State University there are two worlds for black students: a white world [and] a world in which they can do their own black things.

Administrative leadership on minority issues appears to be a complex balancing act. The process of desegregation was competently managed, and relationships between the races have been consistently characterized as positive or improving. There have been very few overt racial incidents. The institution has made some progress in hiring African-American administrators, but its record with faculty has been unimpressive.

Of the 119 positions classified as executive, administrative, or managerial in 1985–1986, 5 were filled by African-Americans. A review of the five years preceding the study provides no clear evidence of progress. The president believes that the university has made very limited progress toward achieving its priority of employing more African-American administrators and faculty members. While the total number in key administrative positions remains small, they constitute a visible and influential part of the campus administrative structure.

Among senior administrators there is both strong support for special interventions to help minority students achieve and a deep-rooted conservatism that holds to the importance of treating everyone the same. The university appears to be reluctant to publicize its success in attracting and serving African-American students, partly because of a concern that the institution might come to be viewed in its prime recruiting territory as a predominantly black institution.

Admissions and Recruitment

Admission practices emphasize position in high school graduating class. Students typically enter with good high school grade-point averages and slightly above average ACT scores. The affirmative action goal of 40 percent African-American set by the Desegregation Monitoring Committee would require that the current proportion attending approximately double. There is a difference of opinion between administrative leadership at Memphis State and SBR staff about the feasibility of this goal.

Senior administrators believe that the existence of community colleges and technical institutes should free Memphis State to become more selective, and there are plans to further increase admission standards. But, as noted by the university president in an interview published in a Memphis newspaper (*The Commercial Appeal*, May 29, 1987, p. A6), during one of the site visits, increases in admission standards cannot cause the university to serve fewer minority students.

The university believes that an alternative to the ACT is necessary for assessing quality in African-American students. Applicants who achieve an 18 on the ACT or a 3.0 high school grade-point average are guaranteed admission. The position of the admissions office is that problems of student performance are a matter of student preparation rather than race. Recruiters work with predominantly African-American schools as diligently as they do with predominantly Anglo ones.

MSU admits proportionately fewer African-Americans than Anglos from their respective applicant pools as first-time freshmen, as indicated in table 8.4.

At the transfer level, the balance swings in favor of African-Americans. The rates suggest the emphasis that is being placed on improving the qualifications of entering students as well as continuing efforts to maintain or improve current ratios of African-American attendance.

Admission to the university is also admission to the college of choice, a policy that contributes significantly to proportional representation across colleges. While there are pressures to increase admission requirements to colleges such as Engineering, currently a student who

TABLE 8.4. Memphis State Admission Rates by Ethnicity, Fall 1985

	FIRST-TIME FRESHMEN		TRANSFERS	
	African-American	Anglo	African-American	Anglo
Applied	585	2,606	290	1,483
Accepted	396	1,895	262	1,180
Percent	67.7	72.7	90.3	79.6

Source: Institutional Research Report, October 1986.

enters the institution and decides on a career in engineering is assigned an adviser in the College of Engineering and is allowed to participate in the college orientation courses without additional requirements. Colleges protect themselves from overenrollment through curricular strategies. The College of Business has increased its mathematics requirement, and the College of Engineering establishes priorities for registration in upper-division engineering classes by grade-point average.

Officers from the Naval Reserve Officers Training Corps (NROTC) program have had substantial success in recruiting students from a school operated by the U.S. Navy in San Diego for enlisted personnel who enter directly from recruit training or from the junior enlisted ranks. The school provides a one-year college preparatory experience during which academic deficiencies are corrected. Among NROTC scholarship students at Memphis State, 44 percent are African-American. They enroll predominantly in engineering, where they are warmly received and earn very high grade-point averages. By contrast, few African-Americans win scholarships in Army or Air Force programs despite constituting a majority of first-year students in the Army program.

Student Financial Aid

Financial aid workshops are offered in area high schools starting in the middle of October and running through early March to counter problems of late applications, but students who need the information the most are the least likely to attend. In 1985–1986, $150,000 in state scholarship funds was available for the first time to recruit minority students. The requirement for eligibility was changed from a minimum score of 26 on the ACT to a minimum score of 20, making approximately the same percentage of African-Americans as Anglos eligible. Students who receive SBR scholarships are expected to give service in return. Scholarship recipients are trained as tutors and encouraged to do tutoring as their service obligation. The process of tutoring helps not only underprepared students but also improves the performance of scholarship recipients.

Early Intervention

In engineering the university works with high schools and junior high schools through the Southeastern Consortium for Minorities in Engineering (SECME). The program involves five major thrusts:

- identifying and encouraging academically talented minority students to pursue college preparatory courses
- enriching and supporting the local school's curriculum in mathematics, science, and the language arts
- strengthening teacher skills through in-service workshops and a summer teacher training program
- providing a guidance program to motivate minority students to prepare for technical careers
- building links with the local community through plant tours, programs for parents, visits to engineering sites, and presentations by minority engineers

The Tennessee Collaborative for Educational Excellence, previously described, serves as the structure for most of the formal activity designed to strengthen the admissions pool. Organized efforts outside the scope of SECME and the Tennessee Collaborative generally are coordinated either through the office of admissions or the office of financial aid.

Advisement and Counseling

The philosophy that African-American students should be treated exactly the same as everyone else applies as much to student support services as it does to academic programs. All students are expected to know about the services and use them, and they were designed for all students and not just for minority students. But the reality in some ways runs counter to this prevailing ethos. Student support services provide an infrastructure through which some special needs are addressed.

A comprehensive center for student development serves students who have not yet picked a major. Counselors assist students during the orientation and registration process and subsequently in the selection of courses and a major. Academic counselors draw upon other center resources, including a career counseling unit, a personal counseling unit, a testing center, and an educational support program (ESP) which helps students "learn how to learn." These services are housed in a common location and supervised by a single administrator, an arrangement that facilitates their use by a predominantly lower-division clientele.

Beyond providing services for all students, the center has organized self-help study groups for African-American students and makes a special effort to ensure that those who join them become aware of all services available under circumstances that encourage their use. Students with a 2.8 or higher grade-point average are encouraged to participate in an African-American scholars group. The career development center sponsors African-American career development workshops. There are also separate organizations, such as a student union and a gospel choir, to help students build a sense of identity—arrangements that have occasioned some adverse faculty reaction.

Residence Life

The university housed about 15 percent of its undergraduates in residence halls in 1986. Plans call for the university to become more residential in character. Residence halls are viewed by university administrators as an aid to recruiting and as asset in promoting the retention and degree achievement of all students. From 25 to 30 percent of students who live in residence halls are African-American, a proportion that exceeds their representation in the undergraduate student body. The university makes an effort to ensure a visible African-American presence among both residence hall staff and advisers. In the past the center for student development conducted programs on minority awareness for residence halls and with the security staff. More recently such programs have been judged to be unnecessary.

ACADEMIC ENVIRONMENT

Good teaching and a caring attitude emerged in our interviews with graduates as important contributors to student achievement. Classes for the most part were small, reflecting the planned absence of large classrooms. But graduates also consistently described differential treatment for African-Americans, not as a function of overt racial incidents but rather inferred from faculty grading behaviors or statements that African-American students should not be expected to achieve academically. One graduate suggested that attitudes "became apparent after the first exam. They did not expect black students to achieve...." She added that instructors gave Anglo students more help and that "white students had a lot more insight about what they needed to learn in order to complete a class successfully." Her comments were qualified by praise for two Anglo instructors in the College of Business and Economics to whom she "would be forever grateful because they had been particularly helpful."

Her perceptions coincided closely with the comments of a university administrator who identified, as potential sources of student perceptions of bias, older faculty members whose services predated integration, part-time faculty members recruited from the community, and full-time faculty members recruited from other universities in the South before Memphis State shifted its recruiting emphasis to a national market.

TABLE 8.5. Full-Time Faculty at Memphis State, Fall 1986

RANK	AFRICAN-AMERICAN (%)	ANGLO (%)	OTHER (%)
Professor	-0-	96.6	3.4
Associate professor	4.9	91.2	3.9
Assistant professor	7.3	86.6	6.1
Instructor	3.8	93.8	2.5

Source: Office of Institutional Research, *Faculty Profiles 1986,* Memphis State University, Spring 1987.

Faculty Characteristics

In 1985, 3.5 percent of the 710 full-time instructional faculty members were African-American. Forty percent were associate professors; the remainder were at the assistant professor or instructor level. Most of the ranked African-American faculty members were in arts and sciences, education, and communication and fine arts. The College of Business and Economics did not have a single ranked African-American and the College of Engineering had one. The distribution of full-time faculty for fall 1986 appears in table 8.5.

While the university exceeded its affirmative action goal of 4 percent for 1986, African-Americans accounted for only 4.3 percent of the total positions and remained unrepresented at the professor level. The number of departments with tenured African-Americans is very small. The academic vice-president has taken the position that if a department can find an African-American faculty member, he will create a position, in preference to saying, "You cannot hire anyone unless you find an African-American." To help offset the lack of African-American faculty members, part of the funds allocated for graduate assistants can be used only for African-American candidates.

The university has an incentive program to recruit African-American faculty members under the terms of the consent decree. The program pays moving expenses, provides released time from teaching, offers an additional allocation for library holdings, and can provide a salary differential. There is a "grow your own" program through which graduates of special promise in high demand areas can be supported through their doctoral program on the condition that they return to the university. At present all the effort is devoted to supporting summer study.

Academic Support Programs and Services

In 1985 the university's approach to working with underprepared students was altered by systemwide *Guidelines* from the SBR. MSU was required to assess students scoring less than 16 on the ACT on a test of basic competencies and to place those judged deficient in a nine-course sequence of special courses in mathematics, English, reading, and study skills. Students were not permitted to skip courses in the sequence. Attendance, including lab, was mandatory. The courses carried college credit recorded on the transcript but not applicable to any degree. Students had to earn at least a C by their second attempt at a remedial or developmental course, or they would be suspended from the university.

Before the *Guidelines*, Memphis State had of course recognized that student preparation was a problem. In 1978 the university had initiated three college-level courses, two in math and one in English, to strengthen the competencies of underprepared students. But the university's efforts, particularly in mathematics, were not viewed as consistent with the competency-based approach taken by the SBR in working with high schools and in reviewing entry-level undergraduate courses. So the SBR made the decision to implement a special program that would operate systemwide with established standards for progress and for exit.

The developmental studies program at MSU reports to the office of academic affairs by state mandate. By university policy, as much responsibility for the program as possible has been assigned to existing staff. Some see this arrangement as part of the university's hope that the program will go away. The first-year plan submitted by the university called for providing instruction in math by regular instructors on split appointment. The mathematics department assigned the sections of developmental studies to their international graduate students. Students in the program could not understand some of their instructors and developed very negative attitudes. SBR staff intervened to require the employment of new instructors with master's degrees and high school teaching experience.

The English faculty, historically better disposed toward remedial education than their colleagues in math, assigned regular faculty on a split assignment during the first year. In the second year, however, they staffed the courses exclusively with part-timers because regular faculty members no longer wanted to teach in the program. When SBR staff took exception to this direction, the university hired four full-time instructors with similar qualifications to those in math. The reading and study skills courses have been taught since the beginning by special full-time faculty members.

Even with the discontinuities resulting from negotiations with the mathematics and English departments, the outcomes of the program seem impressive. An administrator described the performance of students as admirable and counter to the prevailing bias on campus about the impact of academic deficiencies. Student interest and motivation have been positive. Of the 160 students who entered the program in fall 85, 87 percent were still enrolled a year later. This retention rate exceeded the 1983–1984 retention rates for all African-Americans (44 percent) and for all Anglos (48 percent). A March 1987 report to the academic vice-president noted that more than 90 percent of 105 developmental studies students (first-time freshmen admitted with lower than 16 on the ACT composite score) had completed both developmental studies in English and freshman composition with a grade of C or higher. Their success rate compared favorably with the 78 percent successful completion rate for all students attempting freshman composition. Of the 43 developmental studies students who completed both developmental studies math courses, 47 percent completed the level 1 mathematics course with a grade of C or higher, compared with the 30 percent average completion rate for all students attempting level 1 math.

Despite preliminary evidence that it is working better than anyone had anticipated, the university remains unhappy about the program's existence. There is the normal resentment toward a program externally imposed on an organizational culture that has steadfastly resisted special programs and special treatment. But, in addition, a program that serves underprepared students is an unwelcome reminder of the gap between the university's aspirations and its current reality.

The educational support program, though it places no particular emphasis on serving minority students, is among the services emphasized in a university recruiting publication for African-Americans. The program operates under the assumption that every discipline presents learning problems for some or many students and that a learning specialist working closely with a faculty member can diagnose such problems and assist the faculty member in helping students to overcome them. ESP enrolls about 200 students in ten classes. They receive instruction on how to learn closely linked to the content emphasis of their courses. The program also provides instruction in how to take tests, trains tutors, and manages two of the four discipline-oriented learning centers provided by the university. Centers are staffed by a manager, ideally with background in English as a second language, and by graduate students. Faculty members in chemistry and English operate their own learning centers.

SUMMARY

In Tennessee a consent decree emphasizes improved access and participation. A legislative mandate stresses achievement, educational reform, and articulation between the public schools and higher education. State policies and action programs use strategic planning, performance funding, and collaboration with the public schools to influence institutional priorities and keep track of outcomes. There are specific goals and a sophisticated information system for monitoring progress.

African-American students come to MSU because of responsive admission and financial aid practices, proximity to where they live, and low cost. The number of African-Americans in attendance and the community setting make the university a comfortable learning environment. African-Americans succeed academically because of their own efforts, but also because of an institutional culture that has adapted to diversity in student preparation and modes of college attendance. Support services, class scheduling, and teaching practices all consider the part-time working student, who by the senior year becomes the norm.

The most important obstacle to achievement is differential preparation, but the gap appears to be narrowing as a result of aggressive recruiting and an improving public school system in Memphis. Assessment and remediation practices have been strengthened. Learning laboratories and tutorial services have been in place for some time. Student services are sensitive to the needs of African-Americans and increasingly willing to confront the prevailing institutional culture by developing interventions that take into consideration the unique needs of African-Americans as well as those they share in common with all students.

Prior to changes in assessment and remediation, African-American students did not receive systematic information about their readiness for advanced college courses, nor were those with deficiencies required to correct them before enrolling. Faculty members were confronted with substantial differences in preparation and the need to provide extra assistance to African-American students. Under these conditions it is not surprising that graduates and members of the minority community believed that African-American students were receiving differential treatment from a significant proportion of the heavily Anglo faculty. Concerns about stereotyping and lowered expectations were aggravated by the very small number of African-American faculty members.

Administrators have consistently been supportive, in small ways, of efforts to serve African-Americans as long as such efforts did not require highly visible special programs. Faculty members received high marks for their commitment to teaching and for the concern many exhibit for nurturing. Courses in most disciplines reflect and represent African-American culture. Classes are generally small, and teaching is important and respected. There are special programs to improve the recruitment of African-American faculty members and to place more minority graduate assistants in front of classes.

Tennessee encourages institutions to emphasize both diversity and achievement. On balance, Memphis State illustrates as well as any case-study institution how the two can be combined.

9

FLORIDA STATE UNIVERSITY

LOUIS W. BENDER
with the assistance of SANDRA W. RACKLEY

Florida State University (FSU), located in Tallahassee, is one of the two designated "flagship universities" in the University Master Plan of the state university system. A residential, comprehensive, research-oriented institution, it offers undergraduate, graduate, advanced graduate, and professional programs of study through fifteen colleges and schools. FSU awards the baccalaureate degree in ninety-two fields of study, the master's degree in ninety-three, and the doctorate in sixty-five. In the natural sciences, FSU is best known for its basic research programs in physics, nuclear science, chemistry, biology, psychology, meteorology, and oceanography. FSU offers a joint program in engineering with Florida Agricultural and Mechanical University (FAMU), the state system's historically black institution, which is also in Tallahassee.

The fall 1987 main campus enrollment of 24,524 included approximately 4,500 graduate students. FSU also maintains an upper-division and graduate branch campus in Panama City, 100 miles west of Tallahassee. The state context for FSU is discussed as part of the Florida International University case study (chapter 5).

COMMUNITY INFLUENCES

Tallahassee, with a 1986 population of 120,023, is relatively small in comparison with other state population centers. African-Americans represent about 29 percent of the total. While Tallahassee and surrounding Leon County have experienced population growth since 1980, the number of African-Americans has declined. Tallahassee, the state capital, is located in Florida's northern panhandle. The area's economy is based primarily on state government and education.

Louis W. Bender is professor of higher education and director of the State and Regional Higher Education Center, Florida State University. Sandra Rackley is associate dean of undergraduate studies at Florida State University.

Because FSU is largely residential, it is not dependent upon the preparation provided by local county and city school systems. In many ways FSU dominates its environment in a manner not duplicated in more urban settings. FSU is the largest and most prestigious of the institutions located in the city. A high proportion of the business and professional community are graduates. FSU's fine and performing arts programs are the centerpiece of the community's cultural events, and its year-round intercollegiate sports programs produce millions of dollars in revenues for the hospitality industry. As a consequence, a strong symbiotic relationship exists between the university and its local community.

Integration was not as traumatic or adversarial in Tallahassee as in other cities in the state or throughout the South. African-American community leaders describe Tallahassee as a good place for all cultures. The sizable African-American community in the city plays a positive role in the life of students attending the city's colleges and universities.

Florida Agricultural and Mechanical University

Perhaps the most important community influence in terms of African-American participation and achievement in higher education is nearby FAMU. The current level of cooperation between FSU and FAMU took planning, hard work, and external incentives. The development of the 1973 and 1977 higher education desegregation plans sparked considerable debate within the legislature and throughout the state on the appropriate role for FAMU. One proposal argued that FAMU and FSU should be merged; a second called for FAMU to become a branch campus. Other proposals suggested that FAMU be closed or moved to another location in southern Florida. While the issue was a state problem, advocates and supporters of the two institutions were located near the center of the debate, localizing the emotionalism and sentiment and causing strained relations.

When it had been determined that the autonomy of the two institutions would be preserved, the Board of Regents offered incentives for cooperation and then mandated cooperative programs and exchange of faculty. These initiatives achieved only limited results until the legislature authorized a joint program in engineering in 1982. While still in the early stages of development, the FAMU/FSU College of Engineering has grown at a rapid pace and achieved significant African-American representation among students, administrators, and faculty. The success of this joint venture has enhanced cooperation between the two universities in other areas as well.

Students at FSU have social opportunities that would not exist in the absence of FAMU. Cooperative programs between departments, stimulated by the development of the joint College of Engineering, provide academic alternatives for African-American students as well.

Tallahassee Community College

Tallahassee Community College (TCC) provides instruction for students who encounter problems on the required FSU admissions examination. In some cases, FSU encourages student applicants who cannot initially be admitted to FSU (because of an enrollment cap) to become full-time students at TCC and then eventually to transfer to FSU. About 7 percent, or 56 of the A.A. degree graduates, were African-American in 1987, slightly above average for Florida community colleges.

FSU and TCC have a dual enrollment policy which makes it possible for students to attend both institutions concurrently. Relationships in nonacademic areas are also positive, as evidenced by coordination of activity calendars and library usage. There is also an FSU policy that TCC student ID holders may participate in FSU intramural athletics and other student activities. It is not unusual to find TCC students utilizing FSU services and activities as though they were attending both institutions.

STUDENTS

Enrollment caps established by the Board of Regents limited FSU's lower division in the fall of 1987 to 7,266 full-time students. Part-time enrollments accounted for an additional 264, reflecting the emphasis the institution places on full-time study, as well as the size of the population within commuting distance. Table 9.1 compares the characteristics of students enrolling for the period of 1985–1987. The number and proportion of African-American students declined during this period, probably in part as a consequence of increased admissions standards. Less than 40 percent of African-American undergraduate students were male, in contrast with 57 percent of Hispanics, a distribution that mirrors national patterns.

TABLE 9.1. FSU Student Enrollment Characteristics

By Race	Fall 1985		Fall 1986		Fall 1987	
	Number	Percentage of Total	Number	Percentage of Total	Number	Percentage of Total
Anglo	18,734	86.1	19,929	86.1	20,830	84.9
African-American	1,575	7.2	1,576	6.8	1,549	6.3
Hispanic	623	2.9	701	3.0	843	3.4
Asian-American	178	0.8	190	0.8	500	2.0
American Indian	33	0.1	41	0.2	32	0.1
Nonresident alien	559	2.6	689	3.0	688	2.8
Total	21,758		23,138		24,524	

Source: Florida State University Fact Book, 1987–1988.

TABLE 9.2. Public High School Graduation in Florida Compared with FSU Access and Graduation Rates, 1987

	ANGLO (%)	AFRICAN-AMERICAN (%)	HISPANIC (%)
Florida public high school graduation	72.9	17.8	7.8
FTIC applications to FSU	86.4	7.1	4.7
FTIC admissions	87.1	6.8	4.1
FTIC enrollments	89.1	6.5	3.3
Florida CCAD graduation	80.3	5.5	12.5
CCAD admissions	88.4	4.4	6.6
CCAD enrollments	90.8	3.6	5.0
Total enrollments	89.0	6.5	3.4
Baccalaureate degrees	91.4	5.2	2.5

Source: Three-year Trend Analysis of Minority Enrollment and Degrees Conferred in State University System, State University System Board of Regents, Tallahassee, Fla., 1988.

Note: FTIC = first time in college. CCAD = community college associate's degree recipients.

African-American and Hispanic students followed enrollment patterns similar to those of their Anglo colleagues in favoring business and management majors, followed by social sciences, computer and information sciences, engineering, protective sciences, and education.

Table 9.2 places enrollment data for FSU in a system context. Because FSU is designated as a flagship institution and serves a largely residential student body, the comparisons are with statewide data rather than with the city and county as was done with Florida International.

FSU has to work to enroll African-American and Hispanic students. Its isolation from major population centers and the competition from nearby FAMU keep its enrollment of both African-Americans and Hispanics well below statewide averages for high school or community college graduates. The distribution of those earning degrees suggests that while African-Americans are somewhat less likely to persist than Anglos, they stay at ratios similar to those for Hispanics, a different pattern from the one noted for FIU. Of interest in this data as well is the quite low proportion of African-Americans earning transfer degrees from community colleges in a state in which 60 percent of baccalaureate degree candidates are expected to begin in this type of institution.

There are significant differences in the qualification of entering students as a function of race and ethnicity. Overall, African-Americans represented 63 percent of all alternative admissions in 1986–1987, Anglos represented 33 percent, and Hispanics 4 percent. But percentages can be deceiving. For this period, one in every three African-American students admitted did not meet FSU's published admissions criteria. For Anglo students the number was one in every seventy-two.

Retention and Graduation Pattern

FSU has tracked progress and completion rates for FTIC and transfer students since 1976. *The Florida State University Retention File* for September 1988 reported six-year retention rates for FTIC Anglo students of 56 percent. The comparable rate for African-Americans was 45 percent. Students with SAT scores of 800 and above were retained at higher rates regardless of race. African-American students with SAT scores lower than 800 fared better than their Anglo counterparts during the first two years after matriculation, but less well thereafter.

Table 9.3 reports the relationship between test scores and retention and graduation. Beginning with the 1978 fall semester, there was a marked reduction in the number of students from both races admitted with SATs of less than 800. For Anglos the number dropped from 290 in 1978 to 8 in fall 1987. For African-Americans, the decline was from 175 to 17. During this same period, the number of African-American FTIC students entering in the fall semester fell sharply from 312 in 1978 to 151 in 1987, illustrating the impact of changes in admission standards on participation.

Transfer students entering the upper division in 1982 were retained over four years at a 69 percent rate, with 66 percent earning degrees during that period. Retention and graduation patterns were similar to those for FTIC students with 72 percent of Anglos persisting and 70 percent earning degrees, compared with 64 percent persisting and 63 percent earning degrees among African-Americans.

A study of African-American voluntary leavers from the 1985 and 1986 entering classes indicated that off-campus residents were twice as likely to leave as on-campus residents. The on-campus resident population also recorded higher grade-point averages. Among African-

TABLE 9.3. Comparison of SAT Scores with Six-Year Retention and Graduation Rates at FSU

| | PERCENTAGE OF STUDENTS WITH | | | |
| | SAT Less than 800 | | SAT Greater than 800 | |
	Anglo	African-American	Anglo	African-American
Average retention rate	48.6	39.1	59.0	52.5
Average graduation rate	45.9	33.3	54.8	45.8

Source: Office of Budget and Analysis, The Florida State University Retention File, September 1988.

American transfers, out-of-state students were three times as likely to leave as in-state students.

Forty percent of the graduates responding to the survey conducted as a part of this study were of traditional age at the time of graduation, a proportion similar to the one for UCLA graduates and higher than for other case-study institutions. FSU graduates were the most likely to finish degrees in four years or less (54 percent). Seventy-two percent of the graduates had transferred to FSU from another postsecondary institution. Only 19 percent of all graduates reported they were first-generation college-goers, while more than half of the African-American graduates fell in this category (52 percent). The percentage of UCLA graduates who were first-generation college-goers was similar, but in that institution there was little difference as a function of race. Clearly Florida State admits and graduates a different African-American population from the one served by UCLA.

THE UNIVERSITY

FSU's history in baccalaureate programming for minority students is brief indeed. While the doors were not closed to African-American students in the early 1960s, as was the case in some southern states, programming initiatives did not begin until 1967 when the FSU faculty senate requested initiation of an alternative admissions program subsequently entitled Horizons Unlimited. Under the supervision of an advisory board composed of faculty members and administrators, Horizons Unlimited began operation in spring 1968 with a director recruited from FAMU and university funds authorized by the president of FSU. The first class consisted of twenty-five students from socioeconomically disadvantaged backgrounds who were nominated by their high school principal or counselor on the basis of academic promise and potential. Twenty-five faculty members volunteered to serve as mentors and advisers for the first class, providing evidence of a level of commitment that continues to characterize the program today.

Currently, with continuing support from the university budget, the program serves 200 students annually, nearly all of whom are African-American. The philosophy underlying the program recognizes limitations in the academic backgrounds of the students as well as in the complexities of adjusting to university life. Students receive a special early orientation, as well as special faculty advisers, peer group counselors, tutorial services, and financial assistance, in addition to regular federal and state financial aid. Additional financial assistance continues as long as students maintain satisfactory academic achievement records.

Since 1974, FSU has also operated a federally funded special services program directed toward low-income and/or first-generation college students. The program, which provides training in basic skills, counseling, and related support, disproportionately enrolls African-American students.

The Office of Minority Student Affairs sponsors publications and activities to enhance communications between African-American students and other groups within the university community. The office conducts an annual student leadership conference and a five-week program in which professionals and community leaders help students become more effective in classrooms, in student organizations, and in professional life. Also offered are black male enrichment groups, and peer facilitator training for sophomores, juniors, and seniors. Other services include clinics and workshops that teach study and academic survival skills and test taking.

The Student Government Association (SGA) effectively controls approximately $2.4 million derived from an activity and services fee charged to all students. Among the SGA-supported organizations for African-American students are a black student union, a black law student association, a black players guild, and eight Pan-Greek sororities and fraternities. The black student union sponsors films and lectures, soul-food dinners, and a weekly radio program entitled *Soul Plus*. Activities and events are coordinated and sometimes jointly sponsored with the FAMU Student Government Association. A weekly television program, written and directed by African-American students that began under the sponsorship of the black student union, is now a part of WFSU-TV public television. The union also sets up a buddy system for new African-American students at the beginning of each academic year partly to provide peer ombudsman services.

A center for black culture, founded in 1980, operates as a department under the vice-president for academic affairs. It has a university mandate to implement programs of high quality to exhibit a panorama of past, present, and future contributions of African-American people to the local, state, and worldwide community. The center publishes an annual journal which reports on programs, events, honors, and achievements of African-Americans in government, politics and social work, music, dance, drama and theater, science, and community life.

Equity has consistently been one of the top ten goals of university administration, as emphasized in reports to the faculty for more than a decade. Administrators have used strategic planning to establish common goals for affirmative action. The planning process makes explicit the expectation that academic and student affairs staffs will jointly contribute to achievement of goals, regardless of which office exercises formal responsibility.

The Office of Human Resources, headed by an African-American woman with the title assistant to the president, was established in 1980.

The office has been influential in developing awareness and promoting universitywide commitment to increasing the representation of minorities through monitoring, recruitment, hiring, promotion, and retention programs. Annually each college and school must report its plans for increasing employment opportunities and promotion rates for minorities. Plans to increase African-American student enrollment, retention, and academic progress must also be furnished. Reports of progress in carrying out these plans are a prominent part of the president's council agenda during meetings at which priorities and budget allocations are considered.

Human Resources also administers an employee grant in aid program to provide educational and other upward mobility training for minority and female members of both professional and career staffs. University funds support this program, as well as other workshops and related activities throughout the year. The distribution of the university's 1984–1985 administrative work force by race and ethnicity is reported in table 9.4.

FSU has been particularly successful in recruiting African-American professionals, as evidenced by their representation among professional, nonfaculty employees at a level that closely approximates their representation in the FSU student body. The institution has been less successful in recruiting Hispanics.

The Office of Budget and Analysis plays an active role in evaluation of minority initiatives. The original data base for retention studies and related longitudinal analysis was established in the early 1970s. Currently, the university uses a comprehensive student-flow data base to monitor and plan affirmative action initiatives. In 1987, following a study of retention patterns, the university appointed an African-American woman to coordinate retention efforts and monitor student progress.

TABLE 9.4. Comparison of FSU and the Florida State University System Work Force Distribution, 1984-1985

	African-American (%)	Hispanic (%)
FSU:		
Executive, administrative, and managerial	6.9	1.4
Professional, nonfaculty	6.3	1.0
Florida state university system (except FAMU):		
Executive, administrative, and managerial	6.6	2.5
Professional, nonfaculty	6.1	2.7

Source: Florida State University, EEO-6 Report.

Admissions and Recruitment

Before spring 1987 the Board of Regents criteria for admission to the university system as an FTIC freshman were 17 on the ACT or 840 on the SAT and at least a 2.0 high school grade-point average. After that date, the criteria changed to require students with less than a 3.0 high school GPA to qualify on the basis of a sliding scale involving some prescribed combination of test scores and GPA. Students who attained a 3.0 GPA were admissible regardless of test scores. All community college students who earn an A.A. degree are automatically admissible to any university in the state system. Students not meeting these criteria are considered alternative admissions.

Students admitted to FSU by alternative criteria must be under the close supervision of a sponsoring program. The university believes it has an obligation to provide academic support to every student admitted who otherwise might not succeed. With very few exceptions, students admitted by alternative criteria enter either Horizons Unlimited or the Summer Enrichment Program (SEP), which is discussed below.

Most alternative admissions are retained into their second year at a rate 4.5 percent below the student body at large. The majority who do not return for a second year were in academic difficulty during the first year. In fall 1987 a retention system was developed to provide more systematic follow-up for students admitted under alternative criteria as a step toward increasing their academic success.

Early Intervention

The Summer Enrichment Program targets "high-risk students" of three types: (1) minorities with a history of racial discrimination and/or social alienation within the American context; (2) students who perform poorly on traditional measures yet are recommended as having good academic potential for pursuing a college education; and (3) individuals from rural or highly diverse social environments who might find a large university environment overwhelming and detrimental to college success.

The program is offered each summer by a cadre of faculty who live in a residence hall with the sixty participating students. Shared living quarters, the hallmark of the program, are credited with benefitting faculty and students equally. During a two-week session, students receive an introduction to the university as well as instruction in academic and career decision making within a supportive social and academic environment. Program faculty provide instruction in basic skills areas, subsequently help shepherd students through their early terms at the university, and remain familiar allies throughout the college experience.

An evaluation of SEP between 1980 and 1985 revealed that SEP participants maintained a higher retention rate than the average FSU retention rates (which were above national rates). The graduation rate of SEP participants in the 1980 class after four years was 44.4 percent, as compared to the overall rate for the same class of 43.3 percent. The study also compared the SEP participants with a control group that had similar backgrounds but entered the fall term without participating in SEP. SEP participants have consistently performed and persisted better than the control groups.

A new program initiated in 1984 with support of the state's College Reach-Out funds brings fifty minority high school juniors to FSU during the same time as SEP students. This group also lives on campus during the two-week period. The program introduces them to university and campus life and provides workshops on financial aid, career planning, test-taking techniques, self-awareness, and related topics.

Articulation

The Office of Community College and Interinstitutional Relations was established in 1972 to improve the environment FSU offered for transfer students. A special orientation program assists these students making the transition from a two-year campus to the university. An annual faculty-to-faculty articulation workshop brings community college faculty face to face with their departmental counterparts at FSU. The workshop also includes time for community college faculty to visit with students who have transferred to FSU from their college.

Cooperative programs between FSU, FAMU, and TCC permit any full-time student to enroll for one or more courses required by their program of study, at any of the three institutions, with permission from the home institution. The student pays tuition to the home institution at its regular rate and receives credit on the home institution's transcript. Each year about 200 students (most of whom are African-American) take courses at FAMU under the program in such departments as journalism, architecture, and engineering technology, as well as in ethnic studies not offered at FSU.

Advisement and Counseling

All first- and second-year students, with the exception of those in music, dance, and theatre, are assigned to the Division of Undergraduate Studies, which administers the academic and advising programs and coordinates assignment of academic advisers from the teaching faculty. Students who have chosen a major are assigned an adviser from the appropriate field. A special advisement center assists students who are undecided, or who are experiencing academic problems. The division also administers the offices of undergraduate admissions and financial aid, the registrar, and the honors and scholars program.

When an African-American student is admitted to FSU as a freshman or transfer, a letter from the vice-president of student affairs designates a counselor for the student. A comprehensive support network begins to function as soon as the student contacts the counselors. The student also receives a publication entitled *One Step at a Time: A Guide to Success at Florida State University.* The guide advises students to take the following ten steps: (1) Meet the president. (2) Speak the university's lingo. (3) Learn what's academically required. (4) Commit to personal development. (5) Check out the services. (6) Get involved. (7) Meet the minority faculty and staff. (8) Locate administrators. (9) Select a place to worship. (10) Find places for your grooming needs.

In addition, sources of financial assistance for African-American undergraduate students are listed. The student also receives a copy of *Black Involvement at the Florida State University*, a pamphlet introducing African-American professionals on campus and describing support programs and services for African-American students. Students are monitored through an informal network of faculty and counselor communications. They are also served by offices within the student affairs program with designated components that address the needs of African-American students.

Residential Life

FSU provides university housing for 4,000 undergraduates. Although students are not required to reside in university housing, beginning freshmen are strongly encouraged to do so, so that they can take advantage of the advising and developmental programs offered by professional and student staff members. Approximately two-thirds of all African-American undergraduates live in university housing, a ratio that is high when compared to other groups. In some dormitories, students may choose integrated or all-African-American floors. Resident programs emphasize multi-cultural living. Displays, performances, and social events reflect the diverse cultures represented. Soul-food dinners, the Martin Luther King commemoration, Black History Month, and Black Fine Arts Week are among the occasions when African-American culture is spotlighted. Preferred housing is reserved for upper-division transfer students on a proportional basis.

Counting the facilities provided for athletes, sororities and fraternities, and the Southern Scholarship Foundation, in addition to university housing, more than half of all undergraduates live on campus. The eight predominantly African-American sororities and fraternities promote scholarship, community service, and social enrichment. They also provide peer support for tutorial sessions and study groups.

The Southern Scholarship Foundation provides 250 students from rural and disadvantaged backgrounds with a cooperative living program in which residents in each of the fifteen houses share all household duties, including grocery purchasing, menu planning, meal preparation, and other chores necessary for effective operation of the housing unit. Southern Scholarship students have earned a special reputation for their academic achievements, their graduation rates, and subsequent socioeconomic mobility. Many alumni from the program are annual givers to the foundation and also donate services and other assistance.

ACADEMIC ENVIRONMENT

FSU's original initiatives for African-American students resulted from the action of a powerful faculty senate in 1967, a fact that has important implications for the academic environment experienced by current students. From their inception, programs and services intended to enhance minority achievement have reflected both academic and student services participation. An informal network has developed among African-American faculty and administrators to help students whose problems become evident through the university's early alert system or through informal communication. To some outsiders, the FSU environment appears noticeably different from that prevailing on the campuses of many large research universities. A Pulitzer prize-winning education writer for one of Florida's major newspapers, after studying a number of universities, described the climate at FSU as one in which faculty and staff emphasize scholarship and excellence, but where there is also a feeling of warmth characteristic of family and home. A former African-American vice-president for student affairs, Bobby Leach, coined the phrase "comfortability factor" to help explain the need for such an environment, in which students are treated equally and fairly, and different cultural backgrounds are also recognized.

Faculty Characteristics

The affirmative action plan developed in response to the 1973 *Adams V. Richardson* mandate for the state system calls for 3.5 percent of the faculty to be African-American. The actual representation for more than a decade has been 4 percent, slightly more than half the student representation and above the average for research universities nationally. However, full-time faculty for FSU are right at the 3.5 percent target. Hispanics, at 0.3 percent, are significantly underrepresented. The averages within the state university system, excluding FAMU, were 3.4 percent African-American and 1.9 percent Hispanic in 1985. FSU is thus very close to the mean for African-Americans and lags well behind in attracting Hispanics.

In addition to the grant-in-aid program for faculty and staff administered by the Office of University Human Resources, senior faculty volunteers work with junior faculty during their early years to assist them in using university resources to meet the teaching, research, and service requirements for achieving promotion and tenure. The program, which emphasizes assimilation and retention of African-Americans, women, and other minority faculty, served as the genesis for the informal network among African-American administrators and faculty that monitors and provides mentors for students in need of assistance.

Academic Programs

Faculty and administrators seemed generally aware of the challenges African-American undergraduate students face in a predominantly Anglo university environment, but most saw no need for special consideration in the classrooms. While some Anglo faculty members participate in the formal and informal support networks described elsewhere, most were unaware of the academic support and alert systems the university has designed to help African-Americans achieve. Some of these systems are described below.

The budget for Horizons Unlimited includes support for small sections in selected core classes. These classes, while not segregated, are limited to twenty-five to thirty-five students and are scheduled so that Horizons Unlimited students avoid the large lecture sections they would otherwise confront. Math classes for Horizons Unlimited students meet daily rather than in the typical three-sessions-per-week pattern. The two extra class sessions are scheduled for laboratory work or special assistance. As previously noted, retention and graduation rates for Horizons Unlimited students consistently equal or exceed those of the regular student population at FSU.

Many faculty members acknowledge the need to make the curriculum more multicultural and interdisciplinary in response to the increasing representation of African-American, Hispanic, and Asian students, but at the time of the study there had been no major reform initiatives. Informal changes do occur when curricular practices are perceived as potential threats to the campus environment for African-American achievement. An English literature class which included assigned readings laced with the racial epithet "nigger" quickly became the focus of debate in the president's cabinet. Student affairs staff argued that other selections could accomplish instructional goals equally well, while academic representatives argued against any form of censorship. No official action resulted, but the following year, the readings for the class no longer included the offending assignments.

The FAMU/FSU College of Engineering provides professional training without limiting the basic autonomy of either institution. Authorized by the state legislature in 1982, the school now offers baccalaureate programs in chemical, civil, electrical, and mechanical engineering. All four programs have been accredited by the Accreditation Board of Engineering and Technology (ABET). Students may register at either FSU or FAMU and receive a degree in any of the College of Engineering programs. Students must satisfy the admission and general education requirements of the university to which they apply, and the degree is granted by that institution. A new engineering complex, completed in 1987, is located between the two campuses, adjoining a developing state-, county-, and university-sponsored research park.

The 1986–1987 enrollment of 700 students included 24 percent African-Americans and 10 percent other minorities. This is the highest representation of African-American undergraduates in any of FSU's colleges or schools. Recruitment of African-American students and women has been a high priority of the college since its beginning. Faculty hold joint appointments at both FSU and FAMU. The working relationship has been positive and has contributed to growing trust and increasing collaboration between departments in other schools and colleges. FAMU has continued its engineering technology department, which is not affiliated with the joint engineering school.

Among most colleges and schools there is not as much emphasis on recruiting African-American students at the undergraduate as at the graduate level. The College of Arts and Sciences annually sends recruitment letters to eighty-five predominantly African-American colleges and universities throughout the nation, distributes recruitment literature at professional meetings, and offers an array of fellowships and graduate assistantships designated for African-American graduate students. A mailing list of Army, Navy, and Air Force education officers has been developed to aid in recruitment of African-American officers leaving military service.

The results of these and other efforts are evident in the composition of graduate students enrolling at FSU. Almost 30 percent of all first-time African-American graduate students in the state system enroll at FSU, and the university produces nearly 67 percent of all doctoral degrees awarded to this group within the system. The presence of a substantial concentration of African-American graduate students helps in recruitment of high school graduates and provides role models for undergraduates.

Academic Support Programs and Services

The associate dean of undergraduate studies, an African-American woman, maintains an early alert system which focuses on students who were admitted under a waiver policy, who drop below a 2.0 GPA, or who are placed on academic probation. Students are assigned an adviser from among volunteer faculty or administrative staff, most of whom are African-American. Over time, those who volunteer have evolved into an informal support network of concerned professionals who confer with each other regularly. Academic programming and support for African-American students is also provided by academic units.

Most programs and services credited as significant contributors to the baccalaureate success of African-American students at FSU are available to all students regardless of race or ethnicity. Most academic support services and student life development programs are designed to address needs or provide opportunities common to all students. At the same time, formal and informal efforts are directed toward African-American students as a minority in a predominantly white institution.

SUMMARY

Between 1980 and 1986, Florida State's graduation equity score for African-Americans declined from 98 to 50. Institutional data furnished during the study suggested that Florida State had increased its graduation equity score by at least 10 points by fall 1987. During the same period, the proportion of African-Americans enrolled declined from 10 to 7 percent, as admission requirements stiffened and competition for state university–qualified African-American students intensified. The results for African-American students at FSU are similar to those at Florida International. Hispanic students are underrepresented at FSU as a function of the institution's location. Those who attend graduate at rates similar to Anglos, as they do at FIU.

The case suggests that the most important elements accounting for the success of African-American students at Florida State are selectivity, special programs, and the "comfortability of the social environment." Few African-Americans meet the criteria for admission as new freshmen. A very high proportion of the 201 African-Americans admitted in this category in 1987 came in through the heavily minority Horizons Unlimited program, which provides a comprehensive and systematic series of services including outreach, early intervention, transition, and academic support. Alternative sections are provided in key general education courses. An informal network of African-American administrators and faculty members closely monitors and provides mentors for students who experience difficulty.

Transfer students are also highly screened both by the requirement that they attain an associate degree in order to be automatically admissible and by the state CLAST examination which mandates minimum performance in academic skill areas before matriculation as a junior. FSU accords to transfer students many of the special considerations it provides to freshmen. These efforts pay off in the relatively high graduation rates posted by minority and majority transfer students alike.

While historically black FAMU may be regarded by some at FSU as a mixed blessing, it clearly provides an academic and social environment that moderates for some students the impact of attending an institution with marginal minority enrollments. The opportunity to participate in jointly arranged social activities and to attend classes predominantly taught and attended by African-Americans blurs the choice between historically black and predominantly white in a way that is probably beneficial to both, despite concerns about competition for students and faculty. The FAMU/FSU College of Engineering, a joint school mandated by the state legislature, provides a glimpse of an alternative future in which competition for students and fear of losing identity are replaced by programs that combine the strengths of both universities to achieve quality and diversity.

The emphasis upon FAMU's role in contributing to "comfortability" in the environment FSU provides for African-Americans should not overshadow the important steps FSU has taken on its own. Academic and student affairs administrators have been consistently required to make plans and consistently held accountable for the results. Planning and accountability measures are supported by institutional research. A strong affirmative action program has produced a sufficient cadre of African-American administrators and faculty members to provide mentors and advocates for students who need extra help. Careful attention to multicultural programming in cultural events, student life, and residence halls also helps minority students to feel welcome.

Hispanic students at FSU seem to achieve for the same reasons as at FIU. Their characteristics closely resemble the population for whom the culture at FSU was designed. Despite their underrepresentation at FSU, no special efforts appeared to be targeted on them, nor did they seem to be regarded as "minority" in the same sense as African-Americans.

The state has contributed to the positive environment for minorities at FSU through mandates to monitor underrepresented classes, providing a tracking system and requiring feedback and through appropriations to support minority programming. More controversial are mandates for testing which in the judgments of some are a deterrent to participation. There is comparable debate, although less intense or widespread, on the effects of raising admissions criteria. Clearly Florida has been in the vanguard of efforts to balance access and quality. While the resultant policies have not always pleased everyone, few deny Florida's commitment to minority achievement within a strong state university system.

The environment at FSU has its deficiencies as well as its strengths. The proportions and absolute numbers of African-Americans in the undergraduate student body have declined since 1980. Despite this decline there was little evidence that FSU had implemented targeted recruiting or outreach strategies beyond Horizons Unlimited and the Summer Enrichment Program, in both of which numbers are limited because of funding constraints. Nor does the university fully use the Board of Regents waiver policy to increase minority enrollments. To do so would increase the university resources devoted to special programs which remain the major, if not exclusive, academic strategy for helping African-American students succeed.

The organizational culture of FSU, like those of other research universities, remains attuned to a prepared majority population that can succeed without changes in teaching and learning approaches. Faculty members, while "sympathetic" to minority participation, believe that students should adapt to existing curricular and teaching strategies rather than serving as a stimulus for reform. Within this culture, informal networks and special program staff do the best they can, aided by a comfortable environment, and achieve impressive results with a selected group of African-American students, a large proportion of whom are first-generation college-goers. Their best efforts are not sufficient, however, to produce outcomes significantly different from those of other large research institutions with similar faculty cultures.

10

UNIVERSITY OF CALIFORNIA, LOS ANGELES

RICHARD C. RICHARDSON, JR.
with the assistance of PAULA N. LUTOMIRSKI

The University of California, Los Angeles (UCLA) is the largest of nine campuses of the University of California (UC). In 1986–1987 its academic organization included thirteen schools and colleges, seventy academic departments, twenty-three organized research units, and a number of interdisciplinary academic programs offering degrees as well as courses. In all, UCLA offered baccalaureate degrees in ninety-nine subjects, as well as seventy-nine masters programs and doctoral degrees in sixty-three fields. UCLA has received national recognition for the stature of its graduate programs in a wide range of disciplines.

A recent National Conference Board assessment of doctoral departments placed UCLA second only to UC Berkeley among all public universities in the perceived quality of its faculty, and judged thirty departments (of the thirty-two surveyed) to be within the top sixteen, with seventeen of those in the top ten. Of the thirteen schools and colleges at UCLA, only four admit undergraduates. And of the 22,000 undergraduates in the fall of 1986, 19,000 were in the College of Letters and Sciences. UCLA does not have undergraduate schools in business or education.

THE STATE CONTEXT

The California legislature has been a major stimulus for improved opportunities for minorities, establishing its first special higher education programs in 1968. In 1974 the public higher education segments were asked to prepare plans for overcoming ethnic, sexual, and economic underrepresentation in the student bodies of their respective institutions by 1980. Also required was submission of plans to the California Postsecondary Education Commission (CPEC) by 1975 with annual

Paula Lutomirski is director of information management and institutional research at the University of California, Los Angeles.

reports required thereafter. The proportional distribution of California high school graduates was prescribed as the base for assessing degree of underrepresentation. In 1984 the three segments were called upon to develop a plan to strengthen college preparation of low-income and underrepresented minority groups in junior and senior high schools in cooperation with the State Board of Education and the superintendent of public instruction.

Public higher education in California is an enterprise of considerable scope and diversity. In 1985–1986 there were 1.5 million undergraduates enrolled on 108 community college campuses, 19 campuses of California State University (CSU), and 9 campuses of the University of California. The state depends to an unusual degree upon transfers from community colleges as a part of its strategy for guaranteeing access to minority populations. Approximately 50,000 students transfer to the two public university systems each year. The number of transfers from community colleges declined between 1975 and 1985. Minority students were less well represented in transfer cohorts than they were among first-time freshmen.

The basic framework through which this diverse and complex system is coordinated was set forth in the 1960 Master Plan for Higher Education. The most widely known provision of the plan established a tightly prescribed admissions pool through which the UC was limited to the top one-eighth of high school graduating classes and CSU to the top one-third; community colleges were designated to serve the remainder. UC and CSU were also expected to decrease their numbers of lower-division students and increase the upper-division openings available for community college transfers. A 1987 review of the Master Plan confirmed the basic direction of the 1960 document, while calling for renewed emphasis upon unity, equity, quality, and efficiency. The review also emphasized the need for stronger linkages between higher education and the elementary and secondary schools in order to cope more effectively with changing demographics.

CPEC is a citizen board which monitors implementation of the Master Plan, coordinates the efforts of California's colleges and universities, and provides independent nonpartisan policy analysis and recommendations to the governor and legislature. Information, research, and program evaluation are used to place items on the table and to build consensus about the need to address them. In this way the commission, despite its lack of regulatory powers, encourages people to confront issues they might otherwise prefer to avoid. The achievement of minority students has been a major focus of the commission for some time.

Student Financial Aid

Historically the strategy for access in California has been to keep charges low. California Educational Opportunity grants, started in 1969, target educationally disadvantaged students attending public institutions and in particular those attending a community college. Institutional grant programs administered by CSU and community colleges were added in 1982–1983 and in 1984, respectively, to offset fee increases. Under the CSU program, students who do not have their demonstrated need met through Pell or California grants receive an additional award that pays for a portion of the cost of fees. In 1984–1985 more than 37,000 students received state university grant aid totaling more than $12 million.

Between 1973–1974 and 1984–1985 expenditures for state-based student financial aid programs increased in constant dollars by more than 48 percent, from $410 million to $1.4 billion. During this same period the number of undergraduate students increased by 44 percent. In California, as elsewhere, the most important change of the past decade has been increased student dependence on loans. In 1973–1974 loans constituted one-fourth of the available assistance; by 1984–1985 it was just over one-third.

The University of California System

UC implemented the Educational Opportunity Program (EOP) in 1964, four years before the state legislature established similar programs for CSU and the community colleges. More recently the Student Affirmative Action (SAA) program, consisting of several interrelated programs working with targeted students from junior high school through the undergraduate years, has supplemented the work of EOP by increasing the number of minority students eligible for regular admission to the university. Overall direction for achieving undergraduate affirmative action was established by a 1985 five-year plan which set goals for increasing enrollment and graduation rates.

In 1983 only 3.6 percent of African-American and 4 percent of Hispanic high school graduates were eligible to attend UC, in contrast with the 12.5 percent eligibility rate specified in the Master Plan. The comparable figures for California State University were 10 percent for African-Americans and 15 percent for Hispanics, compared with the 33 percent rate anticipated by the Master Plan. About one-half of all African-American and Hispanic first-time students in CSU and UC do not meet regular admission requirements. The number of differentially qualified students admitted from the underrepresented groups is reflected in graduation statistics. In 1986 only one in five special action admission students graduated in five years from UC, and only one in ten from CSU.

COMMUNITY INFLUENCES

Los Angeles County produces approximately 30 percent of high school graduates within the state of California, about 86 percent of whom graduate from public schools. These graduates' chances of attending the University of California in 1985 were about half those of graduates from private schools. Anglo students were more than twice as likely to be enrolled in private schools than African-Americans. Hispanics enrolled in private schools at a point midway between the rates for African-Americans and Anglos, due largely to the influence of the Catholic school system.

The Los Angeles Educational Partnership serves as the main link between schools and the business community. One of its current projects, Focus on Youth, is aimed at preventing dropout. The Southern Christian Leadership Association sponsors Project Ahead, a motivational activity designed to raise the sights of minority students and to assist them in improving educational achievement.

Another community-based program focused on the public schools is Young Black Scholars, which has as its objective graduating from the Los Angeles County high schools, by 1990, 1,000 African-American students who have the necessary grade-point averages and course completion records to make them eligible for admission to the University of California. By contrast, there were only 800 African-American students in the entire state who met these criteria in 1983. The program is sponsored by One Hundred Black Men of Los Angeles, with broad community involvement including UCLA and the Los Angeles Unified School District.

The California Achievement Council, a privately funded statewide effort, funds staff members to work with two area schools performing at low levels and serving predominantly minority populations. The council develops strategies to help the schools raise their achievement levels and hopes that promising initiatives can be picked up by publicly funded agencies.

Public Schools

While students at all the Los Angeles County high schools can get the course work they need to attend the University of California, the number who go on from the schools most minority students attend is very small. The ten high schools with the highest numbers of African-American students in 1984–1985 graduated over 3,000 seniors. Combined, they sent 43 students to UCLA, with two of the ten high schools accounting for more than half of this total. The ten schools with the highest numbers of Hispanic students graduated 4,700 seniors, 55 of whom went to UCLA the following fall as freshmen. Three of the ten schools recorded two-thirds of this total. Thus UCLA receives most of its minority students from predominantly Anglo schools in Los Angeles County or from those that are racially balanced. These schools typically are characterized by strong college preparatory curricula.

Predominantly minority schools record such meager outcomes in part because of the effects of school desegregation. Experienced staff moved from inner cities to suburban schools and were replaced by new faculty or those on emergency credentials. Los Angeles High School, the oldest in the city, illustrates the magnitude of the change with which district teachers and administrators have had to contend. It changed from a predominantly Anglo school in the 1960s, to predominantly African-American in the early 1970s, to its current Latino majority.

The alternative to forced busing within the Los Angeles Unified School District is the Permit with Transportation (PWT) program. Students may elect free travel from their assigned school, provided that the result improves racial balance in the receiving school. African-American students are disproportionately involved in this program because they are more likely than other groups to accept busing in the search for somewhat better schools. In the African-American middle-class residential district served by Crenshaw High School (enrollment 1,700), more than 1,000 students use the PWT program to attend schools with better racial balance in the western part of the county. Their places are taken by students from other attendance districts for whom Crenshaw is a step upward.

The district designates some high schools as magnets and places magnet programs within standard high schools. Areas with high proportions of students from non-English-speaking families are designated as minority linguistic regions, qualifying them for special programs to strengthen language skills. Schools located too far from other schools for busing are designated as "racially isolated," with salary supplements for teachers to combat the flight of experienced teachers from inner-city schools. Faculty members in these schools telephone parents to encourage them to support the academic achievement of their children, and to support other activities focused on student retention and achievement.

Many of the minority students we interviewed said they came to UCLA unprepared for the rigors of college academics because their elementary and high schools were not challenging. Most often the students who made these statements had attended predominantly minority, inner-city schools that enrolled large numbers of students requiring remedial education.

Catholic Schools

The schools operated by the Archdiocese of Los Angeles serve a very diverse student population, 39 percent Hispanic and 10 percent African-American. The Hispanic students attending Catholic schools do not represent a cross section of the Hispanic population in the county. Hispanic immigrants go to the public schools partly because parents from Mexico are not accustomed to sending children to Catholic schools and partly because of financial problems. Hispanic students attending parochial schools have parents with some education, as well as experience, with Catholic schools. They are also more affluent than the parents of children served by the public schools. Many African-American students are non-Catholic and look to the Catholic schools as a way out of the ghetto and a way of expressing opposition to the public schools.

Graduates of Catholic schools cannot be compared with public school graduates because of the more restrictive admission policies of the Archdiocese. While the Catholic schools try to respond as well as they can to the needs of lower-achieving students, they perceive themselves as college preparatory even though not all their students are college-bound. Officials of the Archdiocese believe that their minority graduates are academically indistinguishable from their nonminority counterparts. All the schools in the Archdiocese offer the course patterns necessary to qualify a student to attend the University of California.

Community Colleges

The Los Angeles community college district (LACCD) is the largest in the nation, with nine separate colleges which enrolled more than 93,000 credit students in 1985. Forty-three percent of students attending the district schools are African-American or Hispanic, outnumbering the 39 percent who are Anglo. The ethnic composition of the individual colleges varies widely from 74 percent Anglo at Pierce to 1 percent at Southwest. There are other community college districts which also serve the county, including Pasadena, Santa Monica, Glendale, El Camino, Long Beach, and Compton. With the exception of Compton, which is predominantly African-American, all serve diverse populations similar to those enrolled in the more Anglo LACCD colleges.

The transfer function of many LACCD colleges has been seriously eroded during the last several years. Although large numbers of students continue to transfer, there are disturbing trends. The three predominantly African-American and Hispanic colleges experienced a 38 percent decline in transfers to public universities between 1979 and 1985, while transfers from the three with the lowest enrollments of these groups declined by 25 percent. By contrast, suburban schools recorded increases in transfers during the same six-year period. Accelerating the trend for transfer students to come from suburban institutions is the state policy on "free flow," the community college equivalent to the Permit with Transportation program of the public schools. Under this program students may cross district lines to attend college.

Among LACCD colleges, East Los Angeles has been a particularly important entry point for Hispanics. As a new immigrant population has moved into the community, it has become increasingly difficult to persuade second-generation Hispanics to attend. Pasadena City College, not far north, has a very high transfer rate for Hispanic students, many of whom travel from the area served by East Los Angeles. In 1985 Hispanic students were well represented in the cohort transferring to the UC from Pasadena. But all the students transferring from East Los Angeles (which in that year was more than 80 percent Hispanic) were Anglo.

STUDENTS

About 95 percent of all UCLA undergraduates come from California, with more than half from Los Angeles County alone. Among underrepresented groups, 15 to 20 percent of freshmen come from families with incomes below the poverty level. Almost 45 percent of all undergraduate students at UCLA receive some form of financial aid. Reflecting the emphasis upon full-time study, the average age of the undergraduate population is young, only 21. The expectation is that students will attend full-time. Most students completing a degree accumulate one or two quarters in excess of four years of residency. As an extremely selective but oversubscribed public university, UCLA is under significant pressure from students not admitted.

Over the past decade there has been a significant increase in the proportion of African-Americans, Hispanics, and American Indians among first-time freshmen. In 1975 the representation of these three groups was just under 12 percent. By 1984 the proportion exceeded 23 percent. In 1986, 27 percent of first-time freshmen were from underrepresented groups. An additional 20 percent were Asian-American, and 5 percent were Filipino. In all, 52 percent of the entering class were minority. UCLA and its sister campus at Berkeley have greater minority enrollments by a considerable margin than any other major research university in the country.

Table 10.1 reports the ethnicity of high school graduates for California and Los Angeles County in relation to the proportions that were university-eligible and the representation of these groups among 1984 UCLA first-time freshmen.

In addition to recording significant increases in the proportions of minorities enrolled, the university reduced the number entering through the special admission program to less than 20 percent. Even though most minority first-time freshmen now meet university eligibility requirements, there are still significant differences in preparation between minority and other students. Regular admittees had high school GPAs averaging 3.76 in 1985, in comparison with the 3.41 average for their SAA counterparts. The difference in scholastic aptitude test scores between the two groups averaged over 200 points.

The African-Americans served by UCLA are predominantly middle-class, with third-generation college experience in many instances. An

TABLE 10.1. California Ethnic Proportions, 1983

ETHNIC GROUP	HIGH SCHOOL GRADUATES		UNIVERSITY ELIGIBLE*	UCLA FRESHMEN
	California	*Los Angeles County*		
African-American	9.0	15.5	2.5	8.5
American Indian	0.7	0.4	0.3	0.6
Hispanic	17.9	26.7	6.7	11.7
Asian-American	6.1	7.5	12.2	18.7
Anglo	64.7	48.6	76.6	53.8
Filipino	1.6	1.3	1.8	4.3

Source: Student Affairs Information and Research Office, *UCLA Admission and Retention Trends,* August 1985.

*California public high school graduates

admissions officer noted that "African-Americans who are not from educated families rarely attain the eligibility pool at UCLA." Another staff member added that African-Americans without educated parents "rarely show up at UCLA or if they do, they don't stay long." These perceptions were supported by the results of our graduate survey; all African-Americans who responded were second- or third-generation college-goers.

Asian students were characterized as having a resource base and an immigrant zeal to achieve. Hispanic populations were described as three populations: first-generation college-going native Latinos from East Los Angeles where there are role models and a tradition of people succeeding through education; immigrants from Central and South America who come with a resource base and the expectation of going on to higher education; and immigrants, largely from Mexico, without resources. This last group is no more likely to attend UCLA than first-generation college students from African-American families.

The differences in the preparation of minority and nonminority students at UCLA contribute to the variations in retention rates reported in table 10.2.

Asian-Americans, Anglos, and Filipinos persisted in both the regular and special admission categories at rates that significantly exceed those for all other groups. The differences are particularly noticeable in the special admission category. It is also apparent that far higher proportions of African-Americans and Hispanics entered in the special admission category during this period. Since these data were published, the proportions of special admission African-Americans and Hispanics have diminished and services for first-year students have been strengthened. The gap in retention rates after the first year is now less than eight percentage points. But the difference in graduation rates has not diminished along with the differences in retention rates. In 1986 the five-year graduation rate for non-SAA stu-

TABLE 10.2. Five-Year Retention and Graduation Rates for UCLA Entering Freshman Class of 1980

	REGULAR ADMISSIONS			SPECIAL ADMISSIONS		
		Graduated	Continuing		Graduated	Continuing
ETHNIC GROUP	Number	(%)	(%)	Number	(%)	(%)
African-American	132	46	8	86	17	13
American Indian	10	50	0	1	100	0
Hispanic	234	38	11	42	12	7
Filipino	114	56	8	12	33	17
Asian-American	744	60	9	28	43	0
Anglo	2,765	60	6	149	36	13

Source: UCLA, Office of the Chancellor, Information Management and Institutional Research, *Fall 1988, Persistence and Graduation Information.*

dents was 58.4 percent. By contrast, SAA students graduated at a rate of 34.6 percent. For later cohorts, graduation rates jump 5 to 7 points when the sixth year is taken into consideration.

THE UNIVERSITY ENVIRONMENT

The emphasis on minorities at UCLA dates to 1964–1965 when one of the earliest versions of the Educational Opportunity Program was initiated. It was during this period that the Black Student Union first emerged as well. Even before the era of special programs UCLA had been known for prominent minority graduates. The first African-American Major League baseball player, Jackie Robinson, after whom the baseball stadium is named, was a graduate, as were other important African-American athletes, including Kareem Abdul Jabbar; Arthur Ashe; and Kenny Washington, the first African-American NFL football player. While the history of serving minority students who went on to national prominence was by no means limited to athletes (Ralph Bunche, U.S. delegate to the United Nations, was also a graduate), the athletic programs of the university remain an important part of the tradition of minority achievement at UCLA, especially for African-American students.

Despite its history of serving minority students and despite efforts to provide a supportive academic and social environment, UCLA suffers from the same environmental problems confronted by most large urban universities. The graduates we interviewed had found the size of the university or of their department intimidating. The social setting was described as uncomfortable, especially within the fraternities and sororities. Graduates spoke of racial segregation resulting from students' tendency to interact with people from their own racial or ethnic group.

Minorities in visible leadership positions help to ameliorate the harsher elements of the institutional environment. While they are underrepresented among top management, there are proportionately more minorities at UCLA than elsewhere in the system. African-Americans represented 8 percent of the top 100-plus administrators, or very nearly their proportional representation among high school graduates in California. By contrast, Hispanics were seriously underrepresented, accounting for less than 2 percent of those in senior administrative positions. Among career staff, a category which includes everyone from senior clerk to top management, African-Americans accounted for 20 percent of positions and Hispanics for another 11 percent, exceeding their combined proportion in high school graduating classes but still leaving Hispanics somewhat underrepresented.

Enrollment Management

The University of California system uses a central admissions process. Students may apply to as many campuses in the system as they wish, but they complete one application form and submit it to central processing. Each campus to which the student is applying receives a copy of the application and a computer tape of pertinent information. Each campus may then admit or reject the student. UCLA accepts the best-qualified Anglo and Asian-American students; those less qualified may be admitted to other campuses. During the study, UC by policy admitted all African-American, Hispanic, and American Indian applicants who met eligibility requirements and who applied on time. Students from these categories were immediately offered admission by UCLA.

Under the UC admissions plan the state is divided into service districts, each of which is assigned to one of the campuses. The service area for UCLA is Los Angeles County. While UCLA recruits in a relatively restricted area, recruitment visits are seen as essential because they give the university an opportunity to go after the best-prepared students. Criteria for selecting schools to visit include their history of sending good students and the numbers of minority students they enroll.

The factors contributing to the success experienced by UCLA in recruiting underrepresented minorities has been attributed to six variables in addition to the popularity of the institution and its advantageous geographic location: (1) a unified and supportive administrative base, (2) coordination between early outreach and recruitment efforts, (3) internal monitoring of program and staff effectiveness, (4) diversified outreach staff; (5) placement of interns in targeted schools, and (6) intensive recruitment and preenrollment follow-up programming.

Coordinated management efforts include: (1) regular meetings of program coordinators to share information about schools and about delivery of services to students, (2) the sharing of successful academic counseling techniques, (3) access to a microcomputer data base which provides demographic and academic information on student participants, and (4) use of admissions counselors and evaluators to train staff and to provide frequent updates on UC admissions requirements. Some eighteen different programs share the administrative base and contribute to the cooperative effort.

Among the undergraduate colleges, competition for admission is most severe in engineering. The average GPA for engineering entering freshmen in fall 1985 was 3.89 on a 4.0 scale. The average math scholastic aptitude test score for engineering freshmen was 675. For African-Americans and Hispanics the contrasting grade-point averages and SAT scores were 3.78 and 606, respectively. The higher admission standards for engineering are reflected in the lower proportions of African-Americans and Hispanics enrolled. While underrepresented groups constituted about 18 percent of the undergraduate student body for the university in 1985, they represented only 12 percent of enrollment in the school of engineering. During the last two years, engineering has moved from schoolwide admission requirements to admission requirements on a department-by-department basis. There is some concern about the effect of this change in policy on minority representation in the more highly selective fields such as electrical engineering.

Admission for transfer students is as competitive as it is for freshmen. Transfer students bring with them a minimum grade-point average of 2.6 (3.2 for the School of Engineering and Applied Sciences), although there is some flexibility in the application of this standard to minorities. Test scores are not required for transfer students. Affirmative action figures for new junior enrollments do not exhibit the progress that has been made in the participation rates of first-time freshmen. Between 1975 and 1986 the number of new juniors admitted in the SAA category increased from 12.7 to 15.2 percent (Filipinos are included in this comparison). But almost a quarter of these were in the special admission category. Many believe that aggressive university recruitment of minorities directly from high schools has reduced the proportions of minority students with reasonable academic preparation who begin their postsecondary education in a community college.

Whatever the explanation for the limited gains in the number of underrepresented minorities transferring to UCLA as new juniors, their performance remains satisfactory. The three-year graduation rates for junior SAA regular admissions (55 percent) exceeds the five-year rates for their freshmen regular admission counterparts. For non-SAA regular and special admissions the five-year rates for freshmen are better than three-year rates for juniors, as is the case with SAA special admits, but the differences in all instances are fairly small.

Early Intervention

Programs are categorized as immediate outreach or early outreach. Immediate outreach programs are designed to identify potential applicants from underrepresented groups who are eligible for UC admission. Typical services provided through the immediate outreach program include presentations to high school and community college students and counselors, campus tours, career information days, college motivation nights, admissions counseling, and freshman orientation sessions and seminars.

Early outreach programs, which are designed to expand the pool of eligible minority candidates, have components in both junior and senior high schools. The junior high program, which involves parents as well as students, offers academic advising and role model presentations as well as college and university visits. The senior high program offers similar programs but places increased emphasis on academic services such as tutoring and advising. Student course selection and progress are closely monitored. Student participants are expected to complete college preparatory classes on a schedule which meets university subject requirements before high school graduation.

To encourage cooperation among university faculty, community college faculty, and K-12 teachers, UCLA has created within its graduate school of education the Center for Academic Interinstitutional Programs (CAIP). Every summer more than 1,000 teachers attend the CAIP summer institutes. During the academic year, a crowded program of conferences, seminars, alliances, and workshops keeps the summer institute participants returning to the campus. Hundreds of additional teachers attend workshops organized by the CAIP in their own school districts.

The CAIP functions on the principle that to make a difference in the public schools requires an influence on educational policy. In the six years since its founding, the CAIP's curricular emphasis has developed from writing and mathematics through all the subjects normally graded A to F, and beyond, to work with linguistic minority programs, counselors, and principals. The aim is always to link faculty members at UCLA with their counterparts in the schools, thus providing continuity on the basis of curriculum content.

The Mathematics Diagnostic Testing Project (MDTP) supplies schools (free of charge) with tests for various levels of mathematics, and returns the test scores with indications of curricular weaknesses. The program also provides consultants who work with mathematics teachers to redesign and realign curriculum so that students will proceed faster and will have a clear understanding of the standard of preparation required for success at the postsecondary level.

In 1982 CAIP staff members began administering an English placement examination (formerly called the "UC Subject A Examination") to eleventh-grade students in selected cooperating schools. The papers are graded by UCLA and high school faculty, a procedure that enables high school faculty to learn UCLA's expectations. Students who pass do not have to take the examination again when applying to UCLA; those who fail have the twelfth-grade year to make up deficiencies.

Thanks in large measure to these outreach and recruitment programs, the number of SAA applications from targeted schools has more than doubled, and the number of students admitted has more than tripled. Despite concerted efforts to motivate, inform, advise, and assist SAA students through early and immediate outreach programs, the level of success remains problematic because of: (1) low eligibility rates and underpreparation of SAA students, (2) lack of a large cohort of SAA students who take the appropriate courses in high school, (3) inconsistent selection criteria used by school staff in selecting students for participation in special programs, (4) lack of familiarity with courses required to become UC-eligible among many junior high and middle school counselors, and (5) limited funds for the large number of minority-dominant junior and senior high schools (sixty-four junior high schools and fifty-three high schools) serving the Los Angeles area.

Articulation with Community Colleges

The CAIP is also the home of the Transfer Alliance Program (TAP), involving thirteen local community colleges. UCLA guarantees junior-level admission to students from TAP colleges who have completed core courses with a 3.0 GPA. A program of alliance meetings brings together community college and UCLA faculty to exchange views on curricula, standards, and instructional techniques. Transfer centers to which the university provides staff have also been established at four area colleges. They arrange visits from college representatives and target minorities for special attention.

Orientation and Advising

UCLA provides a three-day orientation program in which most first-time freshmen participate. Fees are reduced for students who are awarded financial aid. During the three days, placement exams (covering English and math or math/chemistry) are administered to students required to take them. The program, staffed by undergraduates, counselors, and other student services staff, provides sessions on choosing a major, degree requirements and degree planning, motivation, study skills, coping with stress, financial aid, and faculty expectations. Adjustment to the social and physical environment of UCLA is also emphasized. Sessions are offered for transfer students as well as for first-time freshmen.

Many minority students receive academic advising and counseling through the Academic Advancement Program (AAP) or the Minority Engineering Program (MEP). Services designed for the general student population often incorporate arrangements for aiding under-represented populations, such as the rap group for African-American students supervised by an African-American psychologist, a Chicano women's group, groups for Asian-American students, and special career days for groups such as the Black Engineering Society.

Residential Life

The problems faced by minority students in finding affordable housing in the affluent communities surrounding UCLA receive special attention in the allocation of dormitory space. A lottery is held for all students who request housing. A number of spaces are held out of the lottery. Highly recruited scholars, athletes, and AAP students are given priority for these spaces as freshmen, because of the major role housing plays in academic adjustment and orientation to college life. Many academic and support programs are built into the residence halls, including tutoring, faculty-in-residence, teaching assistant review sections, and the teaching of some basic skills classes and seminars. Forty-three hundred students currently live on campus.

Because of current pressures, university policy states that 70 percent of the available beds will be assigned to new students, with two-thirds of these being freshmen. Students who receive residence hall space as freshmen must enter their names again in a lottery if they wish to continue in a residence hall for a second year. No preference is given to any set of students for space in the second year. African-Americans and Hispanics are proportionately represented in residence halls during their first year. By the sophomore year, Anglos and Asian-Americans have increased their representation, while the representation of all other groups has declined, as indicated in table 10.3. The university plan is to guarantee housing to all freshmen for two years when additional spaces are constructed. Plans call for an expansion of housing with the goal of having half the students living on campus or within a mile by the year 2000.

Financial Aid

While UCLA is low-cost in terms of tuition and fees (about $1,400 for the academic year for a resident student in 1987–1988), the university provides substantial financial assistance beyond that available through state and federal programs. Financial aid officers use the State University Grant (SUG) program, which awarded over $10 million in aid to UCLA students in 1986–1987, to tailor awards to student needs. SUG funds are extremely flexible and can be given interchangeably with other aid. Under UCLA policy the neediest students receive the most grants.

TABLE 10.3. Student Representation in Residence Halls and among First-Time Freshmen at UCLA, 1985

		PERCENTAGE IN RESIDENCE HALLS	
	FIRST TIME FRESHMEN		
ETHNICITY	(%)	*Freshmen*	*Sophomores*
African-American	9.7	9.4	6.8
American Indian	0.9	0.9	0.7
Hispanic	15.0	14.4	9.3
Asian-American	15.5	14.4	19.1
Filipino	5.8	5.5	4.7
Anglo	50.2	51.8	56.2

Source: UCLA, Student Affairs Information and Research Office, *1985 Ethnic Proportions of Students Who Live in the Residence Halls by Level*, November 1986.

ACADEMIC ENVIRONMENT

The university is currently trying to develop an academic environment which comfortably includes minority students. Past efforts have focused more on adjusting students to the institution through special programs staffed by minority professionals. Staff members feel threatened by efforts to bring the programs into the framework of the College of Letters and Sciences, and they communicate their concerns to students. Threats to the current structure of minority student services quickly get translated into threats to the university's priorities for minorities. A senior administrator noted that universities must reach some maturity in their relationships with minority students to enter into the kind of discussions currently going on at UCLA. In particular, he added, "They must surmount a widespread perception that a quality university cannot afford to enroll too many African-American and Hispanic students."

Academic standards are stressed. As one staff member noted, "We work hard to bring minority students in. We provide them with academic, financial, and social assistance, but in the end they have to meet the standards just like everybody else." A sequence of writing skills courses is offered by the English department for those who do not meet the "very, very high" standards of UCLA faculty. Every student who enters with a score of less than 600 on the English part of the SAT must write two timed essays, and 60 percent of these students are then placed in writing skills courses. The writing skills level of transfer students was identified as a problem, but it is not one that is easily addressed under current state policy, which excludes students from testing if they have completed their first two years in a community college.

The writing program, which includes courses in grammar and expository writing as well as a standard freshman composition course, is offered under the auspices of the English department by carefully selected non-tenure-track faculty. A special summer freshman preparatory program, available in conjunction with all three writing courses, gives double the usual number of hours of classroom time as well as tutorial support for those who opt to enter. Mathematics was not a part of the original remedial program, but the sequence of courses offered now includes intermediate algebra and precalculus.

The attention currently being given to lower-division instruction and to general education requirements is viewed as a promising intervention that has the potential for improving the educational experience for all students. Among the questions being considered in the reform process are whether UCLA should have an ethnic studies requirement and how the ethnic diversity of America, Los Angeles, and UCLA should affect the curriculum.

Faculty

Faculty ethnicity for the three major undergraduate colleges at UCLA is summarized in table 10.4 according to tenure status. While progress in some areas was evident among recent hires, affirmative action efforts at UCLA at the time of the study could best be described as improving slowly. UCLA's record for tenuring Hispanics is approximately at the average for the system, while the record for African-Americans is below the system average.

The effort to recruit minority faculty members who matched the attainments of the existing faculty suffered from the limited pool of minority graduates with the threshold academic qualifications as defined. The screening process for new faculty members called for the best minority and women candidates to be included during initial screening. Final selection, however, was exclusively a function of merit without regard to gender or race. Departments were described as "uncompromising in the demands of those selected as faculty."

Faculty members were not unaware of the importance of hiring minority persons. As one noted, "Every time we've hired persons of color, that has produced classrooms of color. Minority students seek out classes taught by minority faculty members." But his counterpart in another department without a single active Hispanic or African-American faculty member described himself as "furious" because the dean or the chancellor's office made offers involving special compensation to minorities or women identified through the departmental selection process.

To help address the problem of inadequate recruiting pools, UCLA offers dissertation and postdoctoral fellowship programs, and a program designed to guide very able students at the undergraduate level into graduate programs. The university also provides salary support for released time from teaching and for summer research. The data on promotions indicate that minorities are advancing at a normal rate.

TABLE 10.4. Faculty Ethnicity at UCLA According to Tenure Status for Three Colleges

	LETTERS AND SCIENCES		FINE ARTS		ENGINEERING	
	N	%	N	%	N	%
Tenured:						
African-American	5	0.7	1	1.2	1	0.8
Hispanic	19	2.9	3	3.4	1	0.8
Asian	21	3.3	2	2.3	22	18.6
American Indian	0	0	2	2.3	0	0
Total	642		88		118	
Nontenured:						
African-American	9	7.5	4	13.3	0	0
Hispanic	7	5.8	0	0	1	5.8
Asian	4	3.3	2	6.6	2	11.7
American Indian	1	0.8	0	0	0	0
Total	120		30		17	

Source: UCLA, Office of the Chancellor, Information Management and Institutional Research, *Summary of Ethnic and Sex Employment and Utilization Analysis*, 1986.

During the 1960s four ethnic research centers were established, as an alternative to setting up ethnic study departments. A specified number of faculty positions were allotted to each center with the understanding that these positions would be shared with academic departments which would be involved in the search process. Currently six positions are available to each center, but if additional qualified people are identified in the course of a search, they may also be employed. While effective in creating centers of interest for minority faculty, the centers have been less successful in working with the departments where faculty are tenured and promoted. One of the directors commented on the status of three assistant professors affiliated with his center. Each had been told in a friendly way by his respective department that "he could not get tenure by concentrating on minority issues."

Faculty do not appear to play a major role in efforts to increase minority student achievement and often hold low expectations for minority success. A department chair shared his general perception that African-Americans and Hispanics had not been well prepared. Attitudes toward transfer students were similar to those held for minorities. A faculty member described them as "one of our continuing problems" and noted that it was "well they could not be readily identified in classrooms or faculty might have been harder on them." One difference between transfer and minority students, of course, is that the latter can be identified at sight.

Services such as tutoring were provided by some departments to all students, but no special effort was made to target minorities. Students were expected to take the initiative in using available services. One department chair was skeptical about a report that large numbers of minority students enrolled in departmental courses were requesting AAP tutorial assistance since these students were not seeing departmental faculty during scheduled office hours.

Faculty members who were aware of the university's affirmative action efforts often held the view that minority programs had been operating too independently of faculty involvement and that the people administering the programs had by choice kept faculty involvement to a minimum in order to pursue their own agendas. This view was shared by many administrators and contributed to the decision to bring minority programs into the academic center of the college.

Administrators questioned the commitment of academic faculty to helping minority students succeed. The problem was stated succinctly by a senior administrator:

> Commitment develops on two levels. There is first of all a faculty commitment to administrators doing the job. This is relatively easy to obtain. The second level is a faculty commitment to substantial effort on their part and this level of commitment is not nearly so easy to obtain.

The lack of faculty involvement in minority initiatives can be traced to a number of sources. The priorities of the faculty are firmly centered on research and scholarly distinction. Department representatives made this point firmly and very early in conversations with external visitors. A science department assistant chair opened one conversation on concern about minority achievement by commenting that seven of the department's number were members of the National Academy of Sciences and that one had been awarded the Nobel prize two days earlier. In this same department, only one of fifty faculty members was African-American. Women were poorly represented as well.

Additional insights into faculty attitudes were provided by a faculty leader on the university strategic planning committee whose overall objective was described as "beating Berkeley academically as well as on the playing fields." Affirmative action is one of four priorities adopted by this committee. The subcommittee on ethnic diversity planned an affirmative action retreat for faculty members. Faculty reaction to the retreat was characterized by such comments as: "What, again?" "What more is there to say?" "We know the numbers aren't good and the programs don't work."

Academic Support Services

At UCLA the Academic Advancement Program forms the structure within which most services to retain minority students are delivered.

The term "academic advancement" is used in preference to "educational opportunity" to emphasize that the objectives of the program are to strengthen academic performance as well as to increase the number of underrepresented students who remain on campus. Four basic types of services are offered: (1) learning skills assistance, including small group sessions and individual consultation on reading, writing, and study skills such as time management, note taking, and test preparation; (2) summer transitional programs both for first-time freshmen and junior college transfers; (3) advising and counseling sessions, including advising on careers and graduate and professional schools; and (4) tutoring and instructional assistance.

The AAP began in 1963 with thirteen students. By 1985 a program that had been redesigned in the early 1970s to serve 1,700 students was serving 4,500, 30 percent of whom were African-American and 40 percent Hispanic. Although some graduates objected to common views of AAP as a minority-only support program, others found the perception constructive. One noted that the number of minority students in the program was helpful because "you can usually relate to them." After adding that it helped to share difficulties with someone of similar background, she continued, "Sometimes you do feel a little isolated."

The current strategy for modifying university services to minority students is comprehensive and far-reaching. Objectives include: placing the responsibility for improved outcomes at the division level, monitoring progress through the university's comprehensive student information system, establishing coherence and continuity between the tutoring provided to minority students in high schools and community colleges and at UCLA, and moving away from special minority advisory committees to visible minority participation on all committees. Central to the entire plan is integration of the AAP with parallel services within the College of Letters and Sciences as an integral part of the college's administrative structure. This plan is controversial because it threatens the influence of current staff and raises concerns that minority students will be "tossed" into the institution without appropriate support services. To counter these concerns, key leaders sent the message that they recognized the need for distinct programs to serve special populations with special needs.

Cultural diversity, at least in part because of the need to respond to the concerns of AAP students and staff, has remained an important topic on the chancellor's university relations agenda. The decision to focus on cultural diversity helped to bring the entire university together around questions of race and ethnicity and the appropriate role for AAP.

Freshman and Transfer Summer Programs

Under the leadership of AAP staff, UCLA offers two intensive seven-week summer bridge programs with combined enrollments of 700 to

800 students. The Freshman Summer Program (FSP) provides—for freshmen who score below 600 on the College Entrance Examination Board (CEEB) English test or below 530 on the SAT mathematics test—intensive instruction, tutorials, and learning workshops to strengthen writing or mathematical skills. About 95 percent of those enrolled in this program are African-American or Hispanic. The Transfer Summer Program (TSP) is aimed at improving the composition and problem-solving skills and the analytical thinking of community college transfer students. They are prepared for the rigorous academic programs at UCLA through seventeen hours a week of in-class instruction, tutorial assistance, and workshops. Eighty percent of the students in this program are African-American or Hispanic.

In the FSP during the study, students chose between a writing track (social science and writing courses) and a mathematics track (mathematics and computer sciences courses). Under an "adjuncting" concept, students from five sections of English composition were all enrolled in the same political science, geography, history, or psychology section. The content area instructor assigned research papers and essay exams which the English instructor used as vehicles for teaching students how to write. The course in computer science was coordinated with the math course. The TSP also offered regular courses in special format. In both programs, completion of the courses provided units toward graduation.

Students were in class twice as long as they would ordinarily have been there. Tutoring was built into each class. TSP also included a residence hall component with night tutoring and academic advising. The faculty who taught in the summer programs came from several departments of the university.

Beyond intensive instruction and academic support services, the summer programs offer an introduction to cultural, social, and recreational opportunities at UCLA. While dormitory residence is optional, students are encouraged to live on campus to take part in academic and personal counseling sessions and generally to get to know the campus and its facilities under the guidance of live-in counselors.

Minority Engineering Program

The Minority Engineering Program provides support services and academic enrichment for engineering students similar to those provided by AAP for the rest of the university. MEP picks up students during their first contacts with the university and follows them through their academic careers. MEP students arrive on campus three weeks before the beginning of classes, live in dormitories, and have intensive involvement with support staff. Much emphasis is placed upon structuring groups of minority students who will help one another in the learning process after the term begins.

The academic support services offered under MEP are focused through a professional development program with four main objectives: (1) to build a community of minority freshmen that focuses on achieving academic excellence and becomes a source of peer support; (2) to provide extensive, year-long supplementary instruction for minority students; (3) to orient minority students to the university, to assist in their adjustment, and where necessary, to advocate their collective and individual interests; and (4) to monitor students' academic progress and to furnish ongoing academic advising.

CPEC has evaluated the impact of MEP on the retention of engineering students at the four UC campuses where the program was initiated in fall 1982 (the prototype program was developed at California State University, Northridge in 1973). The two-year retention rates for Mexican-American students increased from 51 percent in fall 1981 before the program to 65 percent after. The before and after percentages for African-Americans were 59 and 70 percent. Three years after the program began, 47 percent of all freshmen entering in fall 1982 remained enrolled. The comparable figure for program participants was 60 percent. Among the UC campuses, UCLA had the highest three-year continuation rates for freshmen (71 percent). The before and after comparisons, as well as the disappointing rates for minority students who did not enroll in MEP, provide convincing evidence that the program works.

SUMMARY

Minority students admitted to UCLA are well qualified by any standards most institutions would apply. Their four- and five-year graduation rates are superior to the rates for nonminority students in most urban universities. Yet they do not perform as well as their Anglo and Asian-American colleagues, partly because many have attended less competitive high schools and have entered with lower GPAs and test scores.

UCLA removed the barriers to minority participation before many institutions of its type. A long history of significant achievement contributes to the institution's attractiveness to well-qualified minority students, as does its location close to significant centers of minority culture. But the contribution of the UCLA case to our understanding of minority achievement goes beyond its history and location.

UCLA has for some time maintained meticulous data on the progress and graduation rates of its different student populations. Alone among the case-study institutions, it has routinely studied the effects of waiving admission standards for each racial and ethnic group. From this data UCLA concluded prior to the beginning of this study that minority students who did not meet UC admission standards were unlikely candidates to survive its rigorous academic environment. As an alternative strategy, the university developed systematic and carefully coordinated programs of early intervention and outreach. It also developed bridging strategies and a careful system of continuing support for at-risk student populations. The success of efforts to expand the pool of qualified minority applicants has diminished UCLA's need to admit students who are not qualified in order to meet affirmative action goals.

From the late 1960s through 1986, UCLA relied primarily on special programs and special staff to help minority students overcome preparation gaps and adapt to relatively unchanging academic programs and practices. The current emphasis on bringing special programs into the academic mainstream represents an attempt to engage faculty in adapting academic programs and teaching practices to the needs of an increasingly diverse student body. The composition of the student body at UCLA reflects changing California demographics. The proportion of Anglo students fell below 60 percent in 1986 and seems likely to decline further. Even well-prepared minority students bring different strengths and different cultures than do Anglos.

The move to mainstream programs and services for special populations in an elite university like UCLA clearly has risks, as evidenced by the strong differences of opinion that quickly surfaced. Special programs and special staff have provided underrepresented populations with a sense of identity, academic support, counseling, a physical gathering place on campus, and buffering from some of the more hostile elements in the academic environment. At the same time, they have provided regular faculty members with a convenient rationale for conducting business as usual, despite the increasing diversity of the student body.

The UCLA experiment with adapting its academic culture merits careful attention. In some respects it is a far more interesting development than the special interventions for which the university has received national attention during the past several years. UCLA faces continuing scrutiny from internal and external political interest groups in dealing with issues of balance in an environment in which minority influence on state policy is a present and growing reality.

11

BROOKLYN COLLEGE

PATRICIA CROSSON
with the assistance of DANIEL MAYERS and
ERIC STEINBERG

Access and degree achievement for minority students have played an important role in the history of Brooklyn College. Founded in 1930, during its first thirty years it became one of the most prestigious of the nineteen campuses in the City University of New York (CUNY) system. Free tuition, extremely selective admissions policies, and high standards for graduation characterized the college; minority enrollments remained relatively small. During the open-admissions era in the early 1970s, enrollment doubled, with large enrollment increases recorded for minority students. With the increased emphasis on access came also serious problems with retention and degree achievement.

During the late 1970s, the imposition of tuition and higher admissions standards for four-year colleges in the CUNY system caused declines in enrollment along with stratification of the system. While minorities dominated the community college sector, their proportional enrollments in a number of the senior colleges including Brooklyn fell below their representation in New York City. Concurrently, rates of degree achievement for minority students within the senior colleges gradually improved, although they remained below those for Anglos.

A major fiscal crisis in New York City forced enrollment cuts leading to extensive layoffs among faculty and staff throughout the CUNY system. The effect on morale was devastating. By the late 1970s, Brooklyn College was having difficulty maintaining its proud tradition as a first-class liberal arts college. A new president in 1979 ushered in a less turbulent era. Gradually the declining enrollment stabilized at approximately 14,000 students, and academic preparation improved. The curriculum was strengthened and standards maintained. Concurrently, administrators and faculty members worked to improve the educational

Patricia Crosson is deputy provost at the University of Massachusetts at Amherst. Daniel Mayers (deceased) was dean for institutional development and Eric Steinberg is assistant provost at Brooklyn College.

environment at Brooklyn College to make it more conducive to degree achievement for all students including minorities.

Although it offers masters' and doctoral programs, Brooklyn College is predominately an undergraduate institution with a mission to provide high-quality liberal arts education, primarily to residents of Brooklyn. The institution is organized into three divisions. The College of Liberal Arts and Sciences, by far the largest, offers 100 undergraduate programs to a day-student population. The School of General Studies offers evening undergraduate programs and continuing education. A third division offers all graduate programs.

In its April 28, 1986, issue, *Time Magazine* described Brooklyn College as "one of nine fast-rising and ambitious institutions . . . now challenging the nation's elite schools," and noted, "Brooklyn is providing a first-class education at fourth class prices."

THE STATE ENVIRONMENT

The legislature and the governor view minority success within the educational system as a critical component of a healthy economy for the city and state. They have consistently supported efforts to improve minority participation and achievement at all levels of education. While much attention has been focused on the high schools because of dropout rates and quality problems, state officials have also been concerned about postsecondary education and particularly its influence on access to health, engineering, and other licensed professions in which minority participation has historically been low.

The student financial aid program in New York State is the largest in the nation. In 1984–1985, over 378,000 scholarship and grant awards and 444,000 loans were supported by state appropriations in excess of $1.47 billion. The very important Tuition Assistance Program (TAP) alone makes thousands of noncompetitive, need-based grants each year.

New York also supports five opportunity programs for the educationally and financially disadvantaged: the Higher Education Opportunity Program (HEOP) for students in independent institutions; the Educational Opportunity Program (EOP) for students in the SUNY system; Search for Education, Elevation and Knowledge (SEEK) in the CUNY system; the College Discovery (CD) programs in the community colleges; and the Regents Professional Opportunity Scholarships. These comprehensive programs provide special counseling, tutoring, and remedial course work in addition to financial assistance. A number of other special assistance programs encourage minority and economically disadvantaged students to participate in professional fields.

The first goal in the plan of the Board of Regents of the University of the State of New York (the statewide coordinating board) is access to higher education for all citizens, with special attention to the needs of low-income and minority groups. As part of the planning process, reports and issue papers have focused on minority enrollment and participation in higher education, and on minority access to the licensed professions. The board uses a sometimes controversial program review process to distinguish between what is and is not college-level work (among other quality assurance purposes). Board policy permits remedial and developmental work on a noncredit basis only. Financial aid policies allow students to receive financial aid for five years rather than four.

COMMUNITY SETTING

Brooklyn is the largest of five boroughs in New York City. In 1980, 49 percent of the population was Anglo, 31 percent African-American, and 18 percent Hispanic. Minorities have steadily increased their share of the population. One in four residents was foreign-born in 1980, and 35 percent spoke a language other than English at home. Table 11.1 reports selected educational and economic characteristics from the 1980 census. Brooklyn is highly multiethnic and multicultural. The large numbers of Orthodox Jews, Italian Catholics, African-Americans and Puerto Ricans who have played an important role in the history of Brooklyn College continue to attend, but they have been joined by Eastern European Jews, blacks from Caribbean countries, Cubans, Chinese, Koreans, and many others. For all these groups, Brooklyn College is the logical, low-cost baccalaureate institution. The enrollment of Brooklyn College reflects the multicultural and multiethnic diversity of the city and borough it serves.

TABLE 11.1. Economic and Educational Characteristics of Brooklyn Residents by Race and Ethnicity, 1980

	Anglo	African-American	Hispanic
Median family income	$17,563	$11,574	$8,952
Percentage unemployed, 16 and older	7.1	11.3	12.8
Percentage of families below poverty line	13.2	29.6	40.7
Percentage enrolled in school at age:			
16 and 17	86.9	87.2	79.8
18 and 19	54.0	57.4	43.4
20 and 21	36.5	32.9	23.1

Source: U.S. Bureau of the Census, New York, *Current Population Reports*, 1980.

Many community organizations and groups sponsor programs and activities to encourage youth to attend college. Two large African-American churches that run private schools through the sixth grade hold annual college nights at which many colleges, including Brooklyn, are represented. The Urban League, as part of its efforts to motivate college attendance, helps administer the Mayor's Scholarship Program. The Jack and Jills, a private social club for middle- and upper-class African-Americans, also awards scholarships, many to students who plan to attend historically black or Ivy League Institutions or Brooklyn College as the "at-home" alternative.

Aspira, Inc., a large and influential organization of community leaders, recognizes and encourages Puerto Rican scholars from high school through college. Aspira has a scholarship fund supported by business and industry. The organization also helps to administer the Mayor's Scholarship Program. Aspira Leadership Clubs in fifteen New York high schools provide a sense of community and cultural identity for Puerto Rican and Hispanic youth and raise educational aspirations through the involvement of successful business and community leaders as role models. Aspira keeps in touch with students after they enter college, to provide a support network.

Special arrangements with local businesses and industries provide employment and internship opportunities for the large proportion of students who work either full- or part-time during their undergraduate years. The American Broadcasting Company offers internships and special programs for television majors that lead to long-term career opportunities. Brooklyn College is expected by the business community to produce graduates who will pursue careers in Brooklyn and thus make long-term contributions to the economy and stability of the borough.

The Public School System

The public school system in New York City has three tiers. At the top are specialized high schools such as Bronx Science and Midwood High School, which enroll students from throughout the city on the basis of demonstrated ability and potential in their designated specialty areas. These schools are among the best in the country. In the second tier are the commercial high schools which provide vocational and technical training. These schools have ample resources and are considered to be quite good. The third tier includes the neighborhood district schools which must accept all youth in their assigned area. Third-tier schools are uneven in quality, and many have serious academic problems.

Since CUNY admissions policies define eligibility for the senior colleges on the basis of high school grades *or* rank within the top third of the high school class, large numbers of students who meet the admissions criteria for senior institutions lack adequate preparation for college-level work. Large proportions of students from some high schools who take the CUNY assessment tests fail them.

The City University of New York

The City University of New York, consisting of twelve senior colleges, seven community colleges, a law school, and a medical school, serves a significant proportion of the total public higher education population in the state. Admissions policies, special program initiatives, resource allocation, and special efforts in diagnostic and proficiency testing attest to a long-standing concern with minority access and degree achievement.

The CUNY central office monitors an extensive educational opportunity program under state SEEK funding. In 1983–1984 there were 11,453 students enrolled in SEEK within CUNY institutions. Of this total, 46 percent were African-American and 39 percent Hispanic. Because resources within CUNY not committed to salaries and basic operating costs are scarce, special programs and support services are heavily dependent upon state appropriations.

CUNY administers systemwide diagnostic and assessment tests in reading comprehension, writing skills, and mathematics to all entering students. Brooklyn College adds a speech test to the CUNY required tests. While test results are used primarily for diagnostic purposes, the CUNY Board of Trustees has also mandated that students must meet a prescribed level of proficiency on the tests before entering the upper division. Students who fail to meet the mandated proficiency levels with permissible retakes are not allowed to register beyond sixty credits. A universitywide task force on student retention and academic performance recommended in 1981 that CUNY institutions find ways to improve counseling services and strengthen programs teaching English as a second language.

The CUNY system encourages interinstitutional cooperation and articulation by guaranteeing a place for all city high school graduates who have completed the appropriate curriculum. Similarly, the system guarantees a place in a senior college for all graduates of a CUNY community college who have pursued the appropriate academic transfer program. CUNY guards against competitiveness and duplication by managing the admissions process centrally and designating recruitment and service areas for each institution in the system.

Students are admissible to community colleges in the CUNY system with a high school average of at least 70 or a standing in the top half of their class. Because the population of CUNY community colleges is heavily minority, success in helping minorities earn degrees in New York City depends heavily on transfer. Although formal policies have been in place for several years, only in the last few years have college and system officials made special efforts to facilitate transition from community colleges to senior institutions. Kingsborough Community College is about 20 minutes from Brooklyn College by public transportation and draws students from the same geographical area. Kingsborough works hard to encourage students to participate in the academic transfer programs, and approximately two-thirds of its students go on for baccalaureate work, usually at Brooklyn College.

STUDENTS

Brooklyn College students mirror the diversity of the borough of Brooklyn. Children of first-generation Americans predominated into the 1950s. They were gradually replaced by children of native-born, middle-income, and overwhelmingly Jewish parents. There have always been more Jewish students and fewer African-American and Hispanic students in the college than would be expected from proportions in the surrounding community, but non-Jewish minorities now represent approximately 35 percent of undergraduate students.

Table 11.2 indicates the ethnic composition of the undergraduate student body for 1981 through 1986.

The demographics of the neighborhoods from which Brooklyn College draws the majority of its students, the admissions criteria which are designed to ensure eligibility for the leading graduates of all high schools, and the ability to attract top students because of a reputation for high quality and standards combine to produce a student body at Brooklyn College with an enormous range of academic preparation for college-level work. Many graduates of some of the best high schools in the country come to Brooklyn for an Ivy League experience at commuter college prices. Many others are from some of the worst high schools in the country and, although they meet the criteria for regular admission,

TABLE 11.2. Ethnic Composition of Undergraduate Students at Brooklyn College, 1981–1986

	AMERICAN INDIAN (%)	AFRICAN-AMERICAN (%)	ASIAN-AMERICAN (%)	HISPANIC (%)	ANGLO (%)
1981	1.2	21.4	4.4	7.6	65.4
1982	1.2	19.9	4.0	6.4	68.5
1983	0.9	25.0	5.3	8.3	60.5
1984	1.2	25.2	6.6	9.3	57.6
1986	1.0	23.2	8.2	9.5	55.6

Source: CUNY and Brooklyn College, 1987.

Note: The ethnicity data were collected via the CUNY Ethnic Census, an annual self-reporting questionaire filled in anonymously and voluntarily by students. The percentages are extrapolated to the population.(No data were available for 1985.)

TABLE 11.3. Ethnic Composition of Brooklyn College Graduates, 1983 and 1985

	AMERICAN INDIAN (%)	AFRICAN-AMERICAN (%)	ASIAN (%)	HISPANIC (%)	ANGLO (%)
1983	1.9	19.1	3.9	7.3	65.8
1985	1.1	22.0	5.5	9.0	60.9

Source: CUNY and Brooklyn College, 1987.

Note: The data in this table are based on the CUNY Ethnic Census, an annual self-reporting questionaire filled in anonymously and voluntarily by students. Students were asked if they expected to graduate during the academic year. The percentages are extrapolated to the population.

are far from prepared for college-level work. Still others are part of the SEEK program which admits students on the basis of economic and educational disadvantages.

Table 11.3 reports the ethnic composition of graduates for 1983 and 1985.

The limited data available for Brooklyn College reveal no dramatic discrepancies between minority representation in undergraduate enrollments and minority representation among graduates. Since CUNY stopped collecting and reporting enrollment and graduation data after the 1980 HEGIS survey, it is difficult to compare the data the college furnished from its voluntary ethnic survey with the data available for the other case-study institutions. From the data furnished it does not appear that participation and achievement at Brooklyn College varied as a function of race and ethnicity to the extent that they did in many other case-study institutions.

Our survey of graduates revealed a significant number of first-generation college-goers at Brooklyn. Forty-five percent of the graduates surveyed reported they were the first in their families to attend college, the largest percentage for any of the case-study institutions. Over a fourth of the graduates indicated that one or both of their parents had never completed high school. Only UTEP had a higher proportion of graduates whose parents had not completed high school. At the same time it was clear that Brooklyn graduates were more likely to have pursued a traditional mode of college attendance than might be typical for most commuter colleges. More than a third of the graduates interviewed were in the traditional age range and had never been required to interrupt their college careers. Although some graduates had taken between six and eleven years to graduate, only UCLA and Florida State had higher proportions of students completing their degrees in four years at the age of 22. Brooklyn also had the lowest proportion (45 percent) of transfer students and one of the higher proportions of students who had subsequently gone on to graduate study.

THE UNIVERSITY

Brooklyn College is committed to providing a first-class undergraduate education for a multicultural and ethnically diverse student body. Opinions differ on whether Brooklyn makes any special effort with respect to minority degree achievement. Some believe that the college makes extensive efforts to ensure that all students successfully complete their undergraduate programs with particular attention to minorities. They describe an extensive array of academic and other support services in defense of this position. Others believe that the college is not very supportive of less well prepared minority students because of an overriding concern with academic standards and image. Both groups agree, however, that the commitment to minority degree achievement is much stronger now than it was during the period between 1965 and 1979.

None of the top 10 administrative leaders of the college are from underrepresented minority groups. In the twelve-member middle management grouping of deans and associates, two deans are African-American.

Admissions and Recruitment

Admissions criteria are established by the CUNY Board of Trustees and managed by system officers. Brooklyn College has an office of enrollment management which is responsible at the campus level for admissions, recruitment, and financial aid. Within recruitment parameters established by CUNY, Brooklyn College tries to attract minority students through mailings to students identified through the National Scholarship Service Fund for Minority Students or the National Hispanic Scholars Awards Program. The college participates in college fairs, visits all Brooklyn high schools with college preparatory programs, and sponsors "open-house" events for students throughout the borough whose names appear on high school graduation lists. While these activities are not targeted to minority students, they occur in very multicultural settings.

The most significant financial aid programs for students are supported and operated by the state and/or the CUNY system. Campus-based employment and loan programs are similar to those offered at other institutions. None target minority students as a special group.

Early Intervention

Among the many special programs and collaborative relationships Brooklyn College has entered into with high schools in its immediate neighborhood, the most far-reaching is the operation of Midwood High School. While Midwood serves the section of Brooklyn adjacent to the college, it also attracts well-qualified and highly motivated students from throughout the borough and from other parts of New York City. Midwood offers a general program of studies in English, history, science, math, and foreign languages for ninth- and tenth-grade students. For highly motivated juniors and seniors, Midwood offers the opportunity to study in one of three tracks—medical science, the humanities, or fine and performing arts—in specialized courses taught by Brooklyn College as well as Midwood faculty members. Qualified seniors may use advanced placement courses to complete a full first-year college program. Over 90 percent of recent graduating classes at Midwood have taken advantage of this option.

Brooklyn has also joined other institutions in an ambitious effort to develop an educational park as a model of interaction among educational institutions with different constituencies and different academic missions. Five public institutions which together serve students from kindergarten through college have formed an alliance to foster innovation and broad-scale coordination and cooperation across levels. The School of Education at Brooklyn College has taken an active role in development of the park, which it visualizes ultimately as a network of collaborative programs and activities with a yet-to-be-constructed resource center for pedagogy, curriculum, research results, instructional materials, and faculty development.

Several of the academic support programs described below in this chapter, most notably SEEK and Upward Bound, also have important early outreach and intervention components.

Community College Articulation

It is now fairly easy for students to transfer credit from Kingsborough to Brooklyn College. The two institutions have an effective working relationship and jointly try to ease the transition for students. Together they have developed a program, New Start, to encourage first-time students who experience academic difficulty at Brooklyn to transfer to Kingsborough, make a fresh start, and eventually transfer back to Brooklyn to work toward a baccalaureate degree. Kingsborough provides New Start students with special counseling and support services, and closely monitors academic progress. This model is now being tried by other CUNY senior and community colleges.

Advisement and Counseling

Student affairs at Brooklyn College works to provide a campus environment that allows a healthy respect for differences but is not patronizing toward any ethnic group. A centralized service provides personal and career counseling for all students, although some academic advising, counseling, and career advisement has been decentralized to specific departments or special programs. Personal counseling includes individual casework and group workshops developed to help students, including minorities, who are academically at risk. Career services help students to assess their interests and skills, obtain realistic information about careers, and have occupational experiences through internships and other work opportunities. An active alumni mentoring program helps students move into desired careers.

Student Organizations

Brooklyn College has over 150 academic, athletic, social, and special interest clubs which serve as the primary strategy for bringing students together outside classes. Many of the clubs bring students from different racial or ethnic groups together around common interests such as accounting, math, theater, and chess. Others emphasize ethnicity or culture to provide a comfortable base of support and sense of identity. Among the latter are the Haitian American Students Association, the Dominican Students movement, the Russian American Club, and the Caribbean Students Union. The college supports both types of clubs, but actively encourages those that bring students together across racial and ethnic lines.

The multicultural social environment at Brooklyn College is perhaps best symbolized by the annual County Fair, a day-long community event celebrating ethnic diversity with parades, music, dancing, games, and food booths. It is the second largest ethnic festival in Brooklyn and each year attracts thousands of people to the campus. The fair has been planned and run primarily by student clubs and organizations since 1937. More than seventy-five participating groups were listed on the 1987 program.

Each of the major academic divisions of the college has a student government, and there are elected campus assemblies. For many years student political parties formed along racial and ethnic lines. The two most powerful groups represented Jewish students and students of Caribbean descent. After elections, the party in power distributed student activity fees according to the special interests they represented. Several years ago the college president intervened in support of a system of proportional representation and refused to distribute student fees according to the recommendations of the student assembly. Following several years of controversy and a court suit, the president's view prevailed. The two parties continue, but both are characterized by greater diversity, as is student government overall.

ACADEMIC ENVIRONMENT

The mix of students, a genuinely collegiate atmosphere, and a commitment to undergraduate liberal arts education combine to give Brooklyn

College a distinctive character and ethos. Interviews with recent graduates suggest that students feel a strong identity with and affection for Brooklyn College. The academic environment is exceedingly rich for a commuter institution. There are opportunities to major in about 100 areas, a variety of preprofessional and collaborative professional programs with other institutions, opportunities for involvement in research projects for undergraduates, a number of special internship opportunities, and over fifty masters' and doctoral programs.

Faculty Characteristics

Faculty speak of their commitment to high academic standards and to maintaining the proud reputation of the college. The wide gap between faculty expectations for academic achievement and the actual academic skills and abilities of entering students is a frequent topic of discussion. Faculty members report that they work hard to help students overcome preparation problems but they do not lower standards. They believe that by maintaining the rigor of the academic program and the value of the degree they are providing the best service possible for all students and graduates.

Faculty are involved in the academic support programs of the college. A mentoring program, begun in 1986 when the dean of the college of arts and sciences personally recruited more than ninety faculty members to serve as mentors for 450 students who were considered to be at academic risk, now involves virtually the entire faculty. As of fall 1987, all entering freshmen were assigned to a faculty mentor. Faculty members contact the students, meet with them occasionally, get to know them, "not so much to hover as to care." The program is tied to an early warning system that provides faculty members with printouts of the students' progress. While some students do not use their mentors effectively and some faculty members are far from ideal mentors, the program is important because it shows at least some students that someone cares. Table 11.4 summarizes information about the full- and part-time faculty for fall 1986.

The progress the college has made in recruiting a more diverse faculty is evident from the growing percentages of African-Americans and Hispanics in the lower ranks of full-time faculty. The relationship between the composition of part-time and full-time faculty is much less imbalanced than in many other urban institutions. While the slightly more than 10 percent of full-time faculty who are African-American and Hispanic falls significantly short of the 35 percent in the student body, the representation is nonetheless impressive for the type of selective public institution Brooklyn represents. The figures are more impressive from the perspective of the significant faculty losses (administered under the terms of a collective bargaining agreement) caused by the more than 50 percent reduction in enrollments following the New York City fiscal

TABLE 11.4. Brooklyn College Faculty by Rank, Ethnicity, and Employment Status, 1986

	Anglo (%)	African-American (%)	Hispanic (%)	Asian-American (%)	Total
Full-time:					
Professor	93.1	3.2	1.4	2.3	348
Associate	87.3	6.1	3.7	2.8	213
Assistant	82.2	12.1	3.7	1.9	107
Instructor	92.0	–	8.3	–	12
Lecturer	61.7	23.3	11.7	3.3	60
Subtotal	87.2	6.9	3.4	2.4	741
Part-time:					
Adjunct professor	86.7	6.7	–	6.7	15
Adjunct associate	95.5	4.5	–	–	22
Adjunct assistant	85.2	11.1	–	3.7	54
Adjunct lecturer	82.0	9.0	3.0	6.0	167
Subtotal	84.1	8.9	1.9	5.0	258

Source: Brooklyn College, Affirmative Action Summary Data by Ethnicity, 1986.
Note: This table combines categories from the summary table provided by Brooklyn College.

crisis and the retreat from open admissions, and in light of the historical circumstance that the faculty is over 90 percent tenured.

African-American faculty, however, are not well distributed across academic fields. In 1986, 1 out of every 3 served in the educational services division as staff for the state-funded SEEK program. Of the remaining 33, 13 were in African studies and education. None of the remaining 28 academic units had more than 2, with the exception of English, in which 5 of 74 were African-American. The pattern for the small number of Hispanics was similar. A colloquium funded by the Ford Foundation encourages minority students at Brooklyn to become college teachers.

Academic Programs

Curricular reform has been high on the institutional agenda during the past several years. The desire to improve retention and degree achievement for all students has been an important contributor to this emphasis. The undergraduate curriculum is based on ten core courses required of all students. Core courses focus on cultivating the intellect and imagination, and developing general mental skills. Brooklyn College faculty believe that development of general skills constitutes better preparation for a career than does concentration on vocational skills for any one career. Core courses, including Western culture, art, music, literature, science, and mathematics, are organized into two tiers and may be distributed over the first three years of study. Students must pass the first tier before moving on to the second. One of the core courses focuses on African, Asian, and Latin American cultures. All the core courses also require writing practice and are designed to be coordinated with specific English courses. Development and implementation of the core courses have led to a variety of other curricular adjustments in specific courses and majors and to a renewed attention to course content, instructional practices, and faculty development.

Core requirements were opposed from the outset by some minority students and some faculty members. Many perceive the core as a major stumbling block, a "wall" for large numbers of minority students. Others argue that distribution requirements before the core were just as difficult and that the problems some students (not all of whom are minority) experience with the core simply reflect the very large gap between their academic preparation and the expectations of the faculty.

Once students pass the hurdle of the core, they usually go on to complete their degrees.

Academic Support Programs and Services

Brooklyn College offers a wide range of academic support programs and services. Although not targeted specifically to racial or ethnic groups, all programs serve large numbers of minority students.

The Department of Educational Services (DES), which houses a variety of remedial and counseling services for underprepared students, has come to be viewed as the special department for minority students. DES is a regular academic department with its own faculty and counselors, courses, and elected department chair. DES is the second largest department at Brooklyn College, with forty-eight faculty members. As previously noted, it has a disproportionate number of all minority faculty members employed by the college (eighteen African-Americans and six Hispanics).

The size of the DES faculty expanded rapidly during the early 1970s and contracted just as rapidly at the end of the decade, a clear "last-hired, first-fired" phenomenon. Release of many "last-hired" minority faculty, together with the widespread perception that the remedial work of the department was less worthy than the offerings of other departments, created negative attitudes and considerable tension during the late 1970s. While some of this legacy of ill will remains today, the work of the department is generally considered important to the college. Many of the DES faculty have received tenure and promotion.

The SEEK program, housed in DES, has been in existence for twenty years as a statewide program. Currently about 1,000 SEEK students, 65 percent of whom are African-American and 85 percent non-Jewish minority, attend Brooklyn College. SEEK students get special financial support, usually a combination of Pell and New York State Tuition Assistance Program grants, to fully cover tuition. They also get special stipends to cover the cost of books, transportation, and lunch. SEEK students receive a variety of academic services including tutoring, counseling, and special course work provided by DES. After acceptance by SEEK and admission to Brooklyn College, students take the CUNY assessment tests for diagnostic purposes. Those who fail three of the tests (usually about 45 to 50 percent of students) enter the developmental education program. If they have language problems as well (and about 20 percent do), they also enter the English as a Second Language (ESL) program. SEEK students who fail fewer than three tests are "mainstreamed" into the regular curriculum. They also receive counseling and some orientation courses through DES.

The heart of the program is the one-on-one relationship between students and counselors. Counselors follow their assigned SEEK students throughout their careers at Brooklyn and actually distribute the special stipend checks. They make sure students attend class. All SEEK students participate in a counseling workshop at least during their first semester; for students in the developmental education program, the counseling workshop lasts a full year. A new CUNY-funded program for SEEK prefreshmen brings them to the campus during the summer before their freshman year for special orientation and tutoring sessions. SEEK has occasionally been viewed as tangential to Brooklyn College by college faculty and staff because of its separate funding and close monitoring by CUNY central staff. The academic preparation problems that SEEK students bring to the college when coupled with the faculty's high expectations and standards is almost a formula for failure. SEEK students have experienced considerable difficulty with degree achievement, but in recent years more have made it through to graduation.

The developmental education program, designed primarily for SEEK students, provides a structured two-semester sequence of courses to help students solve problems associated with inadequate academic preparation and pass the CUNY assessment tests so that they may continue their studies at Brooklyn College. Students are grouped together for the first-semester courses: reading; writing; oral communication; and a "gateway" course in social sciences, natural sciences, or humanities. The gateway course provides the substantive material for work in the other courses. During the second semester, students move with the same group to more advanced remedial courses oriented around a different gateway course. At the end of the year, students retake the CUNY assessment tests to determine whether they are eligible to register for core courses.

The college has not been able to reallocate faculty resources rapidly enough to recent years to keep pace with the rapid growth of the need for English as a Second Language courses. Currently from 750 to 1,000 students, including those with remedial needs in English, take ESL courses, as part of a larger set of students with academic preparation problems and those from other countries with excellent academic preparation and a temporary problem with the English language. Special courses are offered for students who fail the reading portion on the assessment test. In addition to the reading courses offered for SEEK and ESL students, there is a noncredit workshop available to all students. The material for courses and exams is taken from the core as a strategy to aid subsequent progress.

Special Services, a unit within DES, is the home for all federally funded Trio programs. While the programs serve all students who are academically disadvantaged, from 80 to 90 percent of participants are non-Jewish minority. A core of tutors, mostly undergraduates, help students with writing, reading, math, and science. Upward Bound, another Trio component, helps fifty students from six high schools in disadvantaged areas prepare for college.

In addition to the programs available through DES, the college of liberal arts and sciences has started several programs to help students who are experiencing difficulty with the core curriculum. Peer tutoring, an academic preparatory program which provides counseling as well as individual and group remedial work, and a writing center with peer tutors from a variety of majors are available. The mathematics department has developed a four-level sequence of overlapping math remedial courses for students who fail the math assessment test. Two levels of remedial algebra and geometry can be combined in various ways depending upon the deficiency and the pace at which a student is able to progress. Between 1,200 and 1,400 students are served in thirty to forty remedial sections each semester. Students taking courses in the remedial math sequence are required to match their in-class hours with participation in a walk-in math workshop staffed by student tutors, many of whom are minority. Students in the mathematics core course (where the failure rate is 30 percent) also use the math workshop.

Minority Access to Research Careers (MARC) is designed to attract the very best students into research-oriented programs in the biomedical sciences. MARC is one of fifty-seven similar centers funded by the U.S. Department of Health. It offers a competitive honors program for minority students who have demonstrated a high level of scholastic ability and an interest in chemical, biological, or biomedical research. Students receive fellowship support, tuition, and travel monies, and participate in activities that help them to become familiar with scientific technology and research methodology. The program is very expensive and affects a relatively small number of students. There are five graduates, twelve current students, and seven faculty members, each of whom receives 30 percent released time for participation.

SUMMARY

Brooklyn, a first-rate liberal arts college, has maintained high standards while increasing the proportions of minority students among its undergraduates and among those who earn a baccalaureate degree. While some caution must be exercised in assessing the level of success because of the absence of comparable data, Brooklyn College would appear to be among the most successful of the case-study institutions in attaining both diversity and achievement.

Location is certainly a factor. Demographic trends in the borough of Brooklyn provide a large multicultural population from which the majority of Brooklyn students are drawn. State influences also play a major role. State officials have consistently linked minority access to postsecondary education and subsequent achievement with a healthy social and economic environment. Significant equal opportunity strategies have been developed, funded, and monitored for all sectors. Thus it has been clear from the outset that all institutions within the state of New York, including the independents, shared responsibility for achieving both quality and diversity. State equal opportunity strategies have been buttressed by a generous, need-based financial aid program that has specifically taken into consideration extra time needed by students who must undergo remediation before beginning a regular college program.

CUNY policies also contribute to student diversity in two ways: first, by specifying grade-point averages or class ranking, without regard to the type of high school attended, as the primary admissions criteria, and second, by providing centralized management of the admissions process through which students are distributed among the CUNY institutions. CUNY monitoring of the state-funded SEEK program for disadvantaged students has brought thousands of minority students to Brooklyn College. CUNY has also managed an extensive system of diagnostic testing and remedial programming to help overcome the serious academic preparation problems experienced by many New York high school graduates.

The importance of state and system influences and an advantageous location should not overshadow the important actions Brooklyn College has taken to improve its learning environment for all students. A core curriculum identifies with clarity Brooklyn's expectations for those it will eventually certify as college graduates. Teaching and mentoring undergraduates is an important and valued faculty activity. Math and English faculty members have accurate information about the preparation of entering students and provide structured alternative experiences that provide flexibility in how students learn, while postlearning assessment provides reasonable assurance of limited variation in what they learn. Student diversity is particularly enhanced through special programs that include the entire range of early outreach, transition, and academic support services essential to providing a high-risk population with a fair opportunity to meet demanding standards for academic success.

The environment at Brooklyn, like that of other case-study institutions, contains negative as well as positive influences. New York City remains a melting pot with a melange of races and ethnicities competing for influence and identity. The contentious and competitive social and economic environment that characterizes the city may be found in student and faculty internal politics as well. At its best, the richness of the multicultural environment flowers in the annual County Fair. At its worst, it shows up in divided sentiment about the motives that produced a core curriculum or the value of a special program that serves a disproportionate number of minority students.

The model proposed in chapter 1 suggests that institutions can combine a commitment to high student achievement with an equally strong emphasis on student diversity. The Brooklyn College case provides considerable support for the model as well as insight into the necessary conditions and probable stresses. Location and external influences are important, as are internal actions and attitudes. Brooklyn College's commitment to achievement for all students has also contributed to the success of African-Americans and Hispanics.

12

CALIFORNIA STATE UNIVERSITY, DOMINGUEZ HILLS

ROBERT T. STOUT
with the assistance of MARGARET BLUE

California State University, Dominguez Hills (CSUDH), located in the city of Carson, is one of the smaller of the nineteen campuses of the California State University. Established in 1960, CSUDH enrolls about 7,000 students, with a full-time equivalency of 5,000. There are five schools: Humanities and Fine Arts; Education; Management; Science, Mathematics, and Technology; and Social and Behavioral Science. There is also the Center for Quality education.

CSUDH is an urban university, serving mature students who commute from throughout the southwestern part of the greater Los Angeles basin. As the campus in the California State University (CSU) most dependent for enrollment on community college transfers, CSUDH serves primarily junior- and senior-level undergraduates and master's degree candidates. It has a student body as diverse as any of the universities in the study.

The 346-acre campus does not have the physical appearance of a typical urban university. It includes athletic fields, the site of the 1986 Olympic Games bicycling competition, a university theatre, a field house and gymnasium, a natural history preserve, and a small number of recently built and attractive apartments which accommodate about 200 students and their families. The tallest building has five stories; most range from one to three. The campus is arranged around large grassy malls, dotted by trees and flower beds. Walkways are broad and uncrowded. Parking lots are on the periphery of the campus. CSUDH is an attractive naturalistic island surrounded by the urban congestion of Los Angeles.

Robert Stout is professor of educational leadership and policy studies at Arizona State University. Margaret Blue is executive assistant to the president at California State University, Dominguez Hills.

The story of how it came to occupy its current site is worth telling. The authorizing legislation "established a state college, to be located in Los Angeles County in the vicinity of the Los Angeles International Airport, to be known as the South Bay State College." Between 1960 and 1962 trustees of the then California State Colleges searched for a suitable site for South Bay State. The leading contender was the city of Rolling Hills Estates, whose mayor proposed a site on the Palos Verdes Peninsula. Beginning in 1962 the trustees appointed staff to South Bay State and authorized curricular planning activity. The academic planning team devised a liberal arts curriculum which stressed interdisciplinary studies, small classes, a core lower-division sequence, and close student-faculty relations.

In July 1962 the trustees changed the name of South Bay State to California State College at Palos Verdes and reaffirmed their support for the site in Rolling Hills. The college opened in 1965 in leased quarters, in the absence of a decision about a permanent site. The indecision was prompted by disagreements among the city of Rolling Hills Estates, other South Bay cities, the California Department of Finance, and legislative leaders. In July 1965 the California State College trustees were told that the Rolling Hills site had been abandoned in favor of eight other potential sites. They decided to make a final decision at their August 1965 session. Between July 1965 and October 1965 the Watts riots occurred, and the governor urged the trustees to choose a site more accessible to the minority populations of southwestern Los Angeles. On October 14, 1965, the trustees chose the current location, Dominguez Hills, situated in the heart of a heavily minority population basin. On March 3, 1966, the trustees changed the name of California State College at Palos Verdes to California State College, Dominguez Hills. On September 12, 1977, CSCDH became California State University, Dominguez Hills.

STATE INFLUENCES

The California State University is composed of nineteen campuses located in major population areas throughout the state. In 1985 CSU received 45,000 students as transfers from community colleges, while 23,000 entered as first-time freshmen. In 1983 about 30 percent of the undergraduates were minority students, with Hispanics and Asian-Americans (at about 10 percent each) together making up the largest part. In 1984 the CSU provided about $15 million in support (financial aid, staff, and administration) for the Educational Opportunity Program (EOP), the umbrella program for activities associated with increasing minority enrollment and graduation.

In January 1986 the Educational Equity Advisory Council, composed of key CSU leadership, issued its report calling for the system to define its institutional as well as its programmatic responsibility for the admission, retention, and graduation of ethnic minority students. The report emphasizes participation, retention, and educational excellence. The report encourages each campus to develop its own plan for meeting these goals and recommends that a share of the educational equity funds be allocated on the basis of competitive proposals.

COMMUNITY SETTING

CSUDH is surrounded by a rich variety of residential housing, industry, and commerce. There is no city named Dominguez, the citizens having voted in 1967 to incorporate as the city of Carson rather than as the city of Dominguez. The service area includes parts of Los Angeles; the beach communities of the Palos Verdes Peninsula; the commercial port community of San Pedro (one of the largest in the world); and the inland communities of Torrance, Compton, and parts of Long Beach. These communities have little in common and few vehicles for cooperation. CSUDH has existed in an environment lacking political and social infrastructures dedicated to its support. In short, it has "been there" but it has not monopolized the attention of the community as have other campuses of the California State University system, partly because CSUDH does not serve a well-delineated geographic area.

The university draws students from wide areas. In 1985 the enrolled students at CSUDH had residence addresses in 418 mail zip codes. The ten highest zip codes of residence only contributed about 2,000 students out of the total enrollment of 7,000. Only four zip codes have 200 or more students in residence. Thus, to describe the "community" of CSUDH is to describe a very major, and changing, portion of one of the largest cities in the world.

For Los Angeles and its immediate suburbs, distance is measured in minutes or hours of driving time rather than in miles. The relatively small number of lower-division students served by the campus arrive from a large number of high schools. The largest portion of entering students, however, are transfers from public community colleges or public four-year institutions. Transfer students come from 20 community colleges and 10 four-year institutions within about a sixty-minute driving radius, but the effective service area is smaller and includes six high schools and ten community colleges. While five different routes of the city bus system have stops at the campus entrance, most students commute by automobile.

Public Schools

Inner-city high schools contribute the largest number of first-time freshmen. The student bodies are diverse, enrollments are large, and life is filled with danger as well as opportunity. In most cases, preparation for college cannot be deemed a dominant mission of these high schools. As one CSUDH graduate said, "The course work was general education in the sense that I didn't take anything that was a college preparatory course per se." In response to a question about how his high school could have given him better preparation, he suggested the need to "stress the importance of academics more than the importance of sports in an inner-city minority high school."

The high schools make an effort to help prepare students for college. We interviewed staff members who were genuinely interested in and concerned about the future of minority youth. Washington Preparatory High School, for example, has received extensive national publicity for its efforts. In addition, we talked with students who wanted to go to college and who thought they were being prepared to do so. The struggle is tough, however. Huge percentages of students in the feeder high schools are poor, and most are minority. While they may be the best students in the school, they are not as well prepared as their competitors from suburban schools. The average combined SAT score among those who took the examination in one of the feeder high schools for CSUDH was in the 700-point range. Such students do not begin college with many academic advantages.

Community Colleges

Most students enter CSUDH from community colleges and other four-year institutions. California community colleges are multipurpose institutions, enrolling students in a wide range of courses and educating widely diverse student bodies. They accommodate part-time adult students, poor students, underprepared students, and students who have uncertain plans. Programs and services are based on the realization that students need special attention. One counselor described the typical student who transferred to a four-year college as a black, female, single parent who aspired to a career in education or business. While never impressively high, the numbers of minority students who transfer from California community colleges to the nineteen-campus California State University have diminished since 1981. Nonetheless, transfer remains a major mission of community colleges in the Los Angeles area.

STUDENT CHARACTERISTICS

In CSUDH's service area there are heavy concentrations of ethnic minorities, both recent immigrants and long-time residents. The second president of CSUDH declared it a "people's university," and others have termed it a crossroads of cultures. The multicultural character of CSUDH is revealed by table 12.1.

TABLE 12.1. Composition of CSUDH Student Body, 1987

RACE or ETHNICITY	PROPORTION
Anglo	38
African-American	32
Hispanic	11
Asian-American and Pacific Islander	12
American Indian	1

Source: Chancellor's Office, California State University, 1987.

While Anglos represent the largest group numerically, their numbers are nearly matched by the enrollment of African-Americans. Hispanics, Asian-Americans, and Pacific Islanders are also well represented. These percentages have been reasonably stable for the past five years, although overall enrollment has declined slightly from a head count of 8,270 in 1983 to 7,869 in 1987.

The student body is older than in many colleges. Only about 3 percent are under age 19, while 15 percent of males and 25 percent of females are age 30 or older. About 65 percent of the undergraduate students are considered full-time, one of the lowest percentages among the CSU campuses. Our survey showed CSUDH to have the lowest proportion (4 percent) of graduates at a traditional age and the highest proportion (25 percent) over 35 among all the case-study institutions. In addition, CSUDH had the lowest proportion of graduates completing a degree within four years (17 percent), and the highest proportions taking more than six years (36 percent) and more than eleven years (13 percent). The majority of graduates (86 percent) had transferred to CSUDH from another institution.

About a third of the graduates in the survey reported they were first-generation college-goers, a moderate proportion for the case-study universities. On the other hand, graduates in the first generation at CSUDH were more likely than most to have parents with less than a high school degree. Sixty-three percent had mothers who had not completed their secondary schooling, while 74 percent had fathers with this level of education. Only Brooklyn College and the University of Texas at El Paso had higher proportions of first-generation graduates in these categories. One graduate commented on CSUDH's mission to serve students from families with little education:

> These people (minority youth in inner-city high schools) are not going to go on in education. Dominguez gets them because it serves an older student ... people who have gone out and got a job and then they come back to Dominguez to finally get a degree. It is very painful for them because they left or graduated from high school with substandard skills, and they have to spend some time bringing their skills back up and it's difficult.

CSUDH students must overcome a number of obstacles, including: underpreparation, multiple responsibilities for family, low incomes, and the need to commute. Work is a major influence on the academic experience. One graduate described a typical day:

> During the time of the year I worked the night shifts on my law enforcement job, I would get off from work at six or seven in the morning, go home and sleep for about three or four hours to ten or eleven o'clock and attend day classes—one or two classes a day—until about three or three-thirty; return home and have dinner with my wife, talk to her for a couple of hours when she arrived home from work; go to sleep for about two or three hours prior to going back to work at ten or eleven o'clock at night.

Despite the obstacles and pain, many minority students see that gaining a degree at CSUDH is something they can manage. Table 12.2 provides information on retention and graduation rates.

The data in table 12.2 are somewhat deceptive because they do not include the number who have not yet graduated but are continuing in college. Most students are part-time. As a consequence, they take fewer courses per semester and "stop out" for periods of time in order to take jobs, raise families, or tend to other matters. Many alternate going to school with employment which allows them to save sufficient money to reenroll. The differences in graduation rates revealed in the data are more gender- than ethnicity-related. Like other multicultural institutions in the study, CSUDH shows fairly minimal race- or ethnicity-related differences in outcomes.

TABLE 12.2. Degree Achievement for Community College Transfers to CSUDH

	First Undergraduate Enrollment in 1980 N	Degree Achieved by 1985	
		N	%
African-American:			
Females	206	98	48
Males	104	36	35
Mexican-American:			
Females	24	12	50
Males	16	5	31
Asian-American:			
Females	16	10	63
Males	13	6	46
Anglo:			
Females	132	70	53
Males	111	50	45

Source: Chancellor's Office, California State University, *Those Who Stay,* 1987.

CSUDH competes for students with twenty or so community colleges, three or four other campuses of its own system, the University of California at Los Angeles (UCLA), and four or five independent institutions, including the University of Southern California. The students in the high schools within its designated service area are predominantly minority, predominantly poor, and not particularly well prepared for college work. The transfer students are perhaps better-prepared, certainly older, and very career-oriented.

THE UNIVERSITY ENVIRONMENT

The move from affluent Palos Verdes to less affluent Carson; the original intent to have a small, interdisciplinary liberal arts college; the press for more professional and preprofessional programs; and the cultural diversity of the surrounding area—all have influenced the development of CSUDH. Currently the part of its mission devoted to serving minority students is being reexamined in order to strengthen it in the face of increasing competition for these students from the other campuses of the CSU system, from UCLA, and from independent universities such as the University of Southern California.

Both the newly appointed president and his predecessor came out of multicultural institutions and have pledged that CSUDH will continue to expand its services to ethnic minorities. This perspective is shared by other top-level administrators as well. Table 12.3 provides information about the ethnic distribution of key administrators. One college dean is African-American and one is Hispanic. Otherwise, the top academic administrators are Anglo.

Beyond continuing the institution's historic emphasis on access and achievement for minority students, CSUDH administrators have identified institutional priorities as increasing quality, capitalizing on the cultural richness of the institution, extending service to the surrounding community, retaining the traditional image of friendliness and commitment to teaching, and strengthening overtures to the Pacific rim economic community. Administrative leaders must also reconcile the current CSU emphasis on standardized modes of operation and more explicit measures of accountability with earlier CSUDH values of faculty autonomy, program entrepreneurship, face-to-face interactions, and a casual orientation toward bureaucratic necessities.

TABLE 12.3. Composition of CSUDH Administrators, 1985

	Anglo	African-American	Hispanic	Asian-American	Native American
Male	31	3	3	0	0
Female	11	5	0	1	0

Source: Head count, local interviews.

Enrollment Management

CSU does not permit constituent universities to recruit in the normal sense of the term. In order to reduce unnecessary competition among campuses, each university has an assigned service area. Many high schools sponsor a "college night" to which any of the campuses may send representatives. However, focused recruiting outside the service area is discouraged. Within this context, CSUDH has an active outreach program. The Office of School and College Relations sends representatives to the high schools and community colleges in the service area. The University Information and Service Center, open eighty hours a week, is located in a very visible place near the main entrance to the campus. Here people can first experience the advertised friendliness and helpfulness of CSUDH, which distinguish it from the larger, less personal environments of sister campuses.

California has specific criteria for admission to any of the California State University campuses. These criteria include required grade-point averages, scores on national examinations, and completion of required high school courses for entering freshmen. Transfers from community colleges must present minimum grade-point averages (2.0) and take prescribed courses to correct any deficiencies. Admission by exception is permitted for students who show promise but who do not present sufficiently good credentials for regular admission. For fall 1985, 115 first-time freshmen were admitted by exception, while 187 were regularly admitted. Of the 115 exceptions, 73 were classified as disadvantaged. In the same year, 966 students were regularly admitted as transfers and 32 were admitted by exception.

In fall 1986 about 300 students entered directly from 20 high schools within the designated service area. Of these, Carson, Banning, Gardena, Narbonne, Lynwood, and Washington sent the greatest numbers of students. Each of these schools has student enrollments which are predominantly or exclusively minority. Students entering as freshmen in 1985 brought median high school grade-point averages of 2.97 on a 4-point scale, or a low B average.

Most new students come from community colleges. Of the six or so in the immediate service area (El Camino, Los Angeles Harbor, Long Beach, Los Angeles Southwest, Compton, Los Angeles City), all have substantial minority enrollments and several are predominantly or exclusively minority. Students who transferred to CSUDH from community colleges brought a median grade-point average of 2.59 on the same 4-point scale.

Predominantly Anglo high schools in the CSUDH service area are becoming smaller, while predominantly minority high schools are growing in size. The percentage of college-bound students from minority high schools is not high. In addition, the transfer rate from community colleges to the CSU is less than 10 percent. Thus, the pool of eligible students, both Anglo and minority, is shrinking. CSUDH has developed three major strategies for dealing with this dilemma. The first emphasizes personal service. The University Information and Service Center, early delivery of admissions materials, personal calls on principals, and the use of faculty in recruiting efforts are examples of this strategy.

A second thrust provides workshops for high school students on such topics as time management, test taking, selecting a college, and choosing a major. These workshops were designed to strengthen recruiting efforts in predominantly Anglo high schools, which are less likely to have extensive programs focused on student development than are those with heavily minority populations.

A third strategy emphasizes intersegmental cooperation among community colleges, the CSU, and the University of California, each of which has a different mission and different admissions standards. In cooperation with Compton Community College, UCLA, and the University of California at Irvine, CSUDH is working to help high schools in the largely African-American city of Compton give better preparation to students who show some potential for college-level work.

The Student Affirmative Action (SAA) office is part of a statewide effort to increase the numbers of regularly admissible, underrepresented minorities. Underrepresented groups within the CSUDH service area include Filipinos, Samoans, Chicanos, other Hispanics, and African-American males. With the exception of the last, the attendance of these groups has risen dramatically during the past decade. Information provided by testing services indicates that students attracted to the university by SAA outreach services may be better-prepared for college work than their non-SAA counterparts. The SAA office emphasizes personalization or "bonding" at each step of the admissions process from identification to matriculation. The staff take pride in their knowledge of each student and closely follow individual progress.

The Equal Opportunity Program recruits students who have financial need and show potential but are not regularly admissible. Program staff recognize that EOP students are not fully prepared to negotiate an impersonal bureaucracy nor to follow a series of required steps in a timely fashion. The success of EOP rests on flexibility and cooperation with other units of the university. EOP provides staff support to the Office of Financial Aid. In return the requests of EOP students are processed quickly. An EOP counselor, cross-trained to evaluate high school transcripts, helps the Office of Admissions and Records at peak times, and EOP applications are processed in a timely manner. When a potential EOP student is identified, program staff use their knowledge and contacts to ensure smooth entry into the university.

The Office of Admissions helps "to teach students to compete with the bureaucracy—how to work it in their favor." Twenty-five percent of all applications are received after the published closing date. Each late applicant is personally interviewed by a member of the admissions staff.

Students not eligible for admission are counseled through the Redirect Program to enroll at a nearby community college. Each is given specific advice about necessary courses and expected performance. Those who take the advice are assured that CSUDH will welcome them if they perform to expectations. In fall 1987, 1,600 students who applied late received assistance from professional staff.

The admissions contract is designed to accommodate applicants who file an application after the published deadline but who appear to meet other requirements. Students can present various forms of unofficial evidence of admissibility. If an admissions officer believes a candidate will meet requirements, the student is allowed to register. Registration is canceled if required documents are not provided by a specified date or if the student does not qualify. In fall 1986, of the 4,000 total applicants, 1,200 were issued contracts. In fall 1987, 1,250 contracts were issued.

CSUDH is also changing recruitment strategies in recognition of the high numbers of potential students who work. Efforts are under way to gain employer support for on-site recruiting through personnel and training offices. Hospitals have also been targeted as employers of persons who could be attracted to the health sciences and newly developed nursing programs. CSUDH perceives its multicultural student body as a source of tremendous vitality and is worried about the increasing competition for the students CSUDH has always served.

Early Intervention

In 1982 the SAA staff recognized that many students in targeted schools were already too far behind or insufficiently motivated to attend college by the time they entered high school. Program Discovery is aimed at students who are eighth graders or younger. Current CSUDH students volunteer to give programs and skits for junior high school students, focused on academic excellence, enrichment, decision making, and the link between work and education. SAA also instituted the "Saturday College" where students as young as 8 receive instruction in science- and technology-related subjects from regular college faculty, while parents are offered workshops in study skills, parenting, child rearing, and securing funds for college costs. About 1,200 students have participated each year since the program began.

The School of Science, Mathematics, and Technology offers a program designed for students in grades 7, 8, and 9. During two 2-week summer sessions, "courses" are offered, for a fee and on a first-come, first-served basis, in such areas as backyard science, marine biology, computer use, photography, and microbes. The dean of the school believes that potential scientists must be identified and coached when they are young. Faculty are now working with elementary school teachers to help them sharpen their content area skills, particularly in mathematics.

During 1986–1987 the School of Humanities and Fine Arts participated in or sponsored almost thirty different events linked to outreach.
These ranged from "preview performances" for high school students
to workshops for teachers, lecture series for the community, and ex-
hibitions and performances in the schools of the area. In fall 1987 an
attractive brochure, called "Consider Us a Resource," was mailed to all
public elementary schools, secondary schools, and community colleges
in the service area. The brochure offers the services of the School of
Arts and Humanities, as well as a speaker's bureau and performances
by university groups.

The Center for Quality Education is designed to provide opportunities for faculty throughout the university to give direct assistance to
local schools and colleges. It is also the academic unit responsible for
teacher preparation. The center has received $270,000 from the Carnegie
Corporation to identify, recruit, and prepare talented minority persons
who wish to become teachers.

Community College Articulation

CSUDH pays careful attention to community colleges because most new
students are transfers. The president has regular meetings with community college presidents. Academic administrators also meet with their
community college counterparts, as do administrators in admissions
and other student services. Jointly staffed transfer centers have been
established to provide careful advice about course planning, financial
aid, and transfer requirements. Community college and CSUDH faculty
meet to develop agreements about appropriate content in courses that
are prerequisite for upper-division work at CSUDH.

Advisement and Counseling

A recently completed educational equity plan aims to provide each
newly admitted student with a faculty mentor, to provide intense and
intrusive support to first-semester students, and to remove bureaucratic
barriers to student progress. Aside from efforts to consolidate and inten-
sify already successful efforts among university support staff (primarily
EOP and SAA), the largest change is the effort to involve substantial
numbers of faculty. Besides acting as mentors, faculty will take very
active roles in advising, admitting, recruiting, and referring students.
The mentoring program has had two years of pilot activity in which volunteer faculty have received training in cross-cultural awareness, active
listening, and self-discovery. Faculty who participated have been evaluated as significantly more effective than untrained faculty in helping
students cope with academic and personal stresses.

The EOP staff also have been active in making contacts with faculty. The objective is to discover what implicit criteria for success exist

in such fields as English, mathematics, psychology, and public administration, and to develop advisement and tutoring programs to prepare students to meet them. EOP staff retain the right to act as advisers to EOP students until the students have completed 80 credits. An EOP student must see an adviser three times each semester and obtain approval to register. EOP staff are able to place a "hold" on registration until students fulfill their obligation to receive advisement.

Student Financial Aid

Financial aid officers, available most evenings until 6:30 p.m., help students fill out application forms, publish articles in the monthly student newspaper, and engage in outreach. In 1985–1986 the unduplicated number of students who received some form of financial aid was 1,729 out of the student body of about 7,000. The aid distribution policy encourages students to accept packages of direct grants combined with loans and work-study assignments. Financial aid officers believe that every eligible student who applies for aid by the deadline receives some assistance.

ACADEMIC ENVIRONMENT

CSUDH was planned primarily as an upper-division and master's institution. Its early mission might be summarized as the provision of a broad liberal arts education to a highly diverse population. Consequently, as some faculty remember it, "We had to learn to be teachers and the students taught us." Subtle shifts in program and mission have occurred during the past ten years. While one basic objective, educating minority students, remains, the educational emphasis on broad integrated majors has given way to more traditional concentrations reflecting student demands. As one faculty member put it, "The creation of the School of Management was the watershed." Within programs, students have shifted from majors traditionally associated with liberal arts and human services (philosophy, sociology, psychology, human services, political science, behavioral science) to more occupation-specific majors such as communications, business, and computer science. CSUDH administrators and faculty are searching for additional ways to respond to these shifts in student demand, in light of the CSU Master Plan which has assigned some of the more attractive possibilities (engineering, for example) to California State University, Long Beach, a campus with an adjacent service area.

The decline in enrollment since 1982 is attributed in part to a shift toward majors not offered by CSUDH, to a decline in the enrollment of African-American students (particularly males) not offset by an increase in Hispanic or Asian-American students, and by a "sizeable erosion" of daytime enrollment. On a short-term basis, additional enrollment decline may be the result of increased standards and the shift from a quarter to a semester system. The consequences of the change in academic calendar for a commuting, part-time student body have been fairly significant. To maintain anticipated graduation schedules, students often must take an additional class each semester over their quarter class load. The burden of additional time falls particularly heavily on students at CSUDH. Many near completion took overloads during the academic year prior to the shift so that they could graduate before implementation of the semester system. This "rush to graduate" produced a larger than average graduating class—and a decline in the normal projected enrollment the following fall semester.

Faculty

The early faculty were in large measure products of the social turmoil of the 1960's. Sometimes described as "peace corps types," they were committed to teaching and service and dedicated to serving students for whom they might "make a real difference." They were optimistic, open to experimentation and interdisciplinary programs, and eager to be academic pioneers. Teaching and program development were prized and rewarded. When asked to describe that period, current faculty leaders say such things as: "Program development was the entrepreneurial game." "We got great satisfaction from kids who made it." "The students really needed us—we saw it every time we went to class." "We were allowed great autonomy." "Talent development was our bag."

Expectations for faculty performance are in transition. While teaching and service were the primary criteria for faculty promotion in the past, research productivity has been emphasized recently under pressures from CSU. Although the reward structure at CSUDH has not changed drastically, the new emphasis on research is viewed with some concern by faculty leaders who helped to found the institution.

The faculty at CSUDH are more diverse than in many state universities, but lag far behind the diversity of the student body. In an institution in which African-Americans represent 32 percent of the undergraduate student body, 8 percent of the tenured faculty and 6 percent of the nontenured, tenure-track faculty are African-American. Hispanic and Asian faculty members, while somewhat underrepresented, are much more nearly proportional to student representation. Interestingly, the proportions of African-Americans and Hispanics among the nontenured, tenure-track faculty are lower than among the tenured faculty, reversing the trends found in most other institutions. The competition for minority faculty members is keen. Institutions like CSUDH are challenged to keep the ones they have already tenured and to add to that number in new hires. About 85 percent of full-time faculty have been granted tenure. This ratio is a little above the average for the other campuses in

TABLE 12.4. CSUDH Faculty Ethnicity According to Tenure

	NUMBER	PERCENT
Tenured:		
African-American	13	6
Hispanic	8	8
Asian	15	8
American Indian	0	0
Non-tenured, tenure track:		
African-American	2	6
Hispanic	1	3
Asian	1	3
American Indian	0	0
Part-time, non-tenure-track:		
African-American	18	11
Hispanic	8	5
Asian	13	8
American Indian	1	1

Source: Chancellor's Office, California State University, 1986.

the California State University. Faculty demographics are summarized in table 12.4.

Faculty members for the most part subscribe to the ethos that students, once admitted, have a right to their best efforts. While the small size of the institution is a contributing factor, in large measure it is individual commitment which drives the orientation. As one of the graduates put it:

> The major difference between [an institution of prior enrollment] and Dominguez Hills was the accessibility of the instructors. At [the other institution] more often than not I sat in a class with 200 students, and all of my questions were answered through teachers' aides. I never really felt my questions were being answered by the person to whom I was responsible. In Dominguez Hills, you know, the average size of the class was 30 students, and instructors were available before the class, after the class, and any time. Office hours were posted and they were adhered to.

Academic Programs

The enrollment decline that began in 1980 and the resultant possibilities of layoffs in some fields clearly influenced faculty thoughts about retention issues. The School of Social and Behavioral Sciences, one of the most vulnerable, decided to focus on general improvements in teaching, on advising, and on activities which bond students to the university. Workshops on teaching an underprepared and heterogeneous clientele gave faculty new insights. Grants for instructional innovations provided incentives to use the insights. Course descriptions were rewritten, and faculty and clerical staff were trained in advisement and in interpersonal relations. The Minority Access to Research Careers (MARC) program paid advanced students to be research assistants. Student retention has been adopted by the dean and faculty as an explicit commitment.

While not under the same enrollment pressures, the School of Science, Mathematics, and Technology has also set student retention as a goal. The school views the diversity of the student body as an advantage because students are not isolated from natural peer groups as sources of networking and support. Among its students, the school must work with those who come with very high grade-point averages from high school but are still unprepared to do college-level work. It is not uncommon for students with a combined verbal and quantitative total of 500 on the SAT to enter with B or better high school average. Faculty must work with such students carefully to convince them that their low initial grades at CSUDH can be overcome and must not be cause for discouragement. Eight faculty members have been given special training and act as advisers to minority students facing academic difficulty. The National Institute of Health funds the Minority Biomedical Research Program, through which twelve students each year are given academic year and summer stipends to assist faculty with research.

Academic Support Programs and Services

Historically, support services at CSUDH were offered under the auspices of special program staff, most notably SAA and EOP. The recently prepared educational equity plan identifies a series of impending changes in retention efforts. The new plan calls for the consolidation and expansion of services under the direction of a newly formed educational support services unit. The planning document notes: "Our EOP and SAA students have always had better retention and graduation rates than our general student body. . . . We have been doing an excellent job with EOP and SAA. It is now time to expand those successes to all students."

In 1977 the CSU established an examination which required students to pass the Junior English Proficiency Test (JEPT) before enrolling for the junior year. Because success records are kept by the institutions, many CSU campuses treated the requirement as one which had to be met prior to graduation. CSUDH, however, has taken a more stringent position. Students who do not pass the exam may enroll for "basic skills" courses and retake the exam as many times as they wish during one year, but they may not enroll for upper-division courses. In 1983 the CSU initiated the Elementary Level Mathematics (ELM) test, which must be passed before a student is eligible to take college algebra courses.

Several services focus on helping students pass the examinations. The Learning Assistance Center (LAC), an all-university unit staffed by two professionals and forty-five to fifty volunteer tutors, provides pretest tutoring. In 1985–1986 the LAC provided some form of service to 1,200 students. The Educational Opportunity Program has developed somewhat more elaborate services for its students, who are required to attend a six-week writing skills workshop prior to admission to the freshman year. Originally offered by the EOP staff (three of whom are graduates of CSUDH), the workshop now has paid staff from the English department and is offered to other entering freshmen as well. In addition, EOP students are required to participate in a three-hour on-campus assessment of academic skills prior to matriculation. The stated policy is: "We don't equivocate on the assessment, but we give them help."

In addition to pretest tutoring, the LAC also provides academic tutoring in any subject on demand. Staff and student tutors offer special programs in listening skills, note taking, and test taking. They "sell" their services through visits to department chairs, faculty groups, and individual classes. Because many of the tutors have previously been recipients of LAC services, their success helps to promote the program. The LAC, under subcontract to the mathematics department, manages the mathematics laboratory, evidence of growing faculty confidence in its services.

SUMMARY

California State University, Dominguez Hills is an integrated urban university. Both students and faculty understand that the institution was designed to offer opportunity to aspiring minority students. Classes tend to be small, faculty are committed to teaching students with highly diverse preparations and learning styles, advisement is plentiful and "intrusive," and CSUDH leaders and faculty members believe in the importance of the institutional mission.

The university community sees enormous strength in the legacy of cultural pluralism. Diversity is celebrated as enriching the life experiences of all participants. CSUDH has a successful history of attracting and helping students who are nontraditional in every sense of the word: ethnic minority, not well prepared, relatively poor, older, working, subject to multiple stresses, and first in the family to go to college.

Some of the success of CSUDH can certainly be attributed to demographic imperatives, given its location in the most culturally diverse section of a culturally diverse metropolitan area. But such an explanation would fall short of describing the extent to which the university has taken charge of its own destiny. However reluctantly in the beginning, CSUDH leaders have accepted the challenge of creating an institution for which there was no extant model.

They did not have to have a model. Of the nineteen campuses in the California State University, CSUDH has been the single campus to have made the most intense commitment to creating a new form of institution. CSUDH has achieved this commitment without benefit of being singled out for the role by any of the power actors in the state legislature, the California Postsecondary Education Commission, or even the CSU chancellor's office. While no institution functions apart from its context, the real story at CSUDH lies within the campus.

Faculty and administrative leadership wanted CSUDH to become the type of institution it has become. Campus leaders over time have understood its mission and have constructed campus policies, procedures, and structures to carry it out. As a result the institution has developed an ethos or culture in which opportunity is given, support is offered, accomplishment is celebrated, and the needs of students are paramount. Faculty and administrators believe that minority students can succeed, and they believe CSUDH has a right to be proud of the contributions it makes to their successes.

There is no single variable or constellation of variables to explain the success CSUDH has experienced in carrying out a mission that was not highly valued within CSU at the time it was first undertaken. The process of constructing an organizational culture that would accomplish the mission has been trial-and-error. No structures or policies existed for emulation. Each structure and each policy was crafted in context and with intent. When some failed, new ones were invented. Throughout, campus leaders paid consistent attention to the mission and its realization. Today CSUDH is an exemplar of the comprehensive and systematic strategies required to transform the culture of a university so that it accommodates both achievement and diversity.

13

UNIVERSITY OF TEXAS AT EL PASO

ALFREDO G. DE LOS SANTOS, JR.
with the assistance of HOWARD C. DAUDISTEL

The University of Texas at El Paso (UTEP), the second oldest campus of the University of Texas system, was created in 1913 as the Texas State School of Mines and Metallurgy. The curriculum was modified in 1927 by the addition of liberal arts courses and a bachelor of arts degree. In 1967, with more than 9,000 students, the institution acquired its current designation as part of the University of Texas system. UTEP includes several colleges: Business Administration, Education, Engineering, Liberal Arts, Nursing and Allied Health, and Science. There is also the Graduate School. Through these divisions, the university offers sixteen baccalaureate degrees, eleven master's degrees, and a doctorate in geological sciences.

Relative isolation from other major universities enhances the interdependence of the university and the region in which it is located. The nearest other campus of the University of Texas system is approximately 300 miles away. The university provides educational opportunities for a large proportion of the state's Hispanic citizens and for residents of northern Mexico as part of its mission. As the only major university on the state's 1,300-mile border with Mexico, UTEP has become increasingly attuned to opportunities for developing educational programs, research, and service activities related to its unique location and clientele.

THE STATE CONTEXT

The population of Texas is projected to be between 19.1 million and 23.1 million by the year 2000, a twenty-year growth rate of between 35 and 63 percent. In 1980 the population was 14.2 million with 21 percent of these of Spanish origin (most of Mexican descent). African-Americans comprised 11.8 percent, and all other groups, excluding Anglos, made

Alfredo de los Santos is vice-chancellor for educational development at Maricopa Community Colleges, Phoenix, Arizona. Howard Daudistel is chair of the department of sociology/anthropology at the University of Texas at El Paso.

up less than 2 percent. The Spanish-origin population tends to be highly concentrated in the younger age groups. While Hispanics make up 21 percent of the total state population, they accounted for about 30 percent of the three youngest age groups. In 1980 only about one-third of Hispanics 25 years of age or older had completed high school, compared to approximately two-thirds of Anglos and one-half of African-Americans.

Hispanics were also seriously underrepresented at all levels of post-secondary education and among graduates. In 1980 they represented only 16.4 percent of the total enrollment in two-year colleges and 11.2 percent of the enrollment in four-year schools. They earned 15.1 percent of the associate and 8.7 percent of the baccalaureate degrees.

The Texas system of higher education is extensive and complex, encompassing thirty-seven public four-year colleges and universities, forty-nine community college districts, one technical institute with four campuses, seven medical schools, two dental schools, and other allied health and nursing units. Twenty-six four-year colleges and universities and six health-related institutions were part of six university systems at the time of the study. The roles, responsibilities, and oversight authority of system administrations varied widely. Public institutions were governed by fifteen separate and relatively autonomous boards of regents, all appointed by the governor. The governor also appoints the board of the technical institute. Each of the state's forty-nine-community college districts is governed by a separate board of trustees, whose members are popularly elected in local districts.

The statewide Coordinating Board provides the umbrella under which this complex array of colleges and universities must operate. The board is advisory to the governor, the legislative budget board, and the legislature; its official functions emphasize coordination and leadership rather than regulation. The board recommends formulas for use in determining legislative appropriations, prescribes a uniform reporting system, collects data, conducts studies needed for policy-making, and approves degree and certificate offerings. While the board is concerned with statewide planning, individual colleges and universities through their respective governing boards exercise considerable autonomy in determining their own priorities and strategies.

The Coordinating Board also has responsibility for implementing the Texas Equal Educational Opportunity Plan for Higher Education, which was inspired by the 1973 *Adams v. Richardson* decision. Overall, the state was significantly short of its affirmative action goals for senior institutions in 1986. Only 4,937 Hispanics were enrolled as first-time freshmen and undergraduate transfers, a number representing 66 percent of the goal. The 2,709 African-American first-time freshmen or undergraduate transfers represented about 53 percent of the plan's goal. In response to the shortfall, the Coordinating Board has sponsored a number of workshops and seminars to assist state institutions in recruitment and retention of minority students.

The Coordinating Board has been designated as a defendant in a lawsuit filed on behalf of several Hispanic organizations and individuals by the Mexican American Legal Defense and Educational Fund (MALDEF). The suit alleges, among other complaints, that policies for approving degree programs have denied minorities access to and participation in quality higher education programs. The approval of new degree programs, especially at the doctoral level, has been an issue for UTEP.

State Financial Aid Programs

The state of Texas provides financial aid programs to students through a number of grants, loans, and scholarships, most of which are administered by the Coordinating Board. These include tuition equalization grants, state student incentive grants, a state college student loan program, a teacher education loan program, and a future teacher loan program, all of which serve many minority students. In 1983 the legislature created the State Scholarship Program for Ethnic Recruitment and appropriated $250,000 for each of the academic years 1984–1985 and 1985–1986. The funds were to be used for scholarships and recruitment of resident minority students enrolling for the first time, either as freshmen or as transfer students.

The University of Texas System

The University of Texas system is made up of seven general academic universities, six health and medical centers, and the Institute of Texan Cultures. The university is governed by the nine-member Board of Regents which is appointed by the governor. As of June 1987, one of the nine regents was Hispanic. There were no minorities among the top ranks of system executives or in the presidencies or vice-presidencies of system institutions, although one has since been appointed.

The enrollment of both Hispanic and African-American undergraduate students in the system has increased over the past decade. In 1976 there were 7,466 Hispanic undergraduate students, or 10.9 percent of the total enrollment. A decade later, the number of Hispanics had more than doubled to 16,023, or 15.4 percent of the total. As indicated in table 13.1, a significant part of this increase occurred because of the changing demographics for UTEP. In 1986 UTEP enrolled about 45 percent of all the Hispanic undergraduates within the system. Systemwide enrollment of African-American undergraduate students had also increased, but not as dramatically as for Hispanics. African-American enrollment would have to nearly triple in order to become proportional to the approximately 12 percent African-American share of the state population in 1980.

While leaders are aware that the system has not met the goals of the Texas Equal Educational Opportunity Plan, they are guardedly

TABLE 13.1. African-American and Hispanic Undergraduates, UTEP and University of Texas System

YEAR	UTEP		UNIVERSITY OF TEXAS SYSTEM	
	Hispanic	African-American	Hispanic	African-American
1976	25.8	1.7	10.9	2.9
1978	38.9	2.0	14.0	3.1
1980	43.8	2.4	14.3	3.4
1982	44.9	1.7	14.2	3.7
1984	50.6	2.3	15.7	4.2
1986	51.3	2.3	15.4	4.0

Source: Statistical Supplement to the Annual Report of the Coordinating Board, Texas College and University System, 1987.

optimistic that race- and ethnicity-related participation issues will be resolved because the directions, particularly for Hispanics, are positive. They are not as optimistic about progress for African-Americans, however, and they acknowledge that improvements will not come fast enough to satisfy many critics.

Top system leaders take an active interest in recruitment and promotion of minority faculty members and administrators, particularly those at the dean level and above. The number of minority faculty continue to increase slowly among the system's institutions, as can be seen in table 13.2. The largest concentration among ranked faculty is at the assistant professor level. In 1980 there were 111 Hispanic faculty members at the professor, associate professor, and assistant professor levels. By 1984 the number had increased to 127, with 56 at the level of assistant professor. The number of Hispanic faculty members would have to increase by a factor of four if they were to be represented proportionately to the Hispanic undergraduates in the University of Texas system.

The situation for African-Americans is worse. African-American faculty are badly underrepresented at all levels, and the situation does not

TABLE 13.2. University of Texas System Faculty Proportions, 1980 and 1984

FACULTY RANK	PERCENTAGE IN 1980		PERCENTAGE IN 1984	
	Hispanic	African-American	Hispanic	African-American
Professor	2.0	0.4	2.1	0.5
Associate professor	2.8	1.4	4.1	1.5
Assistant professor	5.1	2.0	5.7	1.4
Total ranked	3.3	1.2	3.8	1.1
Instructor	3.4	1.8	3.7	1.9
Lecturer	7.0	1.3	4.6	1.7

Source: Statistical Supplement to the Annual Report of the Coordinating Board, Texas College and University System, 1987.

appear to be improving. In fact the number and proportion of ranked faculty declined between 1980 and 1984.

COMMUNITY SETTING

El Paso–Juarez is the third largest metropolitan area on the border between United States and Mexico, with a population in 1985 in excess of 1.3 million. It is a binational, bicultural, bilingual community, in which Mexican, American, and Indian cultures converge. As is true of all border communities, El Paso–Juarez has a unique ambience of cultural, social, and economic interdependence. Citizens on both sides of the border still recall "Black Thursday," the day in 1982 when the Mexican peso plunged, retail stores on both sides of the border went out of business, and unemployment soared to nearly 30 percent.

El Paso's economic base is varied, consisting of defense, agriculture, manufacturing, and retail businesses. In recent years, the economy has been shored up by *las maquiladoras*, American firms building plants in Juarez because cheap labor makes products more competitive with foreign goods. While some criticize these plants, others contend that two to three jobs are created in the United States for every job created by American firms in Mexico.

Poverty continues to be a significant factor all along the border. The per capita average income is extremely low, and an increasing percentage of Spanish-surname families may be found living in poverty as one travels from the California border counties to those of the Texas Lower Valley. In El Paso county 27 percent of families lived in poverty in 1980.

The proportion of Hispanics in the total population of El Paso has continued to increase over the years as indicated in table 13.3. In 1960 people of Spanish origin made up 44 percent of the population. By 1985 Hispanics represented 68 percent. The Spanish-origin population is much younger than the non-Spanish-origin population. Between 1960 and 1980 the number of African-Americans in El Paso County more than doubled, but their proportion of the population increased to only 4 percent.

The position of Hispanics in the community has improved during the last decade, as they have moved steadily upward through the administrative ranks of institutions and businesses. There is now a broader-based understanding of Hispanic issues. A young Chicana lawyer, who was one of the student leaders involved in demanding changes at UTEP in the early 1970s, described some of the changes in Hispanic strategy:

> Fifteen years ago, we would attack, confront publicly. Now we invite the person who can help solve the problem to lunch, outline the problem, and suggest two or three optional solutions. We agree to help implement the one mutually acceptable. Many Chicano professionals

TABLE 13.3. African-American and Spanish-Origin Population, El Paso
County, 1960–1980

YEAR	AFRICAN-AMERICAN	POPULATION (%)	SPANISH ORIGIN[a]	POPULATION (%)
1960	8,571	2.7	136,993	43.6
1970	10,010	2.8	204,349	56.9
1980	18,151	3.8	297,001	61.9

Source: Bureau of Business and Economic Research, Statistical Abstract of El Paso,
Texas, College of Business Administration, UTEP, 1986.

[a] "Spanish origin" is as defined in the Current Population Reports, U.S. Bureau of
the Census, 1970, 1980.

who left El Paso 10–15 years ago in desperation and frustration are now
returning. We understand politically, and we work within the system.
We know how it works and we are moving to change it.

Another Hispanic professional noted the increasing value of education. "[The] Hispanic community is better educated than ever before.
We as a people are more aware of the need for a quality education,
and we understand what the opportunities are for us and our children.
More and more of our children know that they can be doctors, lawyers,
and engineers."

El Paso has many community organizations working to increase the
number of Hispanics who graduate from high school, to improve the
quality of their preparation, and to increase the number who subsequently succeed in postsecondary institutions. The League of United
Latin American Citizens (LULAC) has been instrumental in raising
funds for scholarships, providing financial assistance to children who
need eyeglasses, and sponsoring forums. They sponsor the annual
Youth Leadership Conference, designed to create a network among
the county's Hispanic youth to assist in reducing dropout; encourage
participation in leadership and volunteer activities; and explore issues
and trends affecting young adults in employment, education, training,
personal development, and technology.

The El Paso Inter-religious Sponsoring Organization (EPISO) helps
communities organize around issues, working to increase the knowledge of community members as well as their ability to deal with the
institutions that are supposed to serve them. EPISO members work
with parents and children in the public housing projects and barrios
in the southern parts of El Paso. During spring 1987, EPISO had more
than 400 people enrolled in citizenship classes in eight parishes.

Elementary and Secondary Schools

El Paso County is served by two large and seven small public school districts, enrolling in excess of 120,000 students. Countywide, 75 percent

of all students enrolled in the public schools in 1984–1985 were Hispanic, 3 percent were African-American, and less than 1 percent were Asian-American or American Indian. The Catholic schools had an enrollment in 1986–1987 of 4,500 students, approximately 92 percent Hispanic. More than a decade ago, the high schools had Mexican-American clubs, but now all high school organizations seem to be controlled by Hispanic students. It is no longer unusual, as it was 15 years ago, for the top students to be Hispanic. As a result, an increasing number of Hispanic students are preparing for college, and the students coming from the high schools are much more sophisticated and better prepared academically.

El Paso Community College

El Paso Community College (EPCC) is a multicampus institution offering transfer courses as well as some 150 vocational, technical, and career programs. In addition to serving students at its three campuses, the college offers special classes at public housing projects. Founded in 1971, EPCC is the only community college in UTEP's primary service area. EPCC enrolled in excess of 13,000 students in the fall 1985 semester and sent 95 percent of its transfer students and 100 percent of its associate degree graduates to UTEP. However, the numbers involved are relatively small.

EPCC has been instrumental in broadening the base of education in the community. Before its establishment, few Hispanic parents thought of sending their children to higher education. By 1985, 68 percent of students enrolled were Hispanic. In addition, the administrative staff and the faculty are much more ethnically and racially balanced than is true for the university.

Historically, the relationship between UTEP and EPCC has been less close than their geographic propinquity would suggest. In some ways EPCC has had closer working relationships with New Mexico State University, in Las Cruces approximately 50 miles distant. Recently, with a "semimandate" from above, vice-presidents at UTEP and EPCC have appointed joint task forces of faculty to work on articulation issues. The institutions also cooperated in submitting a joint proposal to the National Science Foundation under the Minorities in Science Improvement Program.

STUDENTS

Over 80 percent of students enrolled at UTEP are residents of El Paso County, while approximately 5 percent come from states other than Texas. Another 4 percent typically come from Mexico, but that percentage has declined recently because of devaluation of the peso. Hispanics make up an increasing proportion of the undergraduate enrollment.

As noted in table 13.1, Hispanics constituted 26 percent of the total undergraduate enrollment in 1976. By 1986 the total number of Hispanic undergraduates had more than doubled to 7,055, making them the majority population. The change in attendance patterns among Hispanic women has been particularly dramatic, rising from 11 percent of total enrollment in 1976 to 26 percent in 1986. Enrollments for African-American undergraduates have fluctuated from year to year since 1976 but do give evidence of modest growth over the decade, from 2.9 percent in 1976 to 4.0 percent in 1986.

Despite the generally favorable picture painted by the growth of minority enrollments, UTEP has not been immune to the affirmative action concerns plaguing other four-year institutions in Texas. The university had an actual goal for 1987–1988 of enrolling 1,379 Hispanics and 133 African-Americans as first-time, full-time freshmen, or undergraduate transfers. They actually enrolled 1,084 Hispanics and 49 African-Americans in the preceding year. Thus UTEP is 13 percentage points above the Texas average in meeting affirmative action goals for Hispanics, while it lags behind in meeting the goals for African-Americans by 16 percentage points.

Our graduate surveys and interviews indicated that the majority of Hispanic students are from middle-class Chicano families. Many are second- or third-generation graduates, often referred to as "UTEPies." About 25 to 30 percent are from families with lower socioeconomic backgrounds and little college-going experience. Fifty-eight percent of the Hispanic graduates we surveyed at UTEP had a primary language other than English, in comparison to 18 percent of the Hispanic graduates at the University of New Mexico (UNM) and 86 percent of those at Florida International University (FIU).

Our survey also suggested nontraditional modes of attendance for Hispanics and non-Hispanics alike. Only 14 percent of graduates were of traditional age, and 70 percent had taken more than four years to complete a degree. In addition, 54 percent had transferred from another postsecondary institution. While transfers represented a very substantial proportion of all graduates, the proportion was lower than for all other case-study institutions except UNM and Brooklyn College.

Retention rates for Hispanic students at the University of Texas at El Paso generally are higher than retention rates for Anglos. From the first year to the second, the retention rate for Hispanic students in the entering class of 1980 was slightly above 60 percent, while the retention rate for Anglos was about 57 percent as reported in table 13.4. For this same cohort, the retention rate from the second year to the third year was about 46 percent for Hispanics, compared to 43 percent for Anglos. This retention pattern continued for the remaining years of the study. When the ethnic groups were disaggregated by gender, Hispanic males had the highest retention rates, followed by Hispanic females, Anglo

TABLE 13.4. Five-Year Cohort Survival Rates at UTEP, Class Entering in 1980

| | Hispanic | | Anglo | |
	Male	Female	Male	Female
Year 1:				
Retain	61.3	61.1	56.0	57.6
Year 2:				
Retain	47.2	45.5	41.7	43.3
Year 3:				
Retain	40.9	36.8	35.5	33.6
Graduate	0.2			0.2
Year 4:				
Retain	32.6	29.9	22.9	24.1
Graduate	3.1	3.9	2.4	6.0
Year 5:				
Retain	21.6	19.3	20.7	14.3
Graduate	10.3	12.1	9.3	13.1

Source: Office of Vice-Chancellor of Educational Development, UTEP.

males, and Anglo females in that order. Retention studies of the entering classes of 1981, 1982, 1983, and 1984 have shown similar results. The number of African-Americans was too small for meaningful reporting.

Cohort survival studies are distorted by student patterns of attendance. Most students alternate periods of full-time college attendance with full-time employment. It is not unusual for students to take a full load one semester only to "step out" for several semesters in order to meet financial and family obligations. While education is a high priority, the privilege of full-time college attendance for four consecutive years is not available to most UTEP students. A faculty member elaborated on this point.

> Work and family obligations dictate when students can take classes. When courses don't fit their work schedules, or when their financial resources are exhausted, many simply stop taking courses until they are able to return. As a result, the average length of time from admission to graduation exceeds six years for many of our students.

Table 13.5 shows that Hispanics earned slightly more than 40 percent of the total number of baccalaureate degrees during the three-year period ending in 1986. In 1985–1986 more Hispanics than Anglos received degrees for the first time. The proportion of degrees received by African-Americans declined during this same period. Clearly, increases in the participation of Hispanics at UTEP have not occurred at the expense of achievement. In 1980 Hispanics represented 43.8 percent of the undergraduate population. Four years later they earned 41.1 percent of the baccalaureate degrees. The comparable statistics for 1982 undergraduate enrollments and 1986 graduations were 44.9 and 43.4 percent. The

TABLE 13.5. Majors Awarding More than Fifty Baccalaureate Degrees at UTEP, 1983–1984 and 1985–1986

	1983–1984			1985–1986		
MAJOR	African-American (%)	Hispanic (%)	Anglo (%)	African-American (%)	Hispanic (%)	Anglo (%)
Business and management	3.7	36.2	48.7	2.8	44.0	43.5
Communications	6.8	42.4	39.0	3.2	54.0	36.5
Education	2.3	49.9	45.7	2.1	53.4	42.9
Engineering	0.9	43.7	25.1	0.4	32.1	31.2
Health sciences	2.7	24.7	71.2	2.2	31.7	65.5
Life sciences	0	59.3	27.1	1.9	61.1	31.5
Physical sciences	0	17.7	53.2	0	13.2	48.0
Protective services	3.6	64.3	31.0	5.7	55.7	37.1
Social sciences	1.5	31.3	59.7	0	41.5	53.8
Total	2.4	41.1	46.0	1.8	43.4	42.7

Source: Higher Education General Information Survey, submitted to the U.S. Department of Education by UTEP.

Note: Foreign students earned 33 percent of all engineering degrees and 38 percent of physical sciences degrees in 1985–1986.

close and positive relationship between increases in participation rates and increases in graduation rates for Hispanics does not appear to hold true for African-Americans, who constituted 3.4 percent of enrollment in 1980 and earned 2.4 percent of degrees four years later. By 1982 their share of enrollment had grown to 3.7 percent, but their share of degrees four years later declined to 1.8 percent.

Almost two-thirds of the degrees conferred each year by UTEP are awarded in four fields: business and management, education, engineering, and the health sciences. As indicated in table 13.5, Hispanics were overrepresented among education graduates, proportionately represented among those earning degrees in business and management, and underrepresented among the engineering and the health sciences graduates in 1985–1986. The underrepresentation among engineering graduates appears to be a function of the high proportion of degrees earned in this field by foreign students. The same cannot be said for health sciences in which a disproportionate number of degrees were earned by Anglos.

Among fields awarding more than 50 but fewer than 100 degrees, Hispanics were best represented in communications, life sciences, and protective services. They were the most seriously underrepresented in the physical sciences. In general, there was good distribution of Hispanics across majors except for the physical sciences and the health sciences. African-American graduates were less well distributed, but interpretation of these figures is difficult because of small numbers.

UNIVERSITY ENVIRONMENT

In its strategic plan, developed in 1985, the university defined its primary mission as meeting the needs of the metropolitan area it serves through instruction, research, and public service. The order in which these traditional university functions were listed was not accidental. In its plan, UTEP emphasized its commitment to creating educational opportunities rather than erecting educational barriers for students whose talents and motivations enabled them to meet the rigorous standards characteristic of university degree programs. The plan also noted university awareness of obligations to the special student constituencies it serves.

UTEP's approach to serving all its students is consistent with the philosophy expressed in its mission statement. The university now provides the services "radical" students were demanding 20 years ago. These include active recruitment of Hispanic students, strong advisement and counseling programs, and tutoring and other academic assistance. The university also gives the parents of high school students financial aid information in English and Spanish, early in the recruitment process.

The university changed executive leadership during the study. The vice-president for academic affairs was named interim president and subsequently given a regular appointment to the post. Under her administration, one of the three senior administrators reporting to the president (dean of students) is Hispanic. The dean of the college of science is also Hispanic, as are some of the incumbents in mid-management positions including financial aid, admissions and records, and co-op placement. As would be expected in a community with the composition of El Paso, many of the secretarial and technical positions were also filled by Hispanics.

Admissions and Recruitment

The university is aggressive in its recruitment programs, particularly in high schools with large numbers of Hispanic students. The efforts of the Office of Undergraduate Recruitment and Scholarships are closely tied to the activities of the Office of Financial Aid. During the fall and early winter the two offices work with high school principals and counseling staff to schedule evening meetings to explain to parents of high school students the types of financial aid available and how to complete the application forms. Meetings are conducted in English and Spanish.

For regular admission, applicants must complete a prescribed course of study including four years of English, three years of mathematics, three years of science, three years of social sciences, and two years of a foreign language. They must also achieve some satisfactory combination of high school standing and scores on the SAT or ACT. For students who graduate in the top quarter of their high school class, any score is acceptable. Students graduating in the second quarter must score a minimum of 700 on the SAT or 15 on the ACT. Students who graduate in the bottom half of their class must score a minimum of 800 on the SAT or 18 on the ACT.

There is a provisional program for students who do not meet regular admissions criteria. Since 1984 the university has admitted a little more than a quarter of its entering freshman class under provisional arrangements. Of the 1874 freshmen admitted for the fall 1987 semester, 29 percent were in the provisional category. Seventy-five percent of these were Hispanic. In order to remove provisional status, a student must earn a C or better in a minimum of three classes that total nine provisional hours of credit. An overall C average must also be maintained in all courses taken. A student who does not clear provisional status during the first semester but who earns at least a 1.5 GPA is given one additional semester to meet the requirements for regular status.

Table 13.6 provides information about success ratios for provisional admittees. During the time the program has been operating, about 39 percent of provisionally admitted freshmen were ineligible to return at the end of the first semester. Approximately the same number met the requirements for removal of provisional status by the end of the first year. By way of contrast, table 13.4 indicated that slightly more than 60 percent of the 1980 Hispanic cohort persisted into the second year, while the figures for Anglos were slightly less than 60 percent.

Clearly, provisional admittees are higher risk, but a substantial and increasing number persist into the second year. Administrators and staff attribute improved results to the academic support programs provided by the university.

TABLE 13.6. Outcomes for Provisionally Admitted Freshmen at UTEP, 1984–1986

YEAR	TOTAL FRESHMEN ADMITTED	PROVISIONAL STATUS		INELIGIBLE AFTER 1ST SEM.		CLEARED IN 1 YEAR	
		N	%	N	%	N	%
1984	2109	583	27.4	227	38.9	205	35.2
1985	1656	524	31.6	202	38.5	207	39.5
1986	1773	484	27.3	192	39.7	201	41.5

Source: Office of Vice-Chancellor of Educational Development, UTEP.

Financial Aid

Hispanic students receive 75 to 80 percent of all available aid. In a community where the unemployment rate hovers around 14 percent and few part-time jobs are available, financial aid is particularly critical during the first year. In addition to federal and state financial aid, the university provides more than 750 scholarships from contributions by local businesses, industry, and civic leadership. One of the major events of the year is a dinner at which donors and student recipients sit together. Despite the best efforts of the university and its surrounding community, the amount of financial aid remains inadequate.

Early Intervention

In 1987 the Chicano Studies Research Center at UTEP, through its School Dropout Research Program, published a directory listing twenty-seven junior high and high school programs aimed at preventing dropouts and encouraging youth to return to school to complete their education. Most of these programs offered some combination of remedial instruction, skills training, part-time employment, and counseling services. The study also concluded that there were "no unified efforts in place to address the problem in an integrated, comprehensive or synergistic manner." The absence of systematic early intervention efforts may reflect the reality that for school districts, as for the university, any activity that occurs is by definition an activity for Hispanics since they constitute the majority of all students.

Apart from the recruiting and financial aid strategies previously described, the university is involved in a small number of focused programs. The College of Engineering offers a program for minorities similar to those described for other case-study institutions. A first-generation Hispanic engineering graduate we interviewed described a summer bridge program as the critical factor in his subsequent success, noting that the friends he made during the summer program were part of a mutual support network throughout his college years. Now employed by a major firm, he spends part of his time visiting high schools in the area encouraging Hispanics to consider the same career he chose.

The faculty in the College of Science have made special efforts to encourage junior high and high school students to enroll in courses that "track" them into science at the university level. Hundreds of students have been brought to campus for weekend science and engineering programs, and public school teachers have been invited to participate in summer laboratory experiences with university faculty. These programs help to socialize first-generation college students into the university culture while building a community environment supportive of higher education.

The Mothers-Daughters Program, jointly sponsored by the YWCA, UTEP, and several local school districts, works with Hispanic girls in the fifth and sixth grades to encourage them to continue their education. The program includes study skills and career awareness for the girls. The mothers discuss parenting skills, the importance of education, and the availability of financial aid. UTEP also works with El Paso Community College to increase retention among sixth, eighth, and tenth graders through Project Accion, a collaborative effort that also involves the El Paso and Ysleta independent school districts and the American College Testing Program.

Community College Articulation

UTEP and El Paso Community College have assigned a priority to efforts aimed at easing the movement of students between the two institutions. One product is a transfer guide designed to acquaint students with freshman and sophomore requirements for degrees offered by the university and to provide them with a list of the courses offered by the community college that satisfy them. A companion publication explains how students can transfer temporarily to EPCC from the university and subsequently return. Faculty members from the two institutions are now working closely together on jointly sponsored articulation committees.

Advisement and Counseling

The university, through its advisement and counseling services, works to socialize students to the culture of the university, to connect them to services, to help them learn about the university's requirements, and to help them find a comfort zone. Good advising is regarded as central to promoting degree attainment, especially among first-generation students.

The university uses a strong career counseling and placement program to take advantage of increased employer interest in hiring Hispanics. Companies see Hispanics as the market of the future and are gearing up now to be ready. A co-op program provides students with work experience related to their majors, as well as significant financial support. Engineering students earn as much as $2,000 per month. Beyond the financial support and work experience, students get to know people who can be helpful to them later in their careers.

Residential Life

The university residence halls are not a significant factor in recruitment and retention of Hispanic students at UTEP, because these students tend to live at home. The university has had difficulty keeping dormitories full. Some have been converted into faculty offices or renovated to serve other functions.

ACADEMIC ENVIRONMENT

The key to understanding the environment UTEP provides for Hispanic student achievement is not captured by a description of its special programs. Most faculty did not feel that UTEP offered many special services for Hispanics who are now in a very real sense "the student body." Hispanic participation and academic success are no longer minority issues; they are teaching and institutional survival issues. An administrator commented that UTEP had become a "special program" for Hispanics. At UTEP the whole has become much greater than the sum of its parts.

Faculty Characteristics

Increases in the numbers of Hispanic faculty have not kept pace with the changing student demographics. Between 1976 and 1984 Hispanic enrollments nearly doubled, from 25.8 to 50.6 percent. During this same period Hispanic representation among ranked faculty members increased from 8.5 to 10.1 percent. To achieve these very modest results, the university filled in excess of 44 percent of the eighteen ranked positions gained during the eight-year period with Hispanics. In 1984 UTEP enrolled 45 percent of the Hispanic students in the University of Texas system, but employed only 32 percent of the ranked Hispanic faculty. Even though there are more Hispanic faculty members at UTEP than at other units in the system, the ratio of Hispanic students to Hispanic faculty members at UTEP remains only slightly above the system average.

Changes in faculty demographics for the period 1977–1984 are reported in table 13.7. The pattern is one of modest growth. The largest numbers of Hispanic faculty are in the lower tenure-track positions. The modest growth at the upper ranks suggests reasonable progres-

TABLE 13.7. UTEP Faculty Proportions, 1977 and 1984

	1977		1984	
	Hispanic	African-American	Hispanic	African-American
Faculty Rank	(%)	(%)	(%)	(%)
Professor	4.3	0.9	5.1	0.9
Associate professor	9.0	0	10.3	0.8
Assistant professor	11.1	0.6	13.6	1.2
Total ranked faculty members	8.5	0.5	10.1	0
Instructors	15.9	0	10.0	0
Lecturer	14.2	0	15.0	0.6

Source: Texas College and University System, Statistical Supplement to the Annual Report of the Coordinating Board.

sion within the tenure and promotion system. The number of African-American faculty members at UTEP has always been very small.

Academic Programs

The Inter-American Science and Humanities Program serves as an initial entry point for Spanish-speaking students who have academic preparation for university work but for whom English is a foreign language. The university library has a large section that houses books, newspapers, films, records, posters, and pamphlets on Mexican-American history and culture. The Chicano Studies Program initiates, coordinates and promotes academic and cultural activities, including community outreach, publications, and sponsorship of lectures, seminars, workshops, conferences and forums that relate to Hispanics. The Minority Biomedical Research Support Program provides research opportunities for undergraduate and graduate students who wish to pursue a career in biomedical research.

Academic Support Services

A wide range of academic support programs are available to all students. An administrator noted that the university had proved its effectiveness in increasing retention rates for underprepared students. Now the focus is on extending the benefits of the lessons learned to the general student body.

The university is particularly proud of its Study Skills and Tutorial Services, which provide a microcomputer learning laboratory; tutoring; test preparation; and special classes in areas such as math, writing, and study techniques. Originally focused to provide study skills for minorities (an African-American vocabulary class and a Chicano writing laboratory), the thrust of the tutorial services program now is generic. Although the majority of the students enrolled are Hispanic, the staff strive to provide a program that is responsive to all students. As one said, "We do not do Chicano tutoring, but we provide good tutoring for Chicanos." During the 1986–1987 academic year, 9,348 students were served through Study Skills and Tutorial Services, a 13 percent increase from the prior year. A continuing goal is to work more closely with the academic departments and to make renewed efforts to integrate tutoring and classroom teaching.

The provisional admission program is credited with reducing attrition rates of students who do not meet regular admission requirements. Provisional admittees attend an orientation at which they receive academic advising as well as information to help them become acquainted with the campus, university policies, and sources of assistance. Students in the program are required to enroll in a free, noncredit class for eight weeks of instruction in the basic skills needed for academic success. Student volunteers, many of whom are former provisional students, work closely with provisional admittees during orientation and study skills classes.

SUMMARY

UTEP, more than most case-study institutions, exhibits a stage 3 profile. Hispanic students now feel that UTEP is their institution. At the same time, the university has difficulty identifying special programs for Hispanics, and most of those that can be identified appear to operate outside the institutional mainstream, with external funding. Understanding this apparent contradiction requires attention to outcomes as well as process. Hispanics and Anglos achieve degrees at comparable rates even though Hispanics are overrepresented among the very large contingent of provisional matriculants. Four out of ten provisionally admitted students will return for a second year, compared with six out of ten of those regularly admitted, despite a special program for provisionals that is fairly minimal compared with those operating in some of the other case-study institutions with outcomes not nearly as positive.

The comparative absence of race- and ethnicity-related differences in degree achievement, as well as the declining difference in survival rates for regular and provisionally admitted students, can be attributed to the level of adaptation evident in the institution's approach to diversity. Learning assistance is routinely available to all students who require it; and many do, as evidenced by the large numbers who participate. The class schedule takes into consideration the nontraditional attendance patterns of many students. UTEP has a considerable amount of experience in helping diversely prepared learners succeed academically, and that experience is increasingly being used to improve the learning environment for all students.

The amount of adaptation that has taken place is remarkable, given the modest changes in the composition of faculty and senior administrators and the mismatch between university aspirations and available resources. Forces influencing the university's adaptation process came from three principal directions. The first was internal and had to do with issues of institutional survival and viability. Between 1976 and 1984, UTEP's enrollment increased by only 139 undergraduates. Since funding for faculty positions is related to enrollment, there would have been a decrease in faculty had there not been an increase of 3400 Hispanics among 1984 enrollees. Changing demographics and the implied threat to institutional viability created an environment within which administrators were encouraged to manage organizational culture through strategic planning, resource allocation, and coordination to ensure that participation for Hispanic students did not improve at the expense of achievement.

State influences, in the form of the Texas Equal Educational Opportunity Plan for Higher Education and the monitoring activities for the Texas Coordinating Board, represented an important external influence on the adaptation process. Increasing Hispanic participation was identified as a state priority and the legislature offered financial incentives for students. State assistance, combined with need-based, federal student financial aid, increased significantly the proportions of low-income Hispanics within the El Paso area who could afford to go on to college. The increasing tide of Hispanic students came just in time to keep the university from experiencing significant enrollment losses; in the process, Hispanics became the majority.

The third and, in the minds of many, most important influence on UTEP's adaptation came from its community setting. While El Paso remains a place where many live in poverty, there is also a substantial and growing Hispanic middle class. Hispanics have assumed leadership roles in politics, business, and the professions, providing both role models and enhanced economic opportunities. Hispanics constitute a large majority in the public and Catholic schools, where they are expected to achieve and go on to college. These changes add up to a well-prepared student population with well-defined expectations about the role of higher education in preparing them for adult roles. These changes also contribute to the community's expectations for UTEP and in the process reinforce state and federal pressures for providing equal educational opportunities.

The factors which provide a positive environment for Hispanic participation and achievement do not have the same effect on the very small African-American population. African-Americans are underrepresented in the student body in comparison with their presence in El Paso County, and achieve degrees at a lower rate than either Anglos or Hispanics. This pattern was also observed among other case-study institutions serving high proportions of Hispanic students.

PART THREE

Assessing Institutional Environments

14

IMPROVING ACCESS
AND ACHIEVEMENT

African-Americans, Hispanics, and American Indians share with other racial and ethnic groups diversity in preparation, value attached to college-going, and patterns of college attendance. They are distributed differently along these dimensions, however, as a consequence of historic discrimination and its correlates of parental education, residential patterns, and socioeconomic status. Differentially prepared students need more and different forms of assistance to meet the standards traditionally expected of college graduates. If such assistance is not available, participation is discouraged and attrition rates soar.

State and institutional policy leaders emphasize access and achievement when they influence colleges to move through three stages of adaptation to serve multicultural students more effectively. In the first stage, institutions remove barriers to participation by adopting recruiting strategies and admissions practices that will ensure that entering classes more accurately reflect the composition of the population from which they are drawn. Institutional efforts work best when supplemented by federal, state, and private efforts to remove economic barriers by providing need-based financial aid.

Policy leaders improve retention by developing the special programs and support services characteristic of the second stage of adaptation. Stage 2 interventions are typically developed under the leadership of student affairs staff and aim at expanding the pool of qualified minority students and assisting the marginally underprepared to find ways of adapting to institutional expectations.

Administrative and faculty leaders move their institutions toward the third stage of adaptation by developing academic programs more reflective of a multicultural society, by using assessment to determine preparation gaps and learning outcomes, and by redesigning the learning process to encourage comparable achievement by more diversely prepared learners. In stage 3 institutions, faculty understand that it is unrealistic and counterproductive to expect students to do all the changing, so they accept primary responsibility for helping more diverse students learn.

Institutional leaders manage organizational cultures to accommodate diversity and achievement by engaging in strategic planning, providing coordination and control, hiring more minority faculty and staff members, and using incentives and rewards to encourage faculty to become more involved in helping racial and ethnic minorities participate and achieve. As institutions move through the stages, their definition of quality changes from an emphasis on reputation and resources that excludes diversity to the recognition that any definition of quality must incorporate diversity to be meaningful in a multicultural society.

The case-study institutions in this book illustrate different stages in the process through which organizational cultures adapt to the challenges and opportunities of becoming increasingly multicultural without reducing standards. In this concluding chapter we draw in detail upon the experiences of the case-study institutions and their state policy environments, within the framework offered by the model, to suggest an approach to encouraging state systems of higher education to recognize the ever-increasing diversity that characterizes our nation as a strength rather than rejecting it as a threat to quality.

USING THE MODEL TO ASSESS AND IMPROVE STATE POLICY ENVIRONMENTS

The model described in chapter 1 can be used as an aid to state and institutional assessment and planning. The first step of a planning process for achieving equity involves identifying the difference between current and desired outcomes for a state's system of higher education. On the basis of this analysis, specific goals can be established for each institution to produce the intended outcomes. As noted in chapter 2, a state must either make a commitment to proportional representation and comparable achievement for its minority populations or accept race and ethnicity as appropriate determinants of the distribution of educational opportunity.

In assigning institutional goals, state policy leaders typically consider such factors as history, location, and mission. While a state may choose to assign some institutions higher participation targets than others, care should be taken to avoid excusing selective institutions from pursuing diversity as well as achievement. Open-access institutions should be encouraged to concern themselves at least as urgently with student achievement as with student participation. For all institutions, including those that have historically served a minority clientele, the realities of a multicultural society require attention to student diversity.

Any institution that receives any form of state support, including independent colleges and universities, should be expected to contribute to state participation goals, and all should make discernible progress toward the participation levels identified for them in the state plan. The retrograde movement, so common in the early 1980s, should be strongly discouraged by state policy instruments similar to those used in the study states. Institutional leaders need to be convinced that progress toward assigned goals is the price of continuing state support without unwanted state intrusions.

The analysis for participation must be repeated for graduation by determining the discrepancies between the racial and ethnic composition of undergraduate enrollments and the composition of graduating classes. Improvements in participation rates must be accompanied by comparable progress toward degrees if state equity outcomes are to include both degree achievement and diversity, rather than trading one for the other. While differing participation targets may be acceptable because of location or mission, there is no similar rationale that justifies racial and ethnic differences in graduation rates. Less well prepared students, who in some states are disproportionately minority, will take longer to graduate and require more learning assistance, but should over time complete college in proportions comparable to their Anglo colleagues.

The methods described in chapter 2 can be used to calculate composite equity scores for enrollment and graduation (the weighted average of the sum of the score times the proportion in the state's population for each group divided by the sum of the proportions for all three groups). The composite equity scores provide an estimate of the degree to which minority students are underrepresented in a state's public four-year, baccalaureate-granting institutions. This same type of analysis can be done for independent institutions within a state, and should be done routinely in states in which the independent sector represents an important part in the state plan for improving access and achievement.

The scores reported in table 14.1 reveal a number of interesting patterns. Only one state, Oklahoma, is in the top quartile of the distribution for both enrollment and graduation rates. Two states, Colorado and South Dakota, are in the bottom quartile for both. Four states—Arkansas, Kentucky, Pennsylvania, and Tennessee—are in the top quartile for enrollment and the bottom quartile for graduation. Four other states—Arizona, Connecticut, New York, and South Carolina—show the reverse pattern, low enrollment and high graduation rates. The pattern of scores suggests the degree to which a state's problem is participation, achievement, or both.

While the composite equity score is a convenient approach to describing a state's overall progress toward equity in higher education, care must be taken to ensure that the performance of one population does not mask the problems of another. Florida appears to be doing reasonably well, with equity scores in the second quartile for both enroll-

TABLE 14.1. U.S. Population Estimates and Composite Equity Scores for African-Americans, Hispanics, and American Indians, 1986

| | 1985 POPULATION ESTIMATE | | | COMPOSITE EQUITY SCORES | |
| | African-Americans (%) | Hispanics (%) | American Indians [a] (%) | | |
State				Enrollment	Graduation
AL	26	1	<1	60	70
AK	3	2	16	41	67
AZ	3	17	6	41	91
AR	17	1	<1	86	52
CA	8	22	<1	45	73
CO	4	12	<1	47	62
CT	8	4	<1	43	100
DE	17	2	<1	66	92
FL	14	10	<1	73	75
GA	27	1	<1	67	67
HI	2	7	[b]	[b]	[b]
IL	15	7	<1	63	61
IN	8	2	<1	70	60
KS	6	3	<1	64	74
KY	7	<1	<1	90	61
LA	30	2	<1	78	74
MD	25	2	<1	75	63
MA	4	3	<1	62	75
MI	14	2	<1	56	63
MS	36	<1	<1	87	67
MO	11	1	<1	53	67
MT	<1	1	5	61	81
NV	7	7	2	53	75
NJ	14	8	<1	71	76
NM	2	38	8	68	89
NY	15	11	<1	32[c]	80[c]
NC	22	1	1	90	73
OH	11	1	<1	58	54
OK	7	2	6	85	79
PA	9	1	<1	81	58
SC	30	1	<1	52	91
SD	<1	1	7	19	46
TN	16	<1	<1	88	62
TX	12	23	<1	65	77
UT	1	4	1	37	65
VA	19	2	<1	73	60
WA	3	3	1	57	79

Note: States listed in this table had populations that were at least 6% African-American, Hispanic, and American Indian in 1986, and reported usable data to HEGIS. Wyoming and the District of Columbia met the population criterion but did not report usable data.

[a] 1980 census data. U.S. Bureau of the Census, *Current Population Reports*, 1980.

[b] In Hawaii, Filipinos and native Hawaiians constitute about 31% of the state's population. According to a 1985 report, they represented about 11% of the enrollment of the University of Hawaii at Manoa and made up about 6% graduates during the period 1977–1984. The two groups are proportionately represented in Hawaii's community colleges.

[c] CUNY data was not reported.

ment and graduation. However, in a composite score, the performance of the Hispanic population (89 for participation and 100 for graduation) conceals the difficulties of the African-American population (62 for enrollment and 58 for graduation). Clearly, in developing statewide strategies, it is critical to look at the performance of each group as well as the composite picture.

In chapter 2 we argued against use of equity scores as a basis for comparisons across states. The characteristics of the populations served are sufficiently different to make such comparisons risky. The primary use of equity scores should be in the diagnosis of a state's problems and in keeping track of progress. However, comparisons using "peer" states may be useful in providing a rough indicator of how effectively a state system is performing for a particular racial or ethnic population. Southeastern states that rely on historically black institutions as part of their strategy for achieving equity might constitute one appropriate peer group. Southwestern and western states could serve a similar purpose for Mexican-Americans. States with large American Indian populations residing on reservations might constitute yet a third.

At a minimum, a state planning process for improving equity should include assessment of current status, identification of specific state and institutional goals, and design of policy instruments through which institutions will be encouraged and supported in efforts to improve. Schedules and accountability procedures are also essential, as is recognition that the planning process is more important than the planning document.

The policy instruments used by study states to improve outcomes for African-American, Hispanic, and American Indian students can be classified according to their point of impact on the three stages identified within the model. The most common policy instrument, and the first chronologically to receive extensive use, was the mandate. For nineteen states, mandates reflect the history of federal efforts to enforce Title VI of the Civil Rights Act of 1964 and the subsequent litigation. Use of mandates also reflects the impatience of groups that have experienced discrimination with less intrusive approaches that appear on the surface to be long-term and uncertain. Mandates present in the study states are listed in table 14.2.

Mandates have been used most commonly to remove barriers to participation among pre–stage 1 institutions. Court-imposed mandates were instrumental in bringing about the desegregation of majority institutions in southern and border states. They have been used in Florida to create an extremely persuasive environment for articulation between two- and four-year institutions. While mandates remove barriers, they do not produce the changes in institutional values and behaviors essential to the retention and graduation of diversely prepared racial and ethnic minorities. The state policy instruments that focus on changing

TABLE 14.2. Mandates

Actor	Action
Court of law	Required studies of the impact of proposed changes in admission requirements on AA/H/AI participation.
	Required Plans for countering the adverse impact of changes in admission requirements on AA/H/AI enrollments.
	Established race- or ethnicity-specific provisions for administering state financial aid programs.
	Required the enhancement of historically AA/H/AI institutions.
Statewide coordinating or governing board	Established criteria and policies for the special admission of AA/H/AI students.
	Developed policies on the status of transfer students with associate degrees.
	Established guidelines for numbering lower-division courses in two- and four-year or institutions.
	Established common academic calendars for two- and four-year institutions.
	Developed policies on the distribution of baccalaureate students between two- and four-year institutions.
	Required institutional compliance with state policies on articulation.
	Established an approved high school course of study for guaranteed admission to a public institution.

Note: AA/H/AI = African-American, Hispanic, and American Indian.

institutions, as distinct from removing barriers to participation, include planning and priority setting, inducements and capacity building, and accountability and evaluation. Table 14.3 reports some of the ways in which the case-study states have emphasized the importance of improving participation and graduation rates for African-American, Hispanic, and American Indian students.

TABLE 14.3. Planning and Priority Setting

Actor	Action
Governor	Placed emphasis upon improving educational opportunities for underrepresented minorities.
Statewide coordinating or governing board	Published a policy statement identifying AA/H/AI participation and achievement as a state priority.
	Developed a statewide plan for improving AA/H/AI participation and achievement, including specific goals, time lines, and funding requirements.
	Conducted regular statewide meetings of administrators involved in affirmative action or opportunity programs.
	Met regularly with representatives from the state board of education (K-12) to plan and coordinate collaborative activities.

Note: AA/H/AI = African-American, Hispanic, and American Indian.

The list, while not exhaustive, suggests some of the actors and actions through which states establish a policy environment that supports institutional efforts to improve the climates they provide for minority participation and graduation. In Michigan a commission on the future of higher education, appointed by the governor, advanced a series of recommendations, many of which were subsequently adopted. In New Mexico the legislature called for a study of issues related to the status of American Indians in higher education. That action led to a similar effort by the University of New Mexico. A committee of the Illinois legislature sponsored a controversial study of access and choice in the Chicago area, leading to a series of studies by the Illinois Board of Higher Education. The California legislature has called upon higher education to improve higher education opportunities for minorities in a series of joint committee reports dating to 1969.

Beyond identifying the issue as important to state policymakers, attainable objectives must be established and roles assigned. Changing outcomes requires coordinated effort among a wide range of institutions, each of which prizes its autonomy. Getting such organizations to act together in pursuit of common objectives requires planning and coordination from an agency perceived to be beyond the arena in which institutions compete for their share of scarce state resources. In addition to encouraging cooperation among postsecondary institutions through a planning process, it is essential that some agencies forge the critical links with state-level K-12 interests, as the Ohio Board of Regents has done.

Institutions favor state policy initiatives that involve them in setting priorities and provide maximum flexibility in deciding how or whether to respond. The California Postsecondary Education Commission and the Illinois Board of Higher Education have long operated on the philosophy that getting items onto institutional agendas through collaborative studies and planning activities is one of the most important strategies through which they encourage recognition of state priorities. Because institutional representatives often favor plans that promise the minimum disruption in current ways of doing business, it is useful to include outspoken advocates for minority interests from the policy community in a format that allows each to temper the influences of the other, as was done by the Arizona Board of Regents in a 1989 planning effort.

Planning and priority setting provide the framework within which other policy instruments are selected and implemented.

Table 14.4 lists examples of state policies designed either to encourage institutions to respond to the priorities in a state plan (inducements) or to develop the capacity for responding (capacity building).

Pennsylvania, California, and New York are among the states that have funded educational opportunity programs that contain elements drawn from all three stages of the model. The Trio programs present in many of the case-study institutions illustrate the use of inducements and capacity building at the federal level. Opportunity programs emphasize outreach, recruitment and financial aid, transition activities, and mentoring and learning assistance. Through these programs, institutions are encouraged to include new populations and to provide the learning support necessary to their success. Opportunity programs also build capacity by bringing onto campuses minority professionals who subsequently provide leadership in helping institutions become better adapted to the new populations their programs have attracted. At UCLA at least two of the key senior minority leaders on campus at the time of the study first became members of the university staff in the 1970s as administrators with the academic advancement program.

New Jersey and Virginia are noted for their use of challenge grants to encourage institutions to address quality and access priorities. Several case-study states have developed programs designed to expand the pool of potential minority faculty members as an inducement for universities to increase the racial and ethnic diversity of faculty members. Most case-study states have taken into consideration the extra time more diversely prepared students require to graduate in establishing guidelines for financial aid. New Jersey has provided incentives to independent institutions, as well as public institutions, to encourage them to offer effective developmental education programs for students assessed as having deficiencies in basic skills. Through this program, the state sends the message that diversity, like quality, should be an important priority for all institutions. Florida and Michigan are among

TABLE 14.4. Inducements and Capacity Building

Actor	Action
Legislature	Provided funding for comprehensive opportunity programs for economically and educationally disadvantaged students.
	Provided grants challenging institutions to improve undergraduate achievement.
	Provided funding for remedial work in four-year institutions.
	Funded a need-based, noncompetitive student financial aid program which, as a minimum, offsets the difference between Pell awards and the costs of attending public institutions.
	Provided entitlement or special scholarship programs targeted for AA/H/AI students.
Statewide coordinating or governing board	Developed statewide strategies for preparing and recruiting more AA/H/AI faculty members.
	Convened discipline-related groups of high school and college faculty members to articulate course competencies.
	Provided leadership and support for collaborative programs to expand the pool of college-bound students in junior high and high schools with high concentrations of AA/H/AI students.

Note: AA/H/AI = African-American, Hispanic, and American Indian.

the states that have provided inducements for institutions to work with the public schools.

Mandates open colleges and universities to minority participation. Planning helps to make equity an institutional priority and defines appropriate strategies for its pursuit. Inducements encourage institutions to seek out and serve students who would be poor risks within their conventional academic programs. Planning is an ongoing process that relies on periodic assessment of progress and the use of resulting information to make mid-course corrections. The policy instruments states have used to assess progress toward planning objectives, as well as to evaluate the effectiveness of inducements and capacity building strategies, appear in table 14.5.

TABLE 14.5. Accountability and Evaluation

ACTOR	ACTION
Court of law	Established goals, timetables, and monitoring procedures for desegregating the state system of higher education.
Legislature	Required assessment for all first-time-in-any-college students.
	Required students to demonstrate proficieny on a standardized test before advancing to upper-division status.
Statewide coordinating or governing board	Supported and monitored the operation of opportunity programs for economically and educationally disadvantaged students.
	Publicly disseminated institution-specific information on participation and degree achievement by race and ethnicity.
	Formally evaluated institutional progress in achieving participation and graduation goals for AA/H/AI students.
	Rewarded institutional success and penalized failure in achieving goals for AA/H/AI participation and graduation.
	Established monitoring procedures to ensure compliance with transfer articulation policies.
	Required colleges and universities to report student performance data to high schools and community colleges.

Note: AA/H/AI = African-American, Hispanic, and American Indian.

Accountability and evaluation policies are designed to track progress toward participation and graduation goals. We have already shown how this can be done using Higher Education General Information Survey (HEGIS) and Integrated Postsecondary Education Data System (IPEDS) data to produce ratio indicators. A growing number of states, including California, Florida, Illinois, New Jersey, and Tennessee, already have in operation, or are developing, student unit record systems that support studies of institutional outcomes more sophisticated than those produced with ratio indicators. Student unit record systems can be used to follow high school graduates and transfer students, and to report their performance to sending institutions.

These systems can also be used to record success rates for developmental programs and to document differences in the times differentially prepared students need to complete their degrees. Through use of student record systems, states can combine the virtues of cohort survival studies with the capability of making comparisons across institutions and with other states.

The information furnished by measures of student participation and progress can be used to inform the public about institutional performance as well as to revise plans and inducements. Public release of institution-specific aggregate student performance data produces criticism from institutional leaders, as is evident from the experience of the Texas Coordinating Board. Perhaps that is the strongest argument for its use. Clearly, colleges and universities like to be well regarded by their constituencies and, when possible, will alter practices to avoid criticism. Public release of performance data gathered to assess the impact of state policy instruments appears to enhance its value as a motivator.

Even more controversial is use of performance data to reward success and penalize failure, as in the Tennessee performance funding program. Few states have moved to follow Tennessee's lead, although the challenge grant programs described above (see Table 14.4, for example) can be seen as a less intrusive variation of performance funding. Challenge grants reward institutions, before the fact, for designing programs judged to have merit in addressing state priorities. But the funds directed to challenge grants might otherwise be appropriated as part of general funding support.

In the past several years, statutes have been passed in Texas, Georgia, and Florida to require assessment of entering college students and to ensure that prescribed performance standards are met before progress to the upper division or before award of an associate degree. Critics point to qualifying rates, which differ significantly as a function of race and ethnicity, as evidence that these quality initiatives impede minority progress. The model suggests an alternate explanation. In order to move toward stage 3, institutions must assure that all students reach comparable levels of performance across the entire range of academic majors. Assessment requirements shift the emphasis from participation, or even graduation in selected majors, to achievement and, for that reason, contribute to the pressures that move institutions toward the adaptive stage. New Jersey, the City University of New York, and Wayne State have adopted their own comprehensive assessment requirements, eliminating the temptation for legislators to act to assure that diversity is not achieved at the expense of quality.

Assessment requirements work best in states like Tennessee and New York where they are supplemented by carefully designed, state-funded learning assistance programs that provide a reasonable opportunity for students with marginal deficiencies to correct them without being required to attend a two-year institution. The provision that learning assistance programs be offered under the auspices of the academic staff within the Tennessee State Board of Regents system places additional pressure on institutions to move toward stage 3 modes of behavior.

Assessment requirements work least well in states like Florida where the legislature made unrealistic assumptions about the time that would be required for public schools to correct preparation problems and then compounded that error by assigning responsibility for all remedial work at the postsecondary level to community colleges, an action that clearly separated responsibility for quality and diversity. The correlates of this approach can be seen in the sharp reduction in participation rates for African-American students in historically Anglo institutions between 1980 and 1988.

Few states have used evaluations of institutional progress in achieving equity goals as the basis for rewards or penalties in the way that Tennessee has currently proposed. Clearly, threatening an institution's resources is the most intrusive action a state can take. As states move from less to more intrusive interventions, the costs in terms of political resistance increase. As one state higher education officer noted during the study, institutions have constituencies; state boards do not. Perhaps this is why accountability measures are less evident and more recent in application than mandates and inducements. Yet accountability measures appear to be an increasingly important component of the policy instruments through which states seek to promote the attention to access and achievement essential to a healthy economy and the continued well-being of a multicultural society.

ASSESSING INSTITUTIONAL ENVIRONMENTS

Institutions follow a process of assessment, goal setting, and intervention similar to the one described for states. The initial step involves assessing outcomes to determine the progress required to attain comparable graduation rates and the enrollment targets assigned within the state plan. Using the procedures outlined in chapter 3, estimates for participation and achievement were calculated for 1980–1986 for all higher education institutions in the United States. The results for selected institutions are presented in table 14.6 for African-Americans and table 14.7 for Hispanics.

Graduation equity scores for the institutions in these two tables exhibited four distinctive patterns related to the one observed in the analysis of state outcomes. The first included institutions that had achieved high graduation equity scores in 1980 and retained those scores in 1986. In the second pattern, institutions made dramatic gains in equity scores. The third pattern involved institutions with equally dramatic losses. A fourth group consisted of institutions that exhibited very low equity graduation scores for both years.

These patterns, when considered in relation to changes in enrollment proportions, suggest four different organizational cultures at work. The first five institutions in both tables had achieved comparable

TABLE 14.6. African-American Participation and Achievement
A Comparison of Equity Outcomes for Selected Institutions Using HEGIS Data

Institution	Graduation Equity Score		Percentage Enrolled		Percentage of State Population
	1980	1986	1980	1986	1985
Clemson University (S.C.)	100	100	2	6	30.3
Longwood College (Va.)	100	100	5	9	19.1
University of North Carolina at Greensboro	100	100	11	11	22.2
Frostburg State College (Md.)	100	100	8	8	24.5
Auburn University at Montgomery (Ala.)	100	100	15	14	26.2
Ramapo College of New Jersey	40	100	5	6	13.6
Citadel Military College of South Carolina	62	100	3	7	30.3
James Madison University	72	100	3	7	19.1
Southern Illinois University	61	93	9	9	15.4
University of California, Berkeley	55	83	4	5	7.9
Francis Marion College (S.C.)	100	58	12	15	30.3
Arkansas State University	100	52	12	9	16.6
Florida State University	98	50	10	7	13.8
California State College, San Bernardino	88	39	14	7	7.9
Glassboro State College (N.J.)	86	42	8	7	13.6
University of Wisconsin–Milwaukee	57	35	7	6	4.3
University of Toledo (Ohio)	35	35	9	6	10.6
University of Michigan at Dearborn	31	34	6	6	13.7
University of Illinois, Chicago	52	30	18	10	15.4
California State College, Stanislaus	57	19	7	6	7.9

TABLE 14.7. Hispanic Participation and Achievement
A Comparison of Equity Outcomes for Selected Institutions Using HEGIS Data

Institution	Graduation Equity Score		Percentage Enrolled		Percentage of State Population
	1980	1986	1980	1986	1985
FIU	100	100	32	43	9.7
Western New Mexico University	100	100	36	43	38.0
Jersey City State College	100	100	13	19	7.6
UTEP	100	100	44	54	22.5
CSUDH	100	100	10	11	22.3
SUNY at New Paltz	58	100	5	5	10.6
California Polytechnic State U., San Luis Obispo	69	100	4	7	22.3
University of California, Berkeley	71	100	4	7	22.3
UCLA	72	100	6	11	22.3
West Texas State University	76	100	6	6	22.5
California State University, Northridge	100	75	9	9	22.3
California State College, Stanislaus	100	73	9	10	22.3
Texas Woman's University	100	72	9	7	22.5
Adams State College of Colorado	96	68	17	25	11.9
University of Nevada at Las Vegas	100	65	3	5	7.4
University of Illinois, Chicago	72	70	9	9	6.5
San Jose State University	64	60	9	7	22.3
New Mexico Inst. of Mining Technology	50	59	9	8	38.0
Angelo State University (Tex.)	73	58	9	11	22.5
Metropolitan State College (Colo.)	66	47	7	7	11.9

graduation rates for both years. Institutions with comparable graduation rates for the minorities they enroll and enrollment proportions close to or exceeding the proportions within their respective state plans have achieved the outcomes associated with the *adaptive stage* of the model presented in chapter 1. From an examination of participation rates, it is clear that none of the institutions listed for African-Americans exhibited such outcomes. Auburn University at Montgomery came the closest. The top four institutions in the table for Hispanics display adaptive outcomes. Depending upon California's expectations for CSUDH, that institution may also be exhibiting adaptive outcomes.

Institutions achieving high graduation equity scores in both years, or making significant gains during the six-year period without loss of enrollment proportions, illustrate the outcomes associated with the *strategic/adaptive stage* of the model. Clemson in table 14.6 and the University of California, Berkeley in both tables graduated high proportions of the minority students they enrolled. While the composition of their students remained significantly different from the composition of their states, the trend lines were in a positive direction. These outcomes suggest strategic planning and careful coordination of institutional programs. The outcomes typifying the *reactive/strategic stage* of the model are illustrated by the third group of institutions, all of which experienced significant declines in graduation equity scores between 1980 and 1986. Many of these institutions also lost proportional enrollments. This pattern of declining enrollment proportions and declining graduation equity scores suggests changes in the characteristics of the minority students attending without compensatory strategies in the learning environment provided by the institution.

A final group of institutions with low graduation equity scores for both 1980 and 1986 reflect the outcomes predicted by the *reactive stage* of the model. Many of these institutions also reported losses in proportional enrollments; none gave evidence of significant gains. The model described in chapter 1 suggests that consistently poor results occur in majority institutions when improving graduation equity scores or proportional enrollments are not addressed in systematic ways as institutional priorities.

Determining the nature of the problem an institution faces by analyzing the pattern of institutional outcomes is a starting point in efforts to understand organizational culture. The distribution of minority students across majors is also an important indicator. Proportional distribution and comparable degree achievement across majors suggest positive changes in the teaching and learning environment provided for underrepresented groups. The concentration of minority groups in a limited number of majors may indicate the creation of programs with different academic standards to insulate the remainder of the institution from the need to adapt to student diversity.

Course-passing rates for individual departments also provide evidence of organizational culture. Of particular importance are the "gate-keeping courses" in math which determine eligibility to enter such fields as science, medicine, and engineering. Differential failing rates, like the uneven distribution of students across majors, provide evidence of outcomes associated with the reactive or reactive/strategic stage of adaptation.

Intervening to Produce Organizational Change

Institutions can use the model as an aid to the selection of appropriate change strategies. From tables 14.6 and 14.7, it is apparent that institutions can have an enrollment problem, an achievement problem, or both. Institutions with enrollment problems need to focus on stage 1 and stage 2 interventions, while those with achievement problems should emphasize interventions from stage 2 and stage 3. Because increases in diversity must occur to generate the pressures for organizational change, institutions with both enrollment and achievement problems need to begin on the stage 1 side of the continuum. Given the necessary resources, there is every reason for institutions to address all three stages concurrently, as do state and federally funded opportunity programs.

Outcomes by themselves are not reliable indicators of stage of adaptation. Institutions may achieve high graduation equity scores because the minority students they serve are little different from their majority clientele. In 1980 several of the campuses of the California State University system exhibited the outcomes associated with stage 3. By 1986 their graduation equity scores and enrollment proportions had dropped significantly, suggesting a reactive/strategic level of adaptation. It seems likely that heavier recruitment of minority students by the University of California system changed the nature of the pool of minority students attending CSU institutions. In the absence of CSU interventions to compensate for differences in the characteristics of entering students, outcomes suffered. From the experiences of California and other states we can infer that adaptation is necessary whenever the characteristics of a student population change significantly.

Stage of adaptation to a new clientele is most accurately revealed by examining institutional practices, the visible evidence of invisible culture. The behaviors associated with the first stage of adaptation within the case-study institutions appear in table 14.8. These behaviors can be used as a checklist to assess the degree to which any institution gives evidence of a culture that has been adapted to reduce barriers to minority participation. Appropriate behaviors for any given institution are a function of mission characteristics and the type of problem suggested by the assessment of outcomes.

TABLE 14.8. Interventions for Increasing Diversity

Activity	Examples
Student recruitment	High schools with high concentrations of AA/H/AI students are priority targets for recruiting efforts.
	Current AA/H/AI students participate in institutional recruiting efforts.
	AA/H/AI students are recruited through the personnel and training offices of employers.
	Outreach staff provide community college transfer students with accurate and timely advice about course planning, financial aid, and other transfer requirements.
Financial aid	College staff conduct workshops in high schools for AA/H/AI students and their parents.
	College staff help prospective AA/H/AI students fill out financial aid forms.
	Institutional resources are used to fund need-based financial aid for AA/H/AI students.
	AA/H/AI students receive a proportional share of scholarships based on merit.
Admissions and scheduling	Undergraduate admission standards are frequently waived to increase enrollments by AA/H/AI students.
	Institution provides open admissions to one or more major academic units.
	Regular admission requires only a specified GPA or class rank for a prescribed distribution of high school classes.
	Admission to the institution is also admission to the major of choice.
	There is a concurrent or cross-registration agreement with an institution enrolling a higher proportion of AA/H/AI students.
	Classes are scheduled so that degrees can be earned through evening attendance only.

Note: AA/H/AI = African-American, Hawaiian, and American Indian.

Stage 1 behaviors are characterized by three major thrusts. The first focuses on increasing the institutional share of the available pool of potential minority college students through recruitment activities targeted at multicultural high schools and community colleges. A second thrust, closely coordinated with the first, provides information and assistance to help eligible minority students qualify for financial aid. Direct assistance with filling out forms is an important part of the process at the University of Texas at El Paso where many of the Hispanic students are first-generation college-goers. Instructions in Spanish, unnecessary for most prospective students, are appreciated by many parents in closely knit Hispanic families. Ensuring that the criteria for awarding merit-based assistance does not exclude high-achieving minority students through inappropriate use of test scores helps Memphis State University remain competitive for the best minority students produced by its region.

A third thrust of stage 1 behaviors emphasizes the use of admissions criteria and class scheduling to include students from underrepresented populations. The approach can be as simple as a commitment to find ways of admitting as many students as possible from working-class families in the tradition of Temple University or as complex as use of multiple criteria to achieve proportional representation at UCLA. The most common approach is to waive admission standards of 5 to 10 percent of the entering class. At Memphis State, admission to the university meant admission to the major. Wayne State scheduled many of its classes so that students could earn degrees through evening attendance.

Through recruitment, financial aid, admission procedures and scheduling, institutions increase the diversity among their students in terms of preparation, value attached to college-going, and mode of college attendance. By removing some of the barriers to diversity along these three dimensions, institutions expand the pool of racial and ethnic minorities who are eligible to attend. Increasing diversity improves participation rates, but adversely impacts achievement as students increasingly differ from those anticipated by prevailing approaches to teaching and advising.

The stage 2 interventions case-study institutions adopted to combat differential retention rates are summarized in table 14.9.

Stage 2 interventions serve two primary objectives. The first is to change students so that they become a better match for the institutional environment. The second is to change the environment, or buffer elements that cannot easily be changed, to make the institution less difficult to negotiate for students who differ in preparation, objectives, or skin color from those traditionally served.

Institutions engage in stage 2 strategies as the result of a planning decision to improve outcomes for minority students. Stage 2 interventions seek to expand the pool of college-ready minority high school graduates, to help first-generation college students and the marginally

TABLE 14.9. Outreach and Student Support Interventions

ACTIVITY	EXAMPLES
Outreach	On-campus summer enrichment programs for AA/H/AI junior high or high school students are conducted as part of an institutionwide outreach program.
	A professional program (e.g., engineering, business) provides instruction in mathematics, science, computers, or communication skills, along with academic advising and summer enrichment for selected AA/H/AI students in the ninth to eleventh grades.
	A collaborative program with high schools identifies promising AA/H/AI sophomores, juniors, and seniors, and strengthens their college readiness through academic enrichment, advising, tutoring, and instruction in test-taking skills.
	A collaborative program with a junior high school enrolling a high proportion of AA/H/AI students provides academic advising, role model presentations, university visits, and parental involvement.
Transition	A special access program provides outreach, counseling, financial support, special course work, and tutoring to a limited number of low income first college students who do not meet regular admission requirements.
	First-time AA/H/AI students are enrolled in the same course sections as others in the same majors, to facilitate networking and mutual assistance.
	Most new students participate in an orientation program that emphasizes cultural sensitivity as part of its content.
	AA/H/AI students are invited to participate in a special orientation, piggybacked on the regular orientation, in which they work intensively with support staff.
	A summer bridge program provides newly admitted AA/H/AI students with courses for college credit, tutorial assistance, study skills, and assistance in academic and career decision making.
Mentoring and advising	Students in danger of failing are identified by an early alert system and receive timely advising and assistance.

TABLE 14.9. (continued)

Activity	Examples
	New students have immediate contact with the orientation and advising programs of their declared majors.
	"Intrusive" academic advising and mentoring is provided to all AA/H/AI students for at least their first year of attendance.
Environment	A cultural center or AA/H/AI student union provides a gathering place for underrepresented groups.
	Institutional publications emphasize the contributions and achievements of AA/H/AI students.
	Campus social, cultural, and educational organizations produce a year-long calendar of programs celebrating the international, multilingual, and multicultural heritages of undergraduate students.
Residence halls	AA/H/AI students receive priority in residence halls.
	Residence halls provide special options or programming for AA/H/AI students (e.g., all AA/H/AI floors, AA/H/AI scholars, etc.).
	A summer bridge program provides a residential experience to introduce newly admitted AA/H/AI students to the institution, as well as providing programs designed to enhance academic success.

Note: AA/H/AI = African-American, Hawaiian, and American Indian.

underprepared get a head start, to strengthen linkages between college study and a subsequent career, and to make the campus environment a more inviting place for students from minority cultures.

Expanding the pool requires collaboration with high schools and junior high schools. Among the case-study institutions, such collaboration took two primary forms. In Philadelphia, PRIME, Incorporated, focused on developing the talent of minority youth in science-related fields in a format that involved community organizations and a consortium of universities, including Temple. This program has been widely emulated. At UCLA an extensive, university wide early outreach program targeted minority-dominant schools in the university's catchment area.

The best transition programs award degree credit in addition to developing support groups, teaching study skills, and providing opportunities for socialization. By awarding six credits during the summer preceding matriculation, UCLA permitted less well prepared students to reduce course loads during the following academic year without falling behind classmates. The transition program at Florida State included most of the components of the UCLA program, but did not award degree credit. Mentoring and advising are especially critical for firstgeneration college students because they lack firsthand experience with the relationship between college course work and a satisfying career. They are also less likely to know the "tricks of the trade" for achieving workable class schedules and more likely to experience problems with course sequencing. As institutions dealing with large numbers of firstgeneration college students, Brooklyn College and CSU provided every entering student with a mentor.

College environment is influenced by location and by the composition of the student body. The proportion of Hispanic students and an adjacent multicultural community provide a comfortable setting for Hispanics at Florida International, the University of Texas at El Paso, and the University of New Mexico. Florida State University, in less culturally diverse Tallahassee, provided all-African-American floors in residence halls and the Black Student Union to help combat cultural isolation for the small proportion of African-American students who attended.

Stage 2 interventions emphasize student characteristics rather than race and ethnicity. However, elimination of race and ethnicity as a basis for organizing services depends upon the success an institution experiences in adapting values and beliefs to stage 3 patterns in which minority cultures are celebrated for the strengths they contribute to a quality educational experience for all students. The stage 3 interventions found among case-study institutions are synthesized in table 14.10.

Stage 3 interventions focus on changing the learning experience to preserve standards without condemning more diversely prepared students to failure. Design of an appropriate learning environment for new clientele requires knowledge about their actual strengths and weaknesses, as contrasted with those anticipated by the prevailing pedagogy and curriculum. In stage 3 institutions, assessment is used to design more relevant learning experiences, not to limit student diversity. At Memphis State, students who demonstrated weaknesses in basic skills areas were placed in a special noncredit learning sequence. Retention of students assigned to the sequence and their subsequent performance in regular credit classes exceeded the results for their classmates who were not required to take the sequence. The University of Texas at El Paso reported similar results.

Any definition of quality that incorporates diversity as a strength presumes a method for judging institutions by the outcomes they produce rather than by the test scores of the students they admit. Value added is not a sufficient indicator; a quality education of minority students must be one in which they meet the same performance standards

TABLE 14.10. Interventions Involving the Academic Program

Activity	Examples
Student assessment	Admission requirements and assessment procedures ensure that students enrolling in entry-level classes have the academic competencies required for success.
	All students must pass an academic skills examination before achieving upper-division status.
Learning assistance	Students identified as lacking the competencies required for entry-level courses receive appropriate instruction in basic skills, academic advising and tutoring.
	Tutoring is widely available to students who need it.
	Assistance with reading, writing, and math skills is available on a walk-in basis.
	Instruction in study skills, note taking, and test preparation is provided to all students as needed.
	Departments offering prerequisite courses for admission to majors have developed approaches to avoid screening out disproportionate numbers of AA/H/AI students.
	Students who need extra assistance in mastering beginning degree-credit skill courses can enroll in sections that provide extra hours of classroom instruction supplemented by tutoring and learning laboratories.
	Students who follow nontraditional patterns of attendance have access to an educational service center that provides counseling, developmental course work, tutoring, critical reading and library research skills, time management, and study skills.
	AA/H/AI students of high scholastic ability participate proportionately in honors programs.
	AA/H/AI undergraduates receive paid internships with faculty members conducting research.
Curriculum content	Courses in AA/H/AI cultures are available to students who wish to take them as electives.
	All students must complete at least one course that focuses on sensitivity to minority cultures.

Note: AA/H/AI = African-American, Hawaiian, and American Indian.

as everyone else. To assure this outcome, students must be assessed after they have completed some common part of their educational program. A growing number of states and systems prescribe such assessment. Even where assessment is not prescribed by a state or system, as at Wayne State, it is being implemented on the initiative of the institution.

Information about the performance levels of entering students and desired exit competencies can be used to alter pedagogy and curriculum to provide diversely prepared students with the all-important "level playing field." Perhaps the least difficult change involves providing more time. Transition programs of the type offered by UCLA are one approach. Additional learning time can also be provided within the framework of a regular credit course, as in the English classes at UCLA that meet five hours a week for three hours of credit. Reducing class size increases the amount of individual attention that can be provided to each student. A four-year program can be scheduled over five years of full-time attendance, an option that has received increasing attention from medical schools and could be implemented at the undergraduate level as well. While part-time students obviously stretch out their time to completion, most of the benefit is lost by the necessity of juggling family and job responsibilities while working on a degree and the resultant shallow contacts with the university.

In addition to time, more diversely prepared students require substantial learning assistance. Tutoring, walk-in learning laboratories, and courses in test taking and study skills are only a few of the forms of learning support that help first-generation college-goers master an environment for which they have scant preparation. All institutions provide learning support services for some students. Stage 3 institutions, like the University of Texas at El Paso, provide them to all students for as long as they are needed. Institutions in stage 1 or stage 2 limit these services, for the most part, to athletes and students who qualify for externally funded, special programs.

The nature of the curriculum and the cultural diversity of those who offer it are also indicators of stage of adaptation. At Brooklyn College, a highly regarded core curriculum incorporates the contributions of all cultures. Ideally, a curriculum that incorporates multicultural values and contributions should be taught by a culturally diverse faculty. African-American graduates of Wayne State described the opportunity to learn from African-American faculty members as one of the most valued dimensions of their undergraduate experience.

Managing Organizational Culture

Progress through the three stages of adaptation is not a matter of luck or an accident. Leaders in the case-study institutions used such management tools as planning and resource allocation to design and implement strategies that over time removed barriers, helped more diversely prepared students to understand and meet academic expectations, and ultimately changed attitudes and values about who should be taught in a quality institution and how. The strategies used in case-study institutions to manage cultures for improved equity are reported in table 14.11.

Strategic planning is a prerequisite to systematic organizational change. UCLA and UTEP identified minority access and achievement as one of a small number of priorities to which discretionary institutional dollars would flow. Academic and support units were then expected to engage in the detailed bottom-up planning essential to translating institutional priorities into action strategies. By contrast, institutions making less progress toward the adaptive stage identified minority access and achievement as one of a longer list of institutional goals, or relied on categorical funds from external sources to determine the direction and scope of institutional efforts.

During the reactive stage, minority programs and services tend to be fragmented because they originate largely in response to discrete external initiatives. As institutions become more systematic in their approaches to diversity and achievement, the activities essential to a coherent learning experience are increasingly coordinated centrally. At UCLA the Academic Advancement Program became part of the College of Letters and Sciences during the study after reporting to student affairs for nearly two decades.

Beyond coordinating efforts related to outreach, transition, advising, and academic support, institutional leaders hold academic and support units accountable for progress toward planned objectives through sophisticated student information systems of the sort operating at Florida State and UCLA. Wayne State was clearly handicapped in its efforts to improve or even understand minority outcomes by the absence of reliable data.

While planning, coordination, and accountability measures are important tools in exposing values and beliefs that interfere with the participation and achievement of African-American, Hispanic, and American Indian students, institutions must also improve the diversity of administrative staffs and faculty members to build the capacity for sustaining the improvements made. The issue is often stated in terms of providing role models for minority youth, but the problem is equally one of providing examples to challenge the stereotypes held by majority faculty and students. Since the pool of minority academic professionals is very small, states such as Tennessee, Florida, California, and New Jersey have devoted significant effort to expanding the pool, in addition to ensuring that their institutions remain competitive for minority academics who are already prepared.

The responsibility for changing learning environments to make them a better fit for a more diverse clientele, while preserving academic

TABLE 14.11. Managing Organizational Culture

Activity	Examples
Strategic planning	Recruiting and graduating more AA/H/AI students is one of the three top priorities of campus administrators.
	Academic and support units have developed goals and action plans for hiring more AA/H/AI staff.
	Academic and support units have developed goals and action plans for increasing enrollment and graduation rates for AA/H/AI students.
	Resource allocation is tied to the strategic planning process.
	Unrestricted dollars are used to support interventions aimed at increasing enrollments and graduation rates for AA/H/AI students.
Coordination and control	Academic affairs and student affairs staffs work closely together in planning and implementing AA/H/AI initiatives.
	A senior administrator has responsibility for coordinating all recruiting, advancement, and retention programs for AA/H/AI students.
	College and discipline-specific information on AA/H/AI enrollment and graduation rates is routinely available.
	Senior administrators regularly monitor information about progress in increasing enrollment and graduation rates of AA/H/AI students.
	Cohort survival studies provide persistence and graduation data disaggregated by race or ethnicity and by transfer or first-time-in-college status.
	Administrators meet regularly with community college counterparts to monitor the effectiveness of articulation policies.
	Cultural awareness sessions are held for administrators, faculty members, and support staff.

TABLE 14.11. (continued)

Activity	Examples
Increasing staff diversity	AA/H/AI administrators are a visible and influential part of campus leadership.
	Recruiting procedures for new faculty members require that the best AA/H/AI candidates be included during initial screening.
	New AA/H/AI faculty are recruited through enriched salary offers, payment of moving expenses, and released time from teaching to support research.
	Positions have been created to recruit AA/H/AI "targets of opportunity" in fields in which openings would not otherwise be available.
	AA/H/AI research centers make joint appointments with academic departments. Positions revert to the center when the incumbent leaves the institution.
	AA/H/AI graduate teaching assistants are aggressively recruited to increase the presence of these groups in the classroom.
	Targeted dissertation and postdoctoral fellowships are used to expand the pool of potential AA/H/AI faculty.
Faculty incentives and support	Grants and released time encourage faculty members to develop strategies for improving student achievement.
	Advising, mentoring, and good teaching are encouraged and rewarded.
	A mentoring program helps untenured AA/H/AI faculty members meet requirements for tenure.
	A "grow-your-own" program supports promising AA/H/AI doctoral students in high-demand fields on condition that they teach for a specified period following completion.

Note: AA/H/AI = African-American, Hawaiian, and American Indian.

standards, cannot and should not be relegated to the small proportion of minority faculty members likely to be present in most majority institutions during the next decade. Majority faculty members dominate the senior ranks as well as the tenure and promotion systems. Ways must be found of enlisting their support in the adaptation process. The case-study institutions used professional development, grants and released time, graduate student support, and mentoring in their efforts to deal with the shortage of minority faculty members, perhaps the single greatest obstacle to achieving the adaptive stage of the model. No institution claimed to have found the answers, but those making the greatest progress emphasized as many of the staff diversity and staff development activities as their resources and mission permitted.

CONCLUSION

Institutions work with three sets of variables in responding to access and quality tensions: student characteristics, the design of the learning experience, and expected performance standards. Varying any one impacts on the other two. If students enter with less preparation but performance standards and the nature of the learning experience remain the same, fewer will graduate. To maintain or improve graduation rates without changing the design of the learning experience in the presence of greater student diversity requires a reduction in performance standards. The learning environment must be redesigned to maintain or improve graduation rates in the presence of greater student diversity without reducing standards.

A learning environment that will help diversely prepared students to succeed can be designed from a study of the experiences of the case-study institutions. Federal, state, and private sources must remove economic barriers. Institutions must collaborate with high schools and junior high schools to improve precollege preparation and motivation. First-generation college students need assistance in making the transition from high school. Marginally prepared students need additional time and additional learning assistance. There must be a way of identifying and correcting preparation gaps as well as an assessment process to ensure that all students are performing at accepted standards by the time they are awarded a degree. Cultural differences must be accepted and valued in the social environment and in the curriculum. These changes will benefit students of all races and ethnicities, but they are particularly critical to marginally prepared, first-generation college students, who are disproportionately from African-American, Hispanic, and American Indian heritages.

The principal obstacle to changing the learning environment to better accommodate diversity and quality is the degree to which current arrangements serve the purposes of those who operate the higher education enterprise. Teaching lower-division students in large lecture classes with little provision for individual assistance finances the lighter teaching loads essential to the conduct of research in institutions that are inadequately funded. Admission standards restrict student diversity to weed out a majority of those who cannot survive an academic environment that places most of the responsibility for learning on the student and provides very limited academic advising and learning assistance. The system is self-serving and self-perpetuating. It is legitimated by definitions of quality shaped around highly selective institutions that have sufficient resources to avoid the compromises in learning environments less affluent institutions must accept.

Those who see advantages to definitions of quality that exclude diversity are not all within the academy. Legislators opposed to raising taxes are pleased to learn that students can be educated more cheaply in community colleges, and thus they are not disposed to question transfer rates which in states like Florida may be only half as high for African-Americans as for other racial or ethnic groups. Chambers of commerce and local business leaders support research as a vital component of economic development. They either do not understand or lack concern about the reduction in emphasis on teaching and learning practices essential to the support of "world-class research" in emerging regional universities.

In this volume we have emphasized the importance of acting on a definition of quality that incorporates diversity by adapting institutional environments so that they enroll and graduate a clientele more nearly reflective of the composition of the society they serve. Some teaching-oriented public institutions without research aspirations and some independent institutions with a strong sense of mission have demonstrated the feasibility of such change. But given the strength of the forces supporting the status quo, it is unlikely that most institutions will respond to the challenge in the absence of significant mandates, inducements, and accountability measures in the state or federal policy environments. It is not that institutional leaders lack vision or commitment. They are, rather, the molders and the prisoners of institutional environments in which wants always exceed resources and in which the underrepresented lack the influence essential to achieve adequate consideration of their needs.

The issue of minority access and achievement is the major item of unfinished business on the nation's policy agenda. We can come to grips with it most effectively by examining state and institutional outcomes for which the established standards are proportional representation and comparable achievement. These standards must be pursued in the context of a state policy environment that is unambiguous in its expectations and in the support it provides for attaining the standards.

REFERENCES

Astin, A. W. 1985. *Achieving Educational Excellence*. San Francisco: Jossey-Bass.

Brint, S., and J. Karabel. 1989. *The Diverted Dream: Community Colleges and the Promise of Educational Opportunity in America, 1900-1985*. New York: Oxford University Press.

Carnegie Council on Policy Studies in Higher Education. 1980. *Three Thousand Futures: The Next Twenty Years for Higher Education*. San Francisco: Jossey-Bass.

Chaffee, E. E. 1985. Three models of strategy. *Academy of Management Review* 10(1): 89–98.

Commission on Minority Participation in Education and American Life. 1988. *One-Third of a Nation*, Washington, D. C.: ACE/Education Commission of the States.

Cyert, R. M. 1985. "The Design of a Creative Academic Organization," in *Frontiers in Innovative and Creative Management*, edited by R. L. Kuhn. Cambridge, Mass.: Ballinger Publishing Company, pp. 301–302.

Deskins, D. R., Jr. 1983. *Minority Recruitment Data*. Totowa, New Jersey: Rowman & Allanheld.

Goodman, P. S., and J. W. Dean. 1982. "Creating Long-Term Organizational Change," in *Change in Organizations*, edited by Paul S. Goodman and Associates, San Francisco: Jossey-Bass Publishers, pp. 226-279.

Hansen, W. L., and J. O. Stampen. 1988. *Balancing Quality and Access in Financing Higher Education*. Baltimore, Md.: National Center for Postsecondary Governance and Finance.

Hsia, J. 1987. "Asian American Students: Ability, Achievement, and Access to Higher Education." Paper presented at the Annual Meeting of the American Educational Research Association.

KUH, G. D., and E. J. WHIT. 1988. *The Invisible Tapestry: Culture in American Colleges and Universities*. ASHE-ERIC Higher Education Report No. 1. Washington, D.C.: Association for the Study of Higher Education.

LINCOLN, Y. S., and E. G. GUBA. 1985. *Naturalistic Inquiry*. Beverly Hills, Calif.: Sage Publications.

MCDONNELL, L. M. 1988. "Policy Design as Instrument Design." Paper presented at the Annual Meeting of the American Political Science Association.

MEHAN, H. 1978. "Structuring School Structure." *Harvard Educational Review* 48: 32–65.

MILES, M. B., and A. M. HUBERMAN. 1984. *Qualitative Data Analysis*. Beverly Hills, Calif.: Sage Publications.

MILLETT, J. D. 1984. *Conflict in Higher Education*. San Francisco: Jossey-Bass.

NEWMAN, F. E. 1985. *Higher Education and the American Resurgence*. Princeton, N.J.: Carnegie Foundation for the Advancement of Teaching.

NOBLIT, G. W. 1986. "The Legacy of Education in the Social Sciences." *Issues in Education* 4: 42–51.

OHIO BOARD OF REGENTS. 1988. *Student Access and Success in Ohio's Higher Education System*. Columbus, Oh.: Ohio Board of Regents.

PALLAS, A. M., G. NATRIELLO, and E. L. MCDILL. 1989. The Changing Nature of the Disadvantaged Population Current Dimensions and Future Trends. *Educational Researcher* 18(5): 16–22.

PFEFFER, J., and G. R. SALANCIK. 1978. *The External Control of Organizations: A Resource Dependence Perspective*. New York: Harper and Row, 69–70.

RIST, R. C. 1970. "Student Social Class and Teacher Expectation: The Self-Fulfilling prophecy in ghetto Education." *Harvard Educational Review* 40: 411–451.

RUDOLPH, F. 1965. *The American College and University*. New York: Alfred A. Knopf.

SCHEIN, E. H. 1985. *Organizational Culture and Leadership*. San Francisco: Jossey-Bass.

SCHLESINGER, A. M., JR. 1986. *The Cycles of American History*. Boston: Houghton Mifflin Company.

SENECA, J. J., and M. K. TAUSSIG, 1987. "Educational Quality, Access, and Tuition Policy at State Universities." *Journal of Higher Education* 58: 25–37.

SPRADLEY, J. R. 1979. *The Ethnographic Interview*. New York: Holt, Rinehart & Winston.

STATE HIGHER EDUCATION EXECUTIVE OFFICERS. 1987. *A Difference of Degrees: State Initiatives to Improve Minority Student Achievement*. Denver, Colo.: SHEEO.

TIERNEY, W. G. 1988. "Organizational Culture in Higher Education: Defining the Essential." *Journal of Higher Education* 59: 2–21.

TINTO, V. 1987. *Leaving College: Rethinking the Causes and Cures of Student Attrition*. Chicago: University of Chicago Press.

TREISMAN, P. U. 1985. "A Study of the Mathematics Performance of Black Students at the University of California, Berkeley." Unpublished manuscript.

U.S. DEPARTMENT OF EDUCATION, NATIONAL CENTER FOR EDUCATION STATISTICS. October 1986. "Financial Statistics of Institutions of Higher Education." Washington D. C.: U.S. Government Printing Office.

WILDAVSKY, A. 1979. *Speaking Truth to Power: The Art and Craft of Policy Analysis*. Boston: Little, Brown, and Company.

——. 1987. "Choosing Preferences by Constructing Institutions: A Cultural Theory of Preference Formation." *American Political Science Review* 81(1): 3–21.

WILLIAMS, J. B., III, editor. 1985. *Desegregating America's Colleges and Universities: Title VI Regulation of Higher Education*. New York: Teachers College Press.

WILLIAMS, J. B., III. 1988. "The State Role in Achieving Equality of Higher Education," in *Toward Black Undergraduate Student Equality in American Higher Education*, edited by M. T. Nettles. New York: Greenwood Press, pp. 149–178.

WILSON, R., and S. E. MELENDEZ. 1987. *Sixth Annual Status Report on Minorities in Higher Education*. Washington, D. C.: American Council on Education. 3.

YIN, R. K. 1988. *Case Study Research: Design and Methods*. Beverly Hills, Calif.: Sage Publications.

RESEARCH TOPIC INDEX

GENERAL INDEX